Albert M Gibson

A Political Crime

The history of the great fraud

Albert M Gibson

A Political Crime
The history of the great fraud

ISBN/EAN: 9783743407398

Manufactured in Europe, USA, Canada, Australia, Japa

Cover: Foto ©ninafisch / pixelio.de

Manufactured and distributed by brebook publishing software (www.brebook.com)

Albert M Gibson

A Political Crime

A

POLITICAL CRIME

THE

HISTORY OF THE GREAT FRAUD

BY

A. M. GIBSON

"The refuge of lies shall be swept away, and the hiding-place of falsehood shall be uncovered." — *J. S. Black, to the Electoral Commission, Feb. 27, 1877.*

NEW YORK
WILLIAM S GOTTSBERGER, PUBLISHER
11 MURRAY STREET
1885

Press of
William S. Gottsberger
New York

CONTENTS

CHAPTER I.

CHAPTER II.

CHAPTER III.

CHAPTER IV.

CHAPTER V.

CHAPTER VI.

CHAPTER VII.

CHAPTER VIII.

CHAPTER IX.

CHAPTER X.

CHAPTER XI.

CHAPTER XII.

CHAPTER XIII.

CHAPTER XIV.

CHAPTER XV.

CHAPTER XVI.

CHAPTER XVII.

CHAPTER XVIII.

APPENDIX.

A POLITICAL CRIME.

CHAPTER I.

The election of Tilden and Hendricks by the people: Sectional prejudices and class interests: The crime of the nineteenth century
admitted by republicans: The patriotism of Mr. Tilden: His
preference for private life: The great labors he had performed
in the service of the State: The irreparable loss to the people of
the United States: The foolhardy attempt to maintain alien governments in the Southern States — their overthrow hailed with joy by
all good people.

On Tuesday, November 7th, 1876, the people of the
United States, by their suffrages, selected for President
and Vice-President, Samuel J. Tilden and Thomas A.
Hendricks, and were deprived of their choice by illegal
methods, bolstered by frauds, perjuries, and forgeries.

Sectional prejudices, engendered by years of violent
political agitation, and intensified by civil war, the excitement of a fiercely contested presidential campaign, and vast
and widely ramifying financial interests, warped the judgment of many good men and constrained them then to
countenance and acquiesce in the acts of politicians bent on
self-aggrandizement, intent upon the gratification of their
ambition, and determined, at all hazards, to perpetuate their
power. Calm reflection, sober reasoning, deliberate consideration in the midst of the wild excitement of that hour
was, perhaps, more than ought to have been expected.

The surprising thing is that within less than a decade an almost complete revulsion in the opinion of the minority should have taken place.

Those who actually participated in the conspiracy to nullify the will of the people, of course, attempt to justify their conduct, but it is indeed seldom that any others appear as the defenders or apologists of the extraordinary means employed to accomplish that crime. This well-nigh universal change in the sentiments of republicans has been naturally evolved, and is another and striking proof of the deep-seated and inherent sense of justice and right which characterizes the American people. It would have been passing strange if this change had not occurred. It would have been cause for wonderment if a people jealous of their liberties, devoted to the principles of constitutional government, reverently believing in the sacred right of local self-government, and treasuring up the glorious traditions of their ancestors had not risen above party prejudices and made manifest their disapproval of the crime of the nineteenth century.

What a monstrous crime it was! And what dire disasters and innumerable woes it would inevitably have led to, if the man who represented the cause of liberty and law, justice and right had not been a true patriot, a great statesman, a wise political philosopher! Humanity would have had cause to mourn had not Samuel J. Tilden possessed a well-poised, evenly-balanced, serene mind; and had not those he represented been consistent and staunch friends of law and order. Had he been an aspiring demagogue, a selfishly-ambitious politician, instead of a broad-minded, far-seeing leader of men, civil war, in all human probability could not have been averted. But he possessed that rare quality of looking beyond the present turmoil and divining

the evolutions of the public conscience. He reposed im-
plicit confidence in the people. Had his advice been
heeded by those who aspired to the leadership of their
party in Congress there would have been no resort to an
extra constitutional tribunal to decide the electoral dispute.
He would have had the House of Representatives plant
itself firmly on its constitutional rights and calmly awaited
the result. The position would have been impregnable.
Desperate as were the men, who were seeking to set aside
the constitutionally-expressed will of the people, they
would not have dared to assume the fearful responsibility of
unsettling the foundations of the government. The timid
Democratic leaders in Congress, disregarded Mr. Tilden's
advice, and accepted the arbitrament of a tribunal so constituted as to leave to the determination by chance the
deciding vote.

How dignified, manly, and self-respecting, was the bearing and conduct of Mr. Tilden during the eventful months
intervening between the 7th of November, 1876, and the
4th of March, 1877! Personally it was not a deprivation
to lose the presidency. Predisposed to the life of a student,
weary of the strife of the forum, possessing ample fortune, caring not for the pomp and circumstance of official
life, Mr. Tilden, at sixty-three years of age, with health en-
feebled by unremitting attention to his clients, private, and
public, and by unselfish labor in the cause of Democratic
institutions and good government, would have greatly preferred the unalloyed pleasure of private life, the communion
with books, the recreation of travel, and the society of congenial friends, to the vast, the more than herculean, labor of
" working out a reform of systems and policies," and extir-
pating "the cancerous growths of false constructions and corrupt practices" during " years of continuous mal-administra-

tion, under the demoralizing influence of intestine war, and
of bad finance." He would not have been content with
"gliding through an official routine." He had "never accepted official service except for a brief period, for a special
, service, and only when the occasion seemed to require . . .
that sacrifice of private preferences to the public welfare."
For forty years, without thought of an official career, he
had "devoted at least as much thought and effort to the
duty of influencing aright the action of the governmental
institutions" of his "country, as to all other objects." He
had acted upon the belief "that there is no instrumentality
in human society so potential in its influence upon man-
kind for good or evil, as the governmental machinery for ,
administering justice, and for making and executing laws.
Not all the eleemosynary institutions of private benevolence
to which philanthropists may devote their lives, are so
fruitful in benefits, as the rescue and preservation of this
machinery from the perversions that make it the instrument
of conspiracy, fraud, and crime, against the most sacred
rights and interests of the people."*

Animated by no selfish considerations he began the war-
fare against official plunderers who held the city and state
of New York in their iron grasp. The labor he performed
in breaking to pieces the Tweed ring was enough to have
broken the health of a physically stronger man. Following
this came the administration of the affairs of the state and
the overthrow of the Canal ring. This latter corrupt combination was the complement of the former. Together
they dominated the politics of the state and exacted tribute
from the commonwealth and its great commercial metropolis. Their combined power to control parties, to dictate

* Mr. Tilden's letter to Chairman N. Y. Dem. State Com. June 10,
1884.

nominations, to influence legislation, and sway the administration of justice, was no secret. In their plenitude of
power they truthfully boasted of their ability to make or
mar the political fortunes of men. They contemptuously
snapped their fingers at their unorganized victims, and, with
the insolence of robber barons of old, sneeringly asked,
"what are you going to do about it?"

The answer in due time was made by Samuel J. Tilden.
It was a titanic struggle. The thieves had millions stolen
from the people. They were entrenched at every point.
They had made governors. They owned legislatures and
courts. The people had to be organized. The control of
party machinery had to be wrenched from the hands of the
robbers and their allies. The municipal government had
to be rescued from the spoilers and the state redeemed.
The moving spirit, the controlling mind, the master hand,
throughout the long and arduous contest for the supremacy
of right, the vindication of justice, was that of Mr. Tilden.

The services Mr. Tilden rendered the great metropolis
and his native State in uprooting, prosecuting, and bringing
to punishment the Tweed ring of the city, and the Canal ring
of the state, of New York made him the most conspicuous reformer of his time. It is one thing to theorize and quite another to perform. His reforms were accomplished in the face
of formidable organized opposition. The degree of acumen,
the power of analysis, the intellectual force, and the skill of
organization and concentration required in these great under-
takings have rarely if ever been found united in one man.
It would have been strange if these remarkable qualifications
and really wonderful performances had not made Mr. Tilden
the candidate of the people in 1876. Public sentiment demanded the redemption and reformation of the Federal government. The people wanted an executive who had the

capacity, the moral courage, the experience, and the persistent determination to restore the administration of the government to its pristine purity and simplicity.

Had Mr. Tilden been installed as President of the United States, corruption in high places would have ceased, the public service would have been reformed, the moral standards of the people would have been elevated, the overgrown civil list would have been pruned of its excrescences, and an effete accounting system adapted to the needs of the government of an infant republic, but soon thereafter abandoned by the mother country whence it was derived, and which long since ceased to be a check on dishonest officials, would have been replaced by one simple and efficient. The great work which he would have accomplished this generation will not see performed. A man of his mental equipment, of his vast and varied experience, of his genius to originate and capacity to execute, of his grasp of details, of his analytical methods, is rarely found.

The men who conspired to defeat the will of the people in 1876 knew what they were about. They knew that if Mr. Tilden became President of the United States the investigations which would follow would be directed by one who was indefatigable, relentless, and perfect master of the art. They knew what the result would be and the effect it would produce on the public mind. Eternal dishonor would have been the portion of many, and permanent retirement to private life the inevitable lot of a still greater number. The Crédit Mobilier exposure, and the half-hearted inquiry by a partisan committee which followed, had brought in a Democratic House of Representatives. The inquiries that body instituted, though unskilfully conducted, and balked at every turn by executive power, resulted in the impeachment of one cabinet officer and the disgrace of two others.* The public indignation thereby aroused was but a foretaste of the storm of popular rage which would have ensued if the all-pervading rottenness and corruption, the almost inevitable result of the long continuance of one party in power, had been completely laid bare.

Class interests dreaded a change. The reformation of abuses, and the administration of governmental affairs for the benefit of the whole people, would "unsettle values" by disturbing "vested rights" in official jobbery. Combinations to deplete the public treasury by means of star-route mail frauds and naval contracts did not want the existing conditions disturbed and past transactions overhauled. They were ready to unite with "syndicates," and the representatives of southern carpet-bag governments, to defy the will of the people, and prevent the installation of the man they had selected for chief magistrate. The power of these organized influences can scarcely be over-estimated. But they would have been as chaff before the wind if the existing administration had been responsive to public sentiment instead of their creature and superserviceable ally. The false counts in Florida and Louisiana were possible only by the countenance and under the protection of the Federal government.

The desperate means, necessary to accomplish the gigantic frauds by which the people of those states were disfranchised, and their verdict at the ballot-box reversed, would not have been resorted to without the sanction of the chief executive of the nation. What bold disregard of constitutional power, what utter contempt of public sentiment it required to sanction such proceedings!

As the war passions and prejudices had died away the disappearance of alien governments in Virginia, Kentucky,

* Belknap, Robeson, and Williams.

Missouri, Texas, North Carolina, Georgia, Alabama, Arkansas, and Mississippi, was hailed with general approval by the northern people. All self-respecting men admitted that the history of these monstrous perversions of the principles of representative government would remain through all time unparalleled as a record of shameless corruption, wholesale official immorality, and political debauchery. While the English language is spoken the words " carpet-bagger" and "scallawag " will be employed to express the contempt which every decent man feels for the alien and native who oppresses, robs, and wrongs a helpless people !

In 1876 " carpet-bag and scallawag " rule dominated in but three states. The Republican party originally had a respectable white following in Florida among the northern settlers who migrated there, after the war, for health and legitimate business pursuits. But the dishonesty of local officials, the corruptibility of legislators, and State officers, the ease with which jobbers carried schemes to increase the debt and rob the state of its public lands, had disgusted this class and arrayed them on the side of the native whites. South Carolina, with the sole exception of Louisiana was afflicted with the most unscrupulous and despicable gang of public plunderers that ever preyed upon any community. The native scoundrels surpassed in loathsomness of private morals, and official dishonesty the product of any other soil. The career of Frank J. Moses cannot be paralleled in the annals of any other people. The two carpet-baggers who are matchless are John J. Patterson and William Pitt Kellogg. They were the Jonathan Wilds of South Carolina and Louisiana carpet-bag politics. But the cleverest of all the "carpet-baggers " was Daniel H. Chamberlain. As Attorney General and Governor of South Carolina he was the associate and master of the most consummate scoundrels that ever fattened off an unfortunate people, and, strange to say, he survives to play in company with respectable people the role of a political moralist and civil-service reformer! That men whose political aims are professedly high, and who proclaim from the house tops their intention to elevate the standard of official life, and purify our politics, should countenance a man like Chamberlain, and fellowship with him, must be accepted as proof that the drift of public morals is from bad to worse!

The pecuniary cost of "carpet-bag and scallawag" rule in the South may be reckoned by the hundreds of millions, but who will undertake to calculate the extent of the degradation of public and private morals resulting therefrom? Where is the adventurous student of social statics who will venture to estimate the effect of the teachings and examples of "carpet-bag and scallawag" leaders upon six millions of people just emerging from the night of slavery, and whose proneness to falsehood, theft, and kindred vices, was therein engendered? Naturally imitative, predisposed to steal and lie, is it strange that negro legislators were the facile tools of their white leaders, and that black men readily became swift witnesses to bolster by perjury the stories of intimidation and outrages invented by unscrupulous rogues to gull the northern masses? Unfortunately the influence for evil of these political adventurers was not confined to the South. Its ever-widening circles ran over the whole land. Could the presence of a Patterson, a Kellogg, a Dorsey, a West, a Conover, in the Senate of the United States fail to have a deleterious effect upon the morals of the Nation thus disgraced?

CHAPTER II.

The preparation for the great fraud begun in 1873–74: The effect of the Black Friday, San Domingo, French Arms, and Crédit-Mobilier inquiries: The public conscience awakened: The Force bill defeated: A new scheme devised to perpetuate the rule of ambitious men: The third-term programme: The twenty-second joint rule and Morton's Electoral-count bill: Grant believed Mr. Tilden was elected: The Electoral-commission bill a revamping of the Federal device of 1800: The inconsistencies of the rulings of the Electoral commission pointed out — one ruling for Florida, another for Louisiana, and still another for Oregon.

As early as 1873–74 some of the Republican leaders saw plainly that, unless Congress conferred extraordinary powers upon the President of the United States, the southern states, still oppressed by carpet-bag governments, would inevitably, and speedily, regain their constitutional rights. It became apparent within less than a year that their party was rapidly losing its hold upon the northern masses and that in the presidential contest of 1876 the result would probably depend upon the electoral votes of several of the reconstructed states. With a fatuity which now seems very remarkable, these leaders failed to perceive that the northern people were becoming disgusted with sectional politics. Three notable scandals during President Grant's first term had made a decided impression on the public mind. Reflecting patriots contemplated with no little uneasiness the revelations made by the Black Friday, the San Domingo, and French Arms investigations. Im-

mediately succeeding the election of 1872 came the as-
tounding disclosures of the Crédit-Mobilier inquiry. No
other event in the political history of the country produced
such immediate and wide-reaching results. The revelations
were indeed startling. Half a score of popular idols were
overturned, or defaced, and otherwise damaged. Not only
was the public confidence shaken in men who had theretofore commanded almost universal respect and esteem, but
the people began to lose faith in the purity, integrity, and
disinterestedness of Republican leaders.

The public conscience thus rudely awakened by these
revelations began, insensibly, to realize the enormity of the
southern, the sectional policy of the Republican party.
This change in sentiment was at first of slow growth. The
passions and prejudices incident to the war for the preservation of the Union befogged the popular mind and the carpet-bag and scallawag rogues systematically originated and
disseminated stories of horrible outrages alleged to have
been perpetrated by southern whites upon negroes and
southern republicans. Their political allies in Congress
converted the Federal government into a propaganda for the
manufacture and dissemination of outrage stories. As Her-
bert Spencer says "every falsehood has some remote connection with the truth." Southern outrage stories originally had
some basis of truth, but nevertheless they were as a rule
monstrous exaggerations and perversions. In certain sec-
tions of the South there were rude communities and the re-
straints of law were slight. The natural effect of alien rule
is to create lawlessness. The carpet-bag and scallawag
rulers were intent upon plunder and the laws they enacted
were a grievous burden upon the people. In a short time
the administration of justice became a mockery and social
order began to give way to anarchy. The wonder is that

the demoralization was not more general and wide reaching. Had the white population been of any other than Anglo-Saxon origin the result of the attempt to fasten negro and carpet-bag rule upon the southern states would have been frightful.

The attempted imposition of ignorant negro and dishonest and corrupt alien white rulers upon a people of Anglo-Saxon lineage was a wicked and foolhardy experiment. The history of the race ought to have taught the authors of the scheme that it was inevitably doomed to failure. But to the very last, men like Oliver P. Morton, George S. Boutwell, Zach Chandler, and Roscoe Conkling, who were personally honest, and who had, and have great intellectual power and patriotic impulses, were determined to prevent by Federal military power the overthrow of these alien governments. They, and the men of less intellect and meaner motives, who followed in their wake, were willing to disregard the warnings of the Fathers of the Republic, and the examples of the past, and bestow the presidency a third time upon General Grant. Preparatory to driving through the famous and infamous Force bill, which the radical leaders of the Republican majority had devised, an attempt was made, in the closing days of the Forty-third Congress, to adopt, in the House of Representatives, a gag rule to deprive the minority of its constitutional rights. This was the first practical step in the third term programme.

Had the Force bill become a law constitutional liberty would have ceased to exist south of Mason and Dixon's line. The rule of the bayonet would have been supreme throughout that entire region. But the skill, the admirable parliamentary tactics, the wonderful endurance of Samuel J. Randall, secured the defeat of the attempt to impose the gag rule on the House, and the Force bill was killed. It was a memorable struggle. For seventy-two hours, Mr. Randall, without sleep, and with only such refreshments as could be hastily swallowed at his desk, marshalled the Democratic minority and by sheer endurance wore out their adversaries. A few years after this gallant fight against the gag rule in the House of Representatives it was resorted to in the British House of Commons to secure the passage of iniquitous legislation against Ireland. The advocacy of such a measure by Mr. Gladstone was a surprise to his American friends.

Failing to pass the Force bill the radical republicans, under the lead of Senator Morton, attempted to accomplish by indirection what that measure was to have enabled them to do—namely: to control the Presidential election of 1876. The election of an overwhelming majority of democrats to the House of Representatives in 1874 ought to have been accepted by the desperate leaders of the hitherto dominant party as notice that the disclosures of the past few years had shaken public confidence in the honesty and unselfishness of Republican statesmanship, and that the country was tired of sectional politics. The campaign of 1874 had been fought by them on the old issues of southern disloyalty and southern outrages. The response of the people was a disapproval of sectionalism, of carpet-bag rule in the South, and a demand for the reformation of abuses in Federal affairs. The overthrow of the Kellogg government in Louisiana, by armed force, on the 14th of September, only a few weeks before the October elections, seemingly increased Democratic majorities in erstwhile Republican strongholds.

The men who had so long wielded power, instead of deriving wisdom from this exhibition of adverse popular feeling, were only made desperate and reckless. They determined at all hazards to defy the unmistakable will of the people. The vast machinery of the Federal government, the almost unlimited financial resources, subject to assessment for political purposes, and the use which they could make of the army, were not enough to satisfy them. They were resolved not only to play the game of politics with loaded dice, but to cheat in the count, if necessary. With this end in view Senator Morton reported from the Committee on Privileges and Elections, January 26, 1875, an Electoral-count bill, and despite the strenuous opposition of the Democratic minority drove it through the Senate in less than thirty days. However, the rules of the House of Representatives prevented any such haste in that body. The attempt to so amend those rules as to allow the majority to gag the minority had been made as the preliminary to rushing through the " Force bill" and had failed.

Morton's Electoral-count bill provided first, that the affirmative action of the two houses of Congress should be required to reject any certificate of electoral votes, and second, if there was " more than one return " from a state " purporting to be the certificate of electoral votes given at the last preceding election for President and Vice-President in such state " only that one should " be counted which the two houses, acting separately shall decide to be the true and valid return." This was just the opposite of the twenty-second joint rule which had been adopted by the Republican majorities of the two houses in 1865 when the purpose was to prevent the counting of any electoral votes from the states lately in rebellion and thereby express congressional disapproval of President Lincoln's plan of reconstruction. That rule provided that " no vote objected to shall be counted except by the concurrent votes of the two houses." This rule was rushed through hastily and secretly January 30, 1865, to supply the place of a joint resolution which had been passed, specifically providing that, Virginia, North Carolina, South Carolina, Georgia, Florida, Alabama, Mississippi, Louisiana, Texas, Arkansas, and Tennessee, were not entitled "to representation in the Electoral college for the choice of President and Vice-President of the United States for the term commencing on the 4th day of March, 1865," and which it was apprehended the President would not approve. However, Mr. Lincoln did approve the bill and sent a message to Congress in which he stated that he had given his approval solely because he believed that the counting of the electoral vote was a matter entirely beyond the province of the Executive, and expressly declaring that he withheld expression " of any judgment of his own on the subject."

The joint rule of 1865 remained in force and under it three electoral counts were had, in 1865, 1869, and 1873. Upon the assembling of the Congress in December, 1875, on motion of Senator Edmunds, the Senate resolved that the rules of that body, and the joint rules of the two houses, except the twenty-second joint rule, heretofore in use, should be continued until otherwise ordered. It had theretofore not been customary for the Senate, whose organization continues from year to year, to formally readopt its rules and reaffirm the continuance of the joint rules. The House which is reorganized every two years does readopt its rules.

The House of Representatives, which assembled and organized on the first Monday in December, 1875, was largely Democratic, and, therefore, if the twenty-second joint rule had been continued in force any electoral votes which that House refused to count would be rejected. The rule made for partisan purposes, and which had served, on three occasions, partisan ends, would no longer answer the probable necessities of partisans, and hence they dispensed

with it.   The effect of the action of the Senate was to leave
the two houses without any pre-arrangement for counting
the electoral votes in February, 1877.   But prior to 1865
there had been no joint rule relating to the subject.   Theretofore the two houses, a short time in advance of the day fixed
by the act of 1792 — the second Wednesday in February —
for the opening and counting of the electoral votes, agreed
merely upon the place of meeting and the order of proceedings.   Various attempts had been made, previous to the adoption of the twenty-second joint rule, by one or the other of
the two houses, to assume the power to determine the validity of electoral votes and to count the same, but there had
been no agreement.   The significant feature of the twenty-
second joint rule is that it recognized the existence of power
in either house to reject electoral votes.   No one before that
time had been venturesome enough to assert that the Constitution did not guarantee to a state the right to its quota of
electoral votes.   An attempt was made, in 1800, and in 1821,
to enact laws which recognized the power of the two
houses to decide upon the regularity of certificates of electoral votes and provided the methods of exercising such
right, but each time there was no agreement.   Political ex-
pediency was the moving cause of the adoption of the
twenty-second joint rule as partisanship was the origin of
the bill reported by Morton and passed through the Senate
in 1875.   The first, was a gross violation of the Constitution,
and, the second, was intended to give the Republican senate
the power to violate the spirit of the Constitution if the
necessity therefor arose.   It was conceived, formulated,
reported to the Senate, and driven through, for no other
purpose than to give that body, which would continue till
after March 4th, 1877, to be controlled by republicans, the
power to compel the counting of the electoral votes certified

to by the governors of the states of Florida, Louisiana, and South Carolina. The act of 1792 required the executive authority of each state to certify the lists of electors who had been appointed. This certification by the state executive authority was the authentication to the President of the Senate and to Congress of the selection and appointment of the electors. The executive authority of the above-named states was in the hands of unscrupulous and daring men. In each of those states there were Returning Boards composed of unprincipled men who would not hesitate to do anything necessary to perpetuate their party in power, provided they were protected and rewarded. If the necessity arose the will of the people of those states could be nullified by returning and certifying as elected candidates for electors for President and Vice-President of the United States who had been repudiated by the people.

It is, therefore, evident that years previous to the Presidential election of 1876 the Republican leaders in Congress anticipated the probability of the people of the United States defeating at the polls the candidates of their party. They were determined to hold on to power regardless of the popular verdict expressed by constitutional methods. Their first attempt to prepare for such a contingency was to pass through the Senate a bill which would authorize the President to exercise directly absolute power whenever he, or rather they chose, in any or all of the southern states. Defeated in this adventure they endeavored to enact an Electoral-count bill which would enable them to count the electoral votes of these southern states regardless of how the majority of the people therein might vote. The two measures were to have been complements of each other, but the former being defeated they did not abandon the latter. Failing, in February, 1875, on account of the near approach

of the dissolution of the Forty-Third Congress, to pass
their bill, they renewed it in 1876, hoping to delude the
Democratic house into accepting their measure. In this
they were disappointed.

Notwithstanding the defeat of the Force bill which was
to have authorized the exercise of unconstitutional power
by the President and the employment of whatever force he
deemed necessary in southern states, they did induce the
President to in effect declare and enforce martial law in
South Carolina pending the election in that state in 1876.
The whole eastern seaboard of the United States was
stripped of soldiers who were quartered in different localities in that state to overawe the people and prevent a fair
and free exercise of the right of suffrage. The proclamation
issued by the President on the 17th of October, 1876, and
the quartering of thirty-three companies of United States
troops in several counties of South Carolina which followed
thereon were indefensible acts. He did these things upon
the mere request of the governor of that state who did not
establish the existence of "insurrection and domestic violence."

It was merely asserted by the governor that "combinations of men against law exist in many counties who
ride up and down by day and by night in arms, murdering
some peaceable citizens and intimidating others," and
that these combinations "cannot be controlled or suppressed by ordinary course of justice." All this might be
true and not constitute the "insurrection and domestic violence" contemplated by the Constitution. But it did furnish
a *pretext* for the employment of the United States troops un-
lawfully on election day and that was all that was wanted.
The laws* of the United States expressly provide that no

* Sec. 2002 R. S. U. S.

person " engaged in the civil, military, or naval service of the United States shall order, bring, keep, or have under his authority or control any troops or armed men at the polls when any general or special election is held in any state, unless it be necessary to repel the armed enemies of the United States, or to keep the peace at the polls." And yet troops were at the polls in many localities in South Carolina, not for the purpose of repelling the armed enemies of the United States or to preserve the peace, but to aid deputy marshals of the United States in making illegal arrests and to intimidate voters.

The Electoral-commission bill was a revamping of the device of the Federal party in 1800 to nullify the will of the people. It was clear to the federalists at that time, as it was to the republicans in 1875, that the democrats would triumph in the approaching presidential contest, unless some extraordinary measures were taken to reverse the people's verdict. The bill of 1800 was the extraordinary and unconstitutional scheme which was to enable the Federal leaders to count in their candidates who, as they clearly foresaw, were doomed to defeat. The people of that period believed that the federalists meant to convert their government from one of limited powers into an absolute despotism. The alien and sedition laws justly excited their fears and moved them to great wrath. The increase of the army, under pretense of repelling the aggressions of the French Republic, but really for the purpose of enabling Hamilton, if he succeeded in creating the opportunity, to strengthen the Federal government, created the gravest apprehensions in the popular mind.

The fourth Presidential election, it was foreseen would, probably, turn upon the result in Pennsylvania, New York, and New Jersey. How striking the parallel between the struggle of 1800 and that of 1876! In Pennsylvania the general election law expired by limitation and the Federal majority in the senate of that state would not consent to its renewal. Hence, the legislature to be chosen that year would have the appointment of Presidential electors. It was a foregone conclusion that the democrats would have a decided majority on joint ballot in this new legislature. The federalists conceived the idea of contesting the choosing of electors for President and Vice-President of the United States by the Legislature of Pennsylvania on the ground that they should be selected by districts notwithstanding the fact that there was no law providing therefor. On the other hand they had an entirely different scheme for New York. The new legislature of that state, chosen in the spring of 1800, was Democratic and upon it devolved the duty of choosing Presidential electors. But the term of the preceding legislature did not expire till the first of July. The federalists of New York, acting upon the advice of *Alexander Hamilton, designed to have the electors chosen by a legislature which ceased to exist before the appointed time for choosing them came round. It was a bold and illegal design which Hamilton euphoniously denominated a justifiable expedient to defeat Jefferson. It did not succeed because the Governor, John Jay,† although a federalist, refused to be a party thereto and declined to call the legislature together for the purpose.

The federalists had a majority in both Houses of Congress, and expecting the new House to be Republican,‡

* Hamilton's Works, vol. vi, p. 438.

† Life and Writings of John Jay, vol. ii, p. 414.

‡ The followers of Jefferson called themselves Republicans. Their opponents nick-named them *Democrats* and insisted that they were the imitators in the new world of the Revolutionists of France. The Jeffersonians adopted the name applied to them by their enemies.

"they deliberately and unscrupulously determined to enact a law which would enable them to win by foul, if compelled to lose by fair, means."* The bill of 1800 provided that on the day before the second Wednesday in February each House should select by ballot six persons, who with the Chief Justice of the United States, or one of the associate justices, should form a Grand Committee which was to "have power to examine and finally decide all disputes" relative to the election of President and Vice-President of the United States. Each House was to choose two tellers who were to receive the certificates of electoral votes and note their contents. Thereupon the Grand Committee having been organized was to take possession of all the documents, certificates of the electors, and all the certificates and other documents transmitted by them, or by the executive authority of any state, and all petitions, exceptions, and memorials against the votes of any of the electors and the persons for whom they had voted, together with all the testimony accompanying the same. The Chief Justice was to act as chairman of the Grand Committee, which was to sit with closed doors and from day to day till it concluded its labors. It could send for persons and papers, administer oaths and punish witnesses for contempt "as fully and absolutely as the Supreme Court may and can do in cases depending therein."

This tribunal unknown to the Constitution was to have the extraordinary power "to inquire, examine, decide, and report upon the constitutional qualifications of persons voted for as President and Vice-President of the United States, upon the constitutional qualifications of the electors appointed by the different states, and whether their appointment was authorized by the state

* McKnight's Electoral System of the United States, p. 263.

legislatures or not; upon all petitions and exceptions against corrupt, illegal conduct of the electors, or force, menace, or improper means used to influence their votes, or against the truth of their returns, or the time, place, or manner of giving their votes." It was, however, provided that there should be no inquiry as to whether each state had her proper quota of electors or whether the electors were chosen by a majority of the votes in his state or district. Whatever the judgment of this Grand Committee might be it was to be a finality.

This bill was unconstitutional beyond a doubt. Every senator and representative then in Congress who had been a member of the Constitutional Convention opposed and denounced it as violative of the letter and spirit of the Constitution. But the desperate federalists who doubted their ability to defeat Thomas Jefferson in the approaching Presidential contest were determined to pass it. They put the bill through the Senate but in the House the wily republicans, with the assistance of John Marshall, succeeded in so amending it as to take away the powers on which its authors in the Senate chiefly relied to accomplish their purposes. The House amendments made the judgment of the Grand Committee revisable by the two Houses and required a concurrent vote to reject any electoral votes. The Senate insisted that a concurrent vote should be necessary to count disputed votes and a non-agreement resulted.

The people having in 1876, by constitutional methods, indicated their choice for President and Vice-President to be, Samuel J. Tilden, and Thomas A. Hendricks, the Republican politicians determined to disregard the people's will, and at the risk of civil war, and in defiance of every principle of justice and right, and in violation of the letter and spirit of the Constitution of the United States, as well as of the

Constitution and laws of three states, to instal their defeated candidates. The Returning Boards of Florida, Louisiana, and South Carolina, flagrantly disregarding the election laws which gave them existence, returned as elected Republican electors for President and Vice-President when in fact in the two first-named states, and, probably, in the third, the Tilden and Hendricks electors were chosen. This monstrous crime, as we shall hereafter demonstrate, was not only instigated by Republican leaders, but the perpetrators thereof were protected and rewarded by the beneficiaries of the frauds, perjuries, and forgeries by which it was accomplished!

The Republican leaders having failed, as their Federal prototypes did, to make unconstitutional provision, beforehand, to count the electoral votes as necessity might dictate, had to fall back on the old bill of 1800. Upon the reassembling of Congress, in December, 1876, there appeared to be a division of views on the part of Republican senators as to the best method of accomplishing the conspiracy to defraud the people which had thus far been successful. Some maintained that it was the constitutional prerogative of the Vice-President to determine all disputes relative to certificates of electoral votes, and to count the same, and declare the result, which declaration was to be accepted as final, conclusive, and irrevocable. Of this number was Oliver P. Morton who, less than a year previous, had reported to, and carried through, the Senate his Electoral-count bill which made the President of the Senate a mere figurehead in counting the electoral votes. It must, therefore, be concluded that Senator Morton's plan, advocated by him as late as the spring of 1876, was either the result of ignorance or of partisan motives. His sudden conversion to the belief that the President of the Senate alone had jurisdiction in determining questions which he maintained, a short time before, was the province of the two Houses of Congress, cannot be accepted as sincere. It was due to the fact that the President of the Senate was a man who would do the bidding of his party.

The purpose of the radical Republican leaders was to assert and maintain the power of the President of the Senate to count the electoral votes. Mr. Morton was the representative of these desperate men who constituted the large majority of their party in the two houses of Congress. But they could not succeed without the support of the President of the United States. He was the master of the situation. A small minority of republicans, and among them some of the strongest men intellectually in Congress, were opposed to the assumption of this extraordinary power by the President of the Senate.

It was well understood that General Grant had the personal belief that Mr. Tilden was elected. He was familiar with the prior history, character, and doings' of the chief actors in the Louisiana transaction, and was fully convinced that the vote of Louisiana belonged to Mr. Tilden. Confirmatory testimony on this subject has become public since the death of General Grant.

Mr. George W. Childs, who was perhaps the most intimate personal friend and confidant of General Grant, in a letter signed by himself containing reminiscences of the General and published on the 5th day of September, 1885, in the Philadelphia *Ledger*, of which he is the proprietor, has made the following statement:

" He was staying with me in Philadelphia during the canvass of the election between Tilden and Hayes, and on the morning of the momentous day after the election, when the returns gave Tilden a majority of all the Electors, he accompanied me to my office. In a few

moments an eminent Republican Senator and one or two other leading Republicans walked in, and they went over the returns. These
leaders, notwithstanding the returns, said, 'Hayes is elected,' an
opinion in which the others coincided. General Grant listened to
them but said nothing. After they had settled the matter in their own
minds he said: ' Gentlemen, it looks to me as if Mr Tilden was
elected.' * * * * Just before General Grant started
on his journey around the world he was spending some days with me,
and at dinner with Mr. A. J. Drexel, Colonel A. K. McClure and
myself, General Grant reviewed the contest for the creation of the
Electoral Commission and the contest before and in the Commission,
very fully and with rare candor, and the chief significance of his view
was in the fact, as he stated it, that he expected from the beginning
until the final judgment that the Electoral vote of Louisiana would be
awarded to Tilden. He spoke of South Carolina and Oregon as
justly belonging to Hayes; of Florida as reasonably doubtful, and of
Louisiana as for Tilden."

Col. A. K. McClure, editor of *The Times* of Philadelphia, says that* Mr. Childs was not only " the most intimate
personal friend General Grant had during the last ten or
fifteen years of his life," but avers that " it is well known
that in grave political complications, Mr. Childs was often
privately and unreservedly consulted by the General."

* PHILA., Sept. 8, 1885.
Dear Sir: In answer to yours, I would say that I have carefully read
the statement of Mr. Childs as to what was said at dinner with General
Grant, before the latter started on his journey around the world. My recollection of the conversation agrees exactly with his.
Mr. Childs was, according to my observation, the most intimate personal friend General Grant had during the last ten or fifteen years of his
life; and it is well known among their acquaintances that even in grave
political complications Mr. Childs was often privately and unreservedly
consulted by the general.
Mr. A. J. Drexel, who was also of the company at dinner, informs me
that he distinctly recalls the conversation upon that occasion. He agrees
that Gen. Grant's part in it was free, unreserved and candid, as was his
wont; and his remark that he expected, from the beginning until the final
judgment, the electoral vote of Louisiana would be awarded to Mr. Tilden, made such a marked impression upon us who heard it that it is not
strange we should agree so closely in our recollection of it.
Yours truly,
A. M. GIBSON, ESQ.   A. K. MCCLURE.

Colonel McClure not only confirms the exact accuracy of Mr. Childs' report of the substance of the conversation which occurred "just before General Grant started on his journey around the world" in the presence of Mr. A. J. Drexel, Mr. Childs, and himself, but adds that since the publication thereof in *The Ledger* and *The Times* Mr. Drexel has informed him that he has a distinct recollection of the language used on that occasion and vouches for the correctness of the version given by Mr. Childs and himself. The conversation on General Grant's part was spontaneous and his statement that "he expected from the beginning until the final judgment, that the electoral vote of Louisiana would be awarded to Mr. Tilden," was candid and unreserved. Those who knew General Grant well know that he talked with the utmost freedom and frankness when alone with his friends.

General Grant's belief as expressed to the Republican leaders in Mr. Childs' private office, "Gentlemen, it looks to me as if Mr. Tilden was elected," was not a transitory impression made by incomplete returns published the morning after the election. It became a conviction which grew and strengthened as the full returns were received and all the facts were developed. The Republican leaders were bent upon carrying things with a high hand in Washington, and they depended upon General Grant to acquiesce in and maintain whatever course they determined upon. Their intention was to have the President of the Senate assume the right to count the electoral votes, and to determine all questions as to disputed certificates of electoral votes. The probability of such a contingency arising, as has already been pointed out, had been contemplated, and at the beginning of the Forty-fourth Congress Senator Edmunds had quietly managed to have the twenty-second joint rule dropped by the Senate. The preparations were made before and after the assembling of Congress in December, 1876, to sustain in debate this assumption of extraordinary power by the President of the Senate. It was confidently proclaimed that the Senate would sustain this programme, and that President Grant would see to it that whoever the President of the Senate declared to be elected was inaugurated and installed as President of the United States. But the conspirators reckoned without their host.

The plan of the Republican leaders to count in Hayes without regard to the House of Representatives never received any encouragement from General Grant. Shortly after Congress met in December he, through Hon. Hamilton Fish, secretary of state, indicated to Hon. Abram S. Hewitt, chairman of the National Democratic Committee, and a member of the House of Representatives, his desire to have a conference with him on the all-absorbing subject of the electoral count. General Grant made known to Mr. Hewitt his purpose to take no action in regard to the contests in Louisiana and South Carolina over their state governments which could be made to look like the expression of executive opinion in regard to the result of the Presidential election in those states. While he refrained from expressing to Mr. Hewitt his judgment upon the acts of the Returning Board in Louisiana he said plainly that they ought to be the subject of a fair and impartial examination. The impression made upon Mr. Hewitt by General Grant was a most favorable one and the report he made to his Democratic colleagues encouraged them to hope for a pacific and favorable solution of the electoral dispute and the defeat of the Republican conspirators.

Mr. Childs states that General Grant sent for him to

come to Washington and talked with him freely on the
subject of the count of the electoral votes and the embarrassing course of the leaders of his party in Congress. He
said to Mr. Childs: "This matter is very complicated, and
the people will not be satisfied unless something is done in
regard to it which will look like justice. Now, he continued, I have spoken of an Electoral Commission and the
leaders of the party are opposed to it, which I am
sorry to see. They say if an Electoral Commission is appointed you might as well count in Mr. Tilden. I would
sooner have Tilden than the republicans should have a
President who could be stigmatized as a fraud. If I were
Mr. Hayes I would not have it, unless it was settled in
some way outside the Senate. This matter is opposed by
the leading republicans in the House and the Senate and
throughout the country."

This statement by Mr. Childs is fully corroborated by
other gentlemen who were cognizant of what occurred at
the National Capital during that period. The interview
General Grant had with Mr. Hewitt caused the republicans great uneasiness and desperate attempts were made
by them to prejudice the mind of the former by misrepre-
senting the latter. The fact that the President sent for a
number of Republican senators to ascertain their views on
the subject of the electoral count, as Mr. Childs states he
did, was well known at the time to many democrats in
Washington. It was no secret to those well informed in
regard to what was going on at the National Capital
that Senator Conkling and the President were in full accord and that the advocates of the ultra Republican programme accused Mr. Conkling of an intention of betraying
his party. He was in a very large measure held responsible for the policy of the President. So firm was the con-

viction, that Senator Conkling could not be trusted to decide the questions of fact and law involved in the electoral
dispute irrespective of the evidence and the truth, that the
Republican senatorial caucus refused to nominate him for
one of the members of the Electoral Commission. This
was the more significant because Mr. Conkling was, according to Mr. Childs, the senator who, at the request of
President Grant, undertook to carry through the Senate
the Electoral Commission bill. Mr. Childs says: "Grant
was the originator of the plan. He sent for Mr. Conkling,
and said with deep earnestness: 'This matter is a serious
one, and the people feel it deeply. I think this Electoral
Commission ought to be appointed.' Conkling answered:
'Mr. President, Senator Morton is opposed to it and to
your efforts: but if you wish the Commission carried, I can
do it.' He said, 'I wish it done.'" The determination
of the Republican caucus to leave Mr. Conkling off the
Commission was extraordinary in view of the fact that he
was a member of the committee that framed the bill and
was the only Republican senator on the committee who
was omitted. He was not made a commissioner because
he was known to be in accord with President Grant and
to coincide with him in the conviction that the vote of
Louisiana rightfully belonged to Mr. Tilden.

It is to be accounted for that notwithstanding this personal conviction that Mr. Tilden was entitled to the election, General Grant should have allowed the influence of
his official position to be used to defeat the will of the
people. The explanation must be found in the unbounded
ascendency which he allowed those whom he believed to
be his friends, to exercise over him. Zachariah Chandler,
the chairman of the Republican National Committee who
was the inspirer of the most violent acts for reversing the

true result of the election, was General Grant's Secretary of the Interior. Mr. Cameron who was deeply involved in the conspiracy was General Grant's Secretary of War, and directed the military movements of the army in aid of the conspirators. Mr. Robeson who was interested in perpetuating the corrupt system by which he became so notorious, was General Grant's Secretary of the Navy.

These men carried with them the whole mass of the Republican party adverse to the opinion of the President, while the parasites who surrounded General Grant could not endure the prospect of terminating the system by which they were fattening. General Grant's personal convictions were smothered under the overwhelming influences which surrounded him.

It might seem incredible that General Grant could be so enthralled were it not for the concurrent testimony of his most intimate friends and supporters which is contained in the eulogiums and reminiscences published since his death.*

That General Grant was susceptible to the influences which surrounded him is the concurrent testimony of those who knew him best.   His acts frequently did not comport

* In the appendix a number of extracts from a great many reminiscences and eulogiums are given in support of the statements made in the text in regard to the influence that often controlled General Grant.   The following eminent gentlemen who were his intimate personal and political friends are quoted: Mr. George W. Childs, Hon. Hamilton Fish, Mr. Jesse Seligman, Hon. Chauncey Depew, Ex-Secretary Robeson, Hon. John A. Logan, Surgeon-General Gunnell of the U. S. Navy, and the following leading Republican newspapers, the New York *Tribune*, the New York *Independent*, the New York *Evening Post*, the Albany *Evening Journal*, the Philadelphia *Press*, the Phila. *Ledger*.   Mr. George W. Childs says: " He showed a great tenacity in sticking to friends longer than he ought to have done.   * * One of his expressions was, 'Never desert a friend under fire!'"   Mr. Jesse Seligman says: " He was so honest himself that he took the word of those about him as fact without question." Hon. Chauncey Depew says: " His great fault as President * * * was his selection of confidants in men."   Hon. John A. Logan says: " He was a most confiding man * * * such confidence * * * being the cause of all the serious trouble I ever knew him to have."

with that innate sense of justice and right which was ordi-
narily one of his most shining characteristics. This yield-
ing to the advice of those who had his confidence, without
thought of the motives which might actuate them, was
his conspicuous weakness. Those he liked were bound
to him by hooks of steel. The consequences of indiscrimi-
nating fidelity are often disagreeable and not infrequently
disastrous. General Grant was fond of attention and not
averse to flattery. He was readily responsive to the ap-
proaches of rich men. He had been very poor and had
borne the embarrassments of poverty with great manliness,
but he was crushed, broken when the possibility of ending
his days in penury actually stared him in the face. He
was a devoted husband and a fond father, and his family
was always first in his thoughts. His was not the metal of
the elder Brutus!

General Grant was no doubt reluctant to disappoint
his political friends. They exerted great influence over
him. But there was a point beyond which he would not
go. He often suffered them to have their own way and
frequently to very nearly compromise his personal honor
and official fame, but his good fortune and hard common
sense generally preserved him from the seemingly inevitable catastrophe. In the whisky frauds his confidence
was shamefully abused by those who owed everything to
him, and his blind confidence nearly involved him in their
dishonor. More than once his reputation was nearly
smirched by his apparently unreasoning faith in the unscrupulous members of the District of Columbia ring. He
would scarcely believe Belknap guilty when he confessed
and begged to be allowed to resign. Grief and affection
impelled him to grant a dishonored friend's petition without reflecting that thereby he shielded him from the right-

eous judgment of a high court of impeachment. He clung to Attorney General Williams despite the demands of outraged public opinion until feminine eccentricities forced a resignation which should have been demanded long previous. His confidence in, and adherence to, George M. Robeson is inexplicable save upon the unsafe rule, "never to desert a friend under fire," which Mr. George W. Childs says was one of his favorite expressions.

The belief of General Grant in the election of Mr. Tilden and his conviction that the electoral votes of Louisiana should have been given to him by the Electoral Commission, are strangely at variance with his approval of the extraordinary partisan conduct of Mr. Cameron, Secretary of War, in ordering troops to Florida and placing them at the disposal of Governor Stearns to be used, as they notoriously were, to assist in the consummation of the grossest frauds. The same is true of Cameron's orders to the commanding general in Louisiana. But when Grant's dispatches to General Sherman are analyzed in the succeeding chapter, it will be seen that while he yielded to the solicitations of his political friends and was willing to go very far in the employment of troops for political purposes, he was reasonably guarded in his orders to the general of the army.

The Republican politicians who were invited to go to Louisiana to witness the count of votes and observe the conduct of the Returning Board, did not observe his injunction "to see that the board of canvassers make a fair count of the votes actually cast." He did not rebuke their partisan and dishonest course. On the contrary, he seemingly approved the report they made justifying the outrageous and indefensible action of the Returning Board by transmitting it to the Senate. But was this an approval of the report or an endorsement of the conduct of its authors? The report and the accompanying ex-parte statements make a printed volume of several hundred pages. Did he read this mass of manuscript? Did he not consider himself merely the medium through whom it was to be transmitted to Congress? That body was in his judgment not only competent but bound to pass upon the evidence affecting the matters in dispute. The Executive was without any other power in the premises than moral influence and the weight of his great office.

General Grant specially requested W. E. Chandler to remain in Florida until the canvass was completed by the state canvassing board, and he did not publicly commend Francis C. Barlow of New York, the one solitary " visiting statesman " who conscientiously endeavored to act upon the instructions of the President " to see that the board of canvassers make a fair count of the votes actually cast." The manly, honest report Mr. Barlow made to the President, giving it as his deliberate judgment that Mr. Tilden was entitled to the electoral votes of Florida, was not sent to the Senate as was that submitted by John Sherman and his colleagues in justification of the monstrous Louisiana frauds.

The ordering of a large military force to Washington before the meeting of Congress, in December 1876, was denounced at the time by democrats and was doubtless believed by them to be an attempt to overawe and intimidate the representatives of the people. That this concentration of troops at the Federal capital had this effect is true. But the representatives of the people ought to have been made of sterner stuff, and in the language of that grand old patriot, Judge Black, ought not to have betrayed the rights of their constituents until the Federal soldiers actually made their appearance in hostile array at the door of the Hall of Representatives. Their ancestors in 1800 were not awed or intimidated by the threats or the preparations made by the federalists to defeat the election of Jefferson. The timidity, the base cowardice, of many Democratic members of Congress in 1876 was exhibited by their silly twaddle, their trembling expressions of fear about Grant arresting and incarcerating them at Fortress Monroe.

It is not my purpose to defend or to impeach the conduct of General Grant. His acts must speak for themselves. He was a silent and patient man, but to those in whom he had the most confidence he confided his convictions in regard to the fraud of 1876, and they have spoken. So far as Mr Childs is concerned it was not his fault that his statement was not published until after General Grant's death. It was prepared several weeks before General Grant died, with the expectation that it would be made public immediately.

The zeal of General Grant's friends to relieve his memory of the odium of participation in the Great Fraud is commendable. It is another evidence of the fact that connection with that monstrous crime, whether direct or indirect, has proved a veritable shirt of Nessus to all participants. A justice of the Supreme Court four days after being a party to the rendition of a partisan and unjust decision of the Electoral Commission in the Louisiana case was impelled, it is to be hoped by a troubled conscience, to write to a friend and express his regret that he could not see his way clear to decide so as "to cure what I fear was a great wrong of the Louisiana Returning Board." *

While Senator Morton maintained that the President

* See letter of Justice W. Strong to Geo. W. Jones, *McKnight's Electoral System of the United States, p.* 108.

of the Senate was the sole repository of judicial functions in counting the electoral votes, Mr. Conkling and a few other Republican senators in accordance with General Grant's wishes, insisted, as Morton had the year before, that the two Houses of Congress must determine whatever disputes might arise in the progress of the count. A select committee of seven was created by a resolution of the House of Representatives to act in conjunction with any similar committee appointed by the Senate, to prepare and report without delay a measure for the removal of differences of opinion as to the proper mode of counting the electoral votes for President and Vice-President of the United States and as to the manner of determining questions which might arise as to the legality and validity of the returns of such votes made by the several states, to the end that the votes should be counted and the result declared, "by a tribunal whose authority none can question and whose decision all will accept as final." This resolution was adopted on December 14, 1876, and on the 18th the Senate responded by creating a select committee composed of seven senators with power "to prepare and report, without unnecessary delay, such a measure, either of a legislative or other character, as may, in their judgment, be best calculated to accomplish the lawful counting of the electoral votes and best disposition of all questions connected therewith, and the true declaration of the result," and also with power "to confer and act with the committee of the House of Representatives." *

The committee thus provided for were on the part of the House, Henry B. Payne, of Ohio, Eppa Hunton, of Virginia, Abram S. Hewitt, of New York, William M. Springer, of Illinois, George W. McCreary, of Iowa, George F.

* Count of Electoral Votes, p. 3

Hoar, of Massachusetts, and George Williard, of Michigan ; and on the part of the Senate, George F. Edmunds, of Vermont, Oliver P. Morton, of Indiana, Frederick T. Frelinghuysen, of New Jersey, Roscoe Conkling, of New York, Allen G. Thurman, of Ohio, Thomas F. Bayard, of Delaware, and Matt. W. Ransom, of North Carolina.

The House committee having the initiative, it would naturally be presumed had a well-defined programme in view and a thoroughly digested and prepared measure ready. But this was not the case. The committee met, organized, and appointed a sub-committee, with William M. Springer as chairman, to prepare a history of Electoral Counts, a work which had already been performed and published by private enterprise. Weeks were dawdled away in this work of supererogation, and the only draft of a bill, which has survived, was one submitted by George W. McCreary, of Iowa, a republican, and which, singularly enough, provided, in express terms, that the commission created by it should go behind the returns, and examine into, and decide upon, the legality and rightfulness of the disputed electoral certificates.

In the meantime the Senate committee was at work, but there was no concert or consultation between, or among, the Democratic members of the two committees. There was absolutely no advice or consultation with the president-elect. A full month elapsed before the result of the House committee's deliberations was reached which was an informal agreement on the McCreary bill. It was not till January 13, 1877, that this inchoate measure was submitted to Mr. Tilden. Meanwhile the Senate committee had reached a conclusion, a Republican minority disagreeing, the Democratic senators, and Senators Edmunds and Conkling, uniting upon a measure drafted by Mr. Edmunds which was a revised edition of the bill of 1800, emasculated of its good provisions, and with all of its bad features retained and some new ones added. The Democratic senators who had given their assent to this revamped Federal device of 1800 not only had not taken into their confidence their fellow-democrats on the House committee, but they had refused to even hint to senatorial colleagues of the same political faith what the outcome of their deliberations was likely to be!

When the Senate committee had agreed upon a measure, which suited two republicans and three democrats, the House committee was invited to a conference. The joint meeting was held, and upon the democrats of the House committee objecting to the Senate committee's bill, the Democratic senators coolly informed them that they were irrevocably committed thereto and would stand by it. One provision they and their Republican colleagues subsequently consented to abandon, namely that which left the selection of the determining vote of the Commission to lot.

To contrast the Democratic leaders in the Congress of 1800 with those of 1876 would not be fair. Intellectually the latter were not comparable to the former. They lacked, also, the convictions, the courage, the experience, and above all the disinterestedness, of their great predecessors. The appointment of the committee of December 14, 1876, by the House of Representatives was a mistake. The proposition embodied in the resolution of that date to create "a tribunal whose authority none can question and whose decision all will accept as final" was an absurdity, as well as an impossibility. The Democratic majority in the House of Representatives ought to have taken its stand upon the Constitution and maintained its position at all hazards. Later it constituted a committee on the powers and privileges of the

House of Representatives in counting the electoral votes. It is a woful pity that this was not done earlier. That committee, on January 12, 1877, reported resolutions affirmative of the coequal powers of the House of Representatives in the counting of the electoral votes and denying the proposed assumption of power by the President of the Senate to determine in regard to disputed returns, and to count the votes as he saw proper. Here was a modest and moderate declaration of constitutional powers and rights on the part of the House and the issue should have been forced. But before these resolutions could, under the rules of the House, be called up for debate, and the great battle for the right begun, the Senate and House committees agreed upon the Electoral Commission.

The strangest thing, probably, that ever occurred in political history was the acceptance by Democratic senators and Representatives of the rehabilitated Federal device of 1800 to count out the candidates the people had selected and to count in the ones the people had repudiated. It was an exhibition of moral cowardice, of political degeneracy, and ignorance of the history of American politics, which ought to cause every intelligent and self-respecting democrat to hang his head in shame! The Electoral-commission bill, modelled on the one of 1800 by Senator Edmunds, did not provide, as that one did, that the constitutional qualifications of the electors for President and Vice-President should be inquired into, examined, decided, and reported upon. The reason for this departure from the original model will appear hereafter.* Instead of the Chief Justice being selected as a presiding officer with a casting vote as in the bill of 1800 four associate justices were taken, two democrats and two republicans, who were to select a fifth.

* See post decisions of Electoral Commission on eligibility of Electors.

The bait held out to the Democratic gudgeons was the possibility of Justice Davis being selected as the fifth judge. Their Republican adversaries were far better informed than they in regard to the character of Judge Davis. Under no possible circumstances could he have been induced to accept. A more honest, upright, and conscientious man never lived and one more averse to assuming political responsibility. It was a constitutional characteristic. On the bench he always sought to evade a square decision if a political question was involved, and an opportunity to dodge the main issue was invariably embraced by him. Happily for Judge Davis, and greatly to the chagrin of the democrats, just as the Electoral-commission bill became a law, enough so-called independent republicans in the Illinois legislature joined with the Democratic members thereof to elect him to the United States Senate. This furnished Judge Davis the excuse, he was longing for, to decline the proffered place on the Electoral Commission. Mr. Justice Bradley was selected as the fifth judge.

The Florida case was the first to be referred to the Electoral Commission, the law providing that the certificates of the electoral votes should be canvassed in the alphabetical order of the states. There were two important questions involved in this case: first, the honesty, the rightfulness, and the legality of the action of the Returning Board in returning as duly chosen, and the governor in certifying the appointment of the Republican electors for that state; and, second, as to whether, Frederick C. Humphreys, one of the electors, so returned and certified, was, under the Constitution, eligible, he being a Federal officeholder at the time and disqualified by Article ii, Sec. i, Paragraph 2, which says, that no "person holding an office of trust or profit under the United States, shall be appointed an elector." The Commission avoided the first issue by deciding eight to seven "that it is not competent under the Constitution and the law, as it existed at the date of the passage of said act, to go into evidence *aliunde* the papers opened by the President of the Senate in the presence of the two Houses to prove that other persons than those regularly certified to by the Governor of the State of Florida, in and according to the determination and declaration of their appointment by the board of state canvassers of said state prior to the time required for the performance of their duties, had been appointed electors, or by counter proof to show that they had not, and that all proceedings of the courts or acts of the legislature or of the executive of Florida subsequent to the casting of the votes of the electors on the prescribed day, are inadmissable for any such purpose."*

Now witness the self-stultification of the Commission in its next solemn utterance!

" As to the objection made to the eligibility of Mr. Humphreys, the Commission is of the opinion that, without reference to the question of the effect of the vote of an ineligible elector, *the evidence* does not show that he held the office of shipping-commissioner on the day when the electors were appointed."*

First, they *decide* that it is not competent for them " to go into evidence *aliunde* the papers opened by the President of the Senate in the presence of the two Houses," that is to say the certificates of the electors: and second, they *admit* that they *did go* into evidence *aliunde* the certificates to prove that Mr. Humphreys was not ineligible! Was there ever a more monstrous perversion of justice self-confessed by a tribunal of eminent and would-be respectable

* Electoral Count, p. 196.

judges, senators, and representatives, sworn on the Holy
Evangelists to "impartially examine and consider all questions submitted, . . . and a true judgment give thereon,
agreeably to the Constitution and the laws !"

Again, notice that they leave undecided in the case of
Humphreys " the question of the effect of the vote of an
ineligible elector." That is to say at that time they had not
made up their minds whether the exact unqualified language
of the Constitution of the United States prohibiting the appointment of a "person holding an office of trust or profit
under the United States " was a bar to counting an electoral
vote or not. In the case of Humphreys they had admitted
proof *aliunde* the certificate to show that he was fit, but it
was probable that there might be some other cases where
the electors might be proved to be ineligible and, therefore,
they reserved their judgment. It required every vote to
which the democrats, on the face of the papers, did not
have an incontestable right, to elect Hayes and Wheeler,
and as they had undertaken the job of counting them in
they did not mean to allow a constitutional prohibition to
stand in the way of accomplishing their undertaking.

When the Louisiana case was reached the partisan majority of the Commission had come to the conclusion that
they could not apply the same principles laid down in the
Florida case. Accordingly, they held " that it is not competent to prove that any of said persons so appointed electors as aforesaid held an office of trust or profit under the
United States at the time when they were appointed, or that
they were ineligible under the laws of the state, or any
other matter offered to be proved *aliunde* the said certificate
and papers."*

* Electoral Count, p. 422.

In this case they endeavored to be consistent and were bold enough to decide that it did not matter whether an elector was disqualified by the Constitution of the United States or that of the State of Louisiana, his vote must be counted anyhow.

Let us examine briefly this decision as to eligibility of electors. The Constitution of the United States concedes to the states representatives in the electoral college equal to the number of their senators and representatives in Congress. But at the same time it absolutely prohibits the appointment by the state of senators and representatives or óther persons holding offices of trust or profit under the United States. The object of this prohibition is apparent. It was to preserve " the purity and freedom " of the electoral college from any possible contamination from the presence of Federal office-holders who might be influenced by their positions under the general government. Moreover, as the fact of the holding of offices of profit or trust under the United States must be notorious there was no necessity of proving that persons held them. The Congress of the United States is as much bound to take notice of the fact of the appointment of persons to office in a case of this kind as it would be to take notice that George F. Edmunds was a Senator of the United States or Joseph Bradley an associate Justice of the Supreme Court of the United States. The people of a state might elect, and the executive authority certify the election of a person who held an office of trust or profit under the United States ignorantly, but, nevertheless, that person so elected and certified, being disqualified, the state must inevitably forfeit that electoral vote. The proposition is plain and simple. The prohibition would not have been inserted in the Constitution if the framers thereof had not intended it to be absolute. They did not insert meaningless or superfluous words in that instrument, much less whole phrases.

Two of the electors returned by the Returning Board as chosen were disqualified by the Constitution of the United States, A. B. Levissee and O. H. Brewster, the one being United States Commissioner and the other Surveyor General of the United States Land Office for the State of Louisiana. They resigned their offices temporarily, absented themselves for a short time from the meeting of the electors, and were substituted for themselves by their colleagues, and then appeared, took part in the proceedings, and voted for Hayes and Wheeler. O. H. Brewster was immediately thereafter reappointed Surveyor General, and Levissee reassumed the functions of United States Commissioner. It is clear, therefore, that the disqualifications of these men could not be removed by their farce of resigning the Federal offices they held.* The question was raised before the Commission that electors for President and Vice-President, being appointed by the states, might be held to be state officers. If they were, then four more of the men, returned by the Returning Board as electors, were disqualified under the constitution of Louisiana, which provides, that "no person shall at the same time hold more than one office." Kellogg was de facto governor of the state, Peter Josephs, J. Henri Burch, and Morris Marks were also officers of the state.

---

* During the count of the electoral votes in 1837 the question of the eligibility of electors was considered by a Senate committee composed of Henry Clay, Silas Wright, and Felix Grundy, who reported that, "The committee are of opinion that the second section of the second article of the Constitution, which declares that 'no senator or representative, or person holding an office of trust or profit under the United States shall be appointed an elector,' ought to be carried in its whole spirit into rigid execution. * * * This provision of the Constitution, it is believed, *excludes* and disqualifies deputy postmasters from the *appointment* of electors ; and the disqualification relates to the *time of appointment*, and that a resignation of the office of deputy postmaster after his appointment as elector, *would not entitle him to vote as elector, under the Constitution.*"

The Commission also decided "that the returning-officers of elections who canvassed the votes at the election for electors in Louisiana were a legally constituted body, by virtue of a constitutional law, and that a vacancy in said body did not vitiate its proceedings." The constitution of Louisiana article 48 prescribes who the returning-officers of elections shall be — to wit: the officers of elections at the different polling places throughout the state. Senator Edmunds on the 16th of March, 1875, declared in the Senate in unequivocal language that the election law creating the Returning Board was in conflict with the constitution of the state. And yet Mr. Commissioner Edmunds on February 16, 1876, voted that the election law of Louisiana creating the Returning Board was not in conflict with the constitution of that state. Representative George F. Hoar made a report to the House of Representatives in 1875 in which he used the following language in regard to the Louisiana Returning Board's conduct in the election of 1874 — "we are all clearly of the opinion that the Returning Board had no right to do anything except to canvass and compile the returns which were lawfully made to them by the local officers, except in cases where they were accompanied by the certificates of the supervisor or commissioner provided in the third section.* Hereafter it will be shown how much more grossly the Returning Board violated the law in 1876 than in 1874, and yet Mr. Commissioner Hoar voted February 16, 1876, that the presidential electors returned as elected by that Returning Board must be accepted as legally elected.

When the Oregon case came before the Electoral Commission the Republican majority had to reverse themselves again and make law to suit the necessity of the occasion.

* H. R. Mis. Doc. No. 261 43d Cong. 2nd Sess. p. 21.

It has been seen that in the Florida case the Commission decided that it was not competent to go into evidence *aliunde* the certificates although they had gone into evidence to show that Frederick C. Humphreys, a Republican elector, at the time of his appointment, did not hold an office of trust or profit under the United States. And, again, that in the Louisiana case they had held that it was not necessary to prove that an elector did not hold an office of trust or profit under the United States, and that the vote of an ineligible elector must be counted the Constitution of the United States to the contrary notwithstanding. It would seem at first glance that these diverse rulings ought to have been sufficient to cover the Oregon case. They were not, because, it was necessary, in order to bring in the Florida and Louisiana electoral votes for Hayes and Wheeler, that the Commission should hold that the persons "regularly certified to by the governor of the state, and according to the determination of their appointment by the returning officers" were the legal electors.* And if this ruling was adhered to in the Oregon case it would compel the counting of one electoral vote of that state for Tilden and Hendricks which would give them the requisite 185 votes and make them President and Vice-President of the United States.

The returning officers of Oregon were, under the law, the Secretary of State and the Governor. J. W. Watts, one of the Republican candidates for presidential elector, was a postmaster at the time of his election and therefore disqualified under the Constitution of the United States. The Secretary of State held that a disqualified person could not be chosen to an office, and therefore certified that his opponent, who had received a less number of votes, was elected. The Governor coincided and the certificate of election, or appoint-

* Electoral Count, p. 422.

ment, was given to E. A. Cronin, a Tilden elector. Cronin
gave his vote for Tilden and Hendricks in due form and forwarded one copy of his certificate to that fact to the President
of the Senate, deposited another with the judge of the United
States district court, and carried the third to Washington
and delivered it to the President of the Senate. He had
needlessly gone through the form of organizing an electoral
college which neither the Constitution nor the laws of the
United States require, and for that purpose had appointed
two persons to act with him. Nevertheless, his vote for
Samuel J. Tilden, for President, and for Thomas A. Hendricks, for Vice-President, was regularly before the two
Houses of Congress and was, according·to the decision of
the Commission in the Florida and Louisiana cases,
a legal vote and should have been so determined and
counted.*

But the Commission found a way out of the dilemma by
deciding " that the secretary of state did canvass the returns
in the case before us, and thereby ascertained that J. C.
Cartwright, W. H. Odell, and J. W. Watts had a majority
of all the votes given for electors, and had the highest number of votes for that office, and by the express language of
the statute those persons are ' deemed elected.' " And they
further held " that the refusal or failure of the Governor of
Oregon to sign the certificate of the election of the persons

* " By the statute of Oregon, the process of appointing an elector is a
series of steps, from the ballot-box up to the certification by the Governor and
Secretary of State ; these steps are specifically described, and there is no
act, prior to the last, at which the appointment is declared to be complete.
* * * In judging such a case the Commission precluded themselves from
any interference with such a lawfully-appointed elector by their acceptance
of the fraudulent returns of the Louisiana returning officers, and by their
decision in the Louisiana case, above quoted that ' it is not competent to
prove that other persons than those regularly certified to by the governor
of the state, and according to the determination of their *appointment* by the
returning officers for elections, were appointed electors.' "
McKnights Electoral System of the United States, pp. 106-7.

so elected does not have the effect of defeating their appointment as such electors."*

In making this decision the Commission suppressed facts, misstated the law of Oregon, and were guilty *suggestionis falsi*. They failed to state that the secretary of state certified to the governor that E. A. Cronin had been elected and that J. W. Watts had not; they misquoted the law by not stating that the secretary of state and the governor constitute the returning officers and they had held, in the Louisiana case, that an elector is not appointed in the language of the Constitution until he has received the certificate of the governor " according to the determination of... appointment by the returning officers." They suggested a falsehood by so wording their decision as to leave the impression that the secretary of state had certified to the governor that Watts was elected.

Notwithstanding the rule laid down by the Commission that evidence *aliunde* the certificates was not competent, the evidence of the Postmaster-General was taken to show that Watts had resigned his place as postmaster.

If receiving " the highest number of votes " was, as the Commission held in this case, evidence that the electors were to be " deemed elected " how about the Democratic electors of Florida and Louisiana ? The former had a clear majority of 91 over their opponents, and the latter nearly 8000 majority ! But is it not needless to indicate further the inconsistencies, the perversions of law, and the self-confessed stultifications of the partisan majority of the Electoral Commission ? There were in all nine Republican electors who were disqualified by the Constitution of the United States—they being Federal office-holders. In only the cases of Florida, Louisiana, and Oregon could the question of

* Electoral Count, p. 640.

the eligibility be brought before the Commission and in each the decision was radically different.*

Let us now turn to the preliminary scenes in this drama of fraud and follow step by step the conspiracy to nullify the will of the people which resulted in the crime of the Century.

---

* Three of the Republican members of the Electoral Commission were constrained by public opinion to make at different times a defense of the extraordinary decisions of the partisan majority. Mr. Justice Strong frankly admitted that he feared that a great wrong had been done in the Louisiana case. Mr. Justice Bradley claimed that he had serious doubts in the Florida case and asserted that he wrote and rewrote several opinions. He, however, came to the conclusion that the act of a sovereign state expressed through the regularly constituted authorities thereof having jurisdiction of the matter could not be inquired into by Congress or in other words that evidence *aliunde* the governor's certificate could not be taken by the Electoral Commission which merely exercised such powers as the two Houses of Congress possessed. Mr. Commissioner Hoar based his defense upon the same grounds and insisted that the determination of the Commission maintained the sovereignty of the states in its true consitutional sense, and claimed that this assertion and maintenance of state rights would stand as a bulwark against the natural tendency toward centralization of power in Congress. But it is noteworthy that not one of the Republican members of the Commission have attempted to explain and reconcile the manifest inconsistencies of the different rulings of that body. It is also worthy of note that no defense of the rightfulness of the decisions has been attempted. The justifications which have been essayed are based upon purely technical grounds. The fact that three of the majority have been constrained to attempt a defense of their conduct shows that they recognize the rightfulness of the popular condemnation of their acts. Mr. Justice Miller admitted with Mr. Justice Strong that the ballots in the boxes in Louisiana elected the Tilden electors, but he did not go so far as his colleague did and concede the probable commission of a great wrong by the Returning Board in counting in the Hayes electors.

The Republican leaders being compelled to accept the dictum of General Grant and agree to an Electoral Commission won in the end by the sacrifice of their consciences. It was not a very great sacrifice.

CHAPTER III.

The conspiracy hatched: The preliminary preparations by W. E. Chandler: The emissaries from the departments at Washington: Hayes admitted his defeat after Zach. Chandler claimed his election: The situation in Florida: The canvassing board without judicial powers: The talk with President Grant over Jay Gould's private wire: The orders issued to the military: Grant's dispatches analyzed: The Republican visiting statesmen disregarded the President's instructions: They prevented a fair count of the votes actually cast.

On the night of Tuesday, November 7th, 1876, tidings of disasters came from every quarter to the rooms of the National Republican Committee in the Fifth Avenue Hotel, New York City. Long before the dawn of the succeeding morning the members of the committee and the throng of anxious inquirers had sought repose with the conviction that their party had met its Waterloo. Just after the last of the managers had left William E. Chandler arrived from New Hampshire.* He found only a few clerks in the committee rooms, who quickly told him what the situation seemed to be. The chairman, the secretary, everybody, had gone away believing that victory perched on the banners of their adversaries. Mr. Chandler took up the dispatches and read them through. The outlook was indeed desperate.

---

* " I wish to state here that when I arrived at the Fifth Avenue Hotel before daylight on the morning of the 8th of November, I found the committee rooms vacant; everybody had gone to bed. There was no one at the hotel (meaning the committee rooms) except a clerk." W. E. Chandler's testimony, H. R. Mis. Doc. No. 21, 45th Cong., 3d Sess. p 527.

Later telegrams only confirmed the earlier bad news.   The only comforting account came from the New York *Times* office, which was to the effect that the democrats claimed as absolutely certain but 184 electoral votes.   But on the other hand Chandler could only figure out for Hayes 166 electoral votes.   There were 369 electors and if the democrats were certain of 184 they only needed one more to give them a majority of all the electoral votes.   The republicans only having sure 166 required nineteen votes to make a majority.

It was clear that the nineteen votes must come from Florida, Louisiana, and South Carolina.   Here then was the opportunity to retrieve disaster.   Chandler's plan of operations was instantly conceived and the execution thereof immediately begun.   He dictated and had sent in his own name and in that of the Chairman, Zach Chandler, dispatches to the governors* of Florida, Louisiana, and South Carolina which inspired them with hope but left no doubt that upon the result of the counting in their respective states the seating of Hayes depended.   These were followed by other telegrams of like import to men in the same states. Before noon the next day the news from the Pacific

---

* The following were the dispatches — to Florida — "The presidential election depends on the vote of Florida, and the democrats will try and wrest it from us.   Watch it and hasten returns.   Answer immediately" — Also — " Hayes defeated without Florida.   Do not be cheated in returns.   Answer when sure."

To Louisiana — " The presidential election depends on the vote of Louisiana, and the democrats will try and wrest it from you.   Watch it and hasten returns.   Answer immediately."

To South Carolina — " Hayes is elected if we have carried South Carolina, Florida, and Louisiana.   Can you hold your state?   Answer immediately."

These dispatches bear date Nov. 7, but W. E. Chandler testified to the Potter committee that they were " really written and sent on the morning of the 8th."   He arrived at the Fifth Avenue Hotel after midnight of the 7th.

H. R. Mis. Doc. No. 31, 45th *Cong.* 3d *Sess. p.* 526, *also No.* 42 *Mis. Doc.* 44th *Cong.* 2d *Sess. of H. R., p.* 434.

coast confirmed the dispatches of the previous night which said California and Nevada had been carried by the democrats.

When Zach. Chandler, and others, who had left the night before dispirited and hopeless, returned to the committee rooms the next morning they found W. E. Chandler, who quickly explained the situation and outlined his scheme. It was in brief, first, to unequivocally claim the election of Hayes and persist in claiming it; second, bold and skilful men, who could be depended on under all circumstances, must be immediately sent to Florida, Louisiana, and South Carolina; third, ample means must be provided for all contingencies; fourth, communication must be opened with the President and Secretary of War as soon as possible and ample protection by the military secured for the Returning Boards. The New York *Times* had, at his suggestion, that morning claimed the election of Hayes and Wheeler on the assertion that Florida, Louisiana, and South Carolina had been carried by the republicans.

Mr. Chandler proposed to take charge of the work in Florida, and to go thither at once. A credit must be opened for him at the Centennial Bank of Philadelphia,* whose officers were his friends and could be trusted to keep accounts which would not prove troublesome in the future. He selected Florida as the scene of his operations because he knew the powers of the board of canvassers of that state were simply ministerial and great delicacy and ingenuity of management, as well as bold, decisive conduct might be required to accomplish their purposes. In Louisiana and South Carolina there were many bold, unscrupulous, and resourceful men who might be relied on in any emergency, provided they were encouraged by the presence of promi-

* H. R. Mis. Doc. No. 31, 45th Cong. 3d Sess. p. 471.

nent northern republicans who could speak authoritatively of the future, and provided, also, the authorities in Washington spoke in no uncertain tones and emphasized their utterances with the proper display of military power.

Zachariah Chandler was bold and unscrupulous, if not resourceful. If his lethargic mind could not have originated the scheme so quickly devised by the more active brain of the New Hampshire Chandler, it could comprehend all the details. A man of tremendous energy and perfect fearlessness, Zach. Chandler would not have hesitated if the undertaking had embraced the nullification of the expressed will of the people of a dozen instead of only three states. As the members of the National committee and the local party managers of New York City gathered at the headquarters, Wednesday, they were informed of the exigencies of the situation, and the desperate measures necessary to bring Mr. Hayes in. The chairman had promptly sent the famous but untruthful dispatch, to which he undeviatingly adhered, "Hayes has 185 electoral votes and is elected." That day and night the arrangements for men and means to be sent to Florida, Louisiana, and South Carolina were made, and before Thursday evening they were on their way. W. E. Chandler left Wednesday night for Florida, and from Lynchburg, Va., wrote the following letter to Zach. Chandler under cover to M. A. Clancy:*

"THE ARLINGTON,

"*Lynchburg, Va.*, Nov. 9, 1876.

"My Dear Sir: Please think over and guard every possible contingency in all the states. Ascertain what the laws of every Hayes

H. R. Mis. Doc. No. 31, 45th Cong. 3d Sess. p. 526.

state are about vacancies. There is danger of some form being neglected, especially in Oregon, which is so far away, and has a Democratic governor. Will Senator Edmunds give his best thought to this
subject and notify every Hayes state what precautions to adopt — to
search their state laws carefully and obey them literally ?

"Colorado must be specially looked after, and the danger of bribery
of the legislature guarded against.

"I got delayed over night and shall omit Raleigh, but want to see
Chamberlain about Oranges before eating the latter. [Florida before
reaching there.] I will telegraph Clancy, and will sign 'Everett
Chase' and you may telegraph me same way, care the governors, and
sign Clancy, and not Z. C., *and don't telegraph unless necessary.* Remember Crapsey was to telegraph J. J. Ridenour, 5th Ave. You left
that off the cipher."

Thomas J. Brady,* with a force of special agents of the
Post-office Department, followed Mr. Chandler, bearing also
a sum of money for immediate use. The Department of
Justice ordered its available detectives to report to Chandler at the earliest moment in Tallahassee. William A.
Cook, of Washington, at Chandler's suggestion, was sent to
Columbia, South Carolina, to overlook operations at that
point, and messengers were dispatched to New Orleans,
bearing sinews of war, and intelligence that representative
men would follow immediately. There was absolute silence
preserved about these movements. The telegraph was resorted to only in cases of necessity, as W. E. Chandler had
advised.

The reiterated dispatch of Zach. Chandler, "Hayes
has 185 electoral votes and is elected" was interpreted
by Hayes himself as without serious significance. In
an interview published in the Cincinnati papers,† Thursday

* H. R. Mis. Doc. No. 31, Part 4, 45th Cong. 3d Sess. p. 59.
† N. Y. Sun, Nov. 9, 1876. Dispatch from Cincinnati.

morning, the defeated candidate said : " I think we are defeated in spite of recent good news. I am of the opinion
that the democrats have carried the country and elected
Tilden, as it now seems necessary for the republicans to
carry all the states, not set down as doubtful, to secure even
a majority of one. I don't think encouraging dispatches
ought to be given to the public now, because, they might
mislead enthusiastic friends to bet on the election and lose
their money. I do heartily deprecate these dispatches."

Although Mr. Hayes indulged in some hypocritical utterances about his sorrow for the fate of " the poor colored
men of the South," whom he so readily abandoned later, to
secure the presidency, he was, doubtless, sincere when he
admitted in this interview his defeat and deprecated the
dispatches coming from the chairman of the National committee. At that time he did not know and probably did
not dream of the object the desperate party leaders had in
view.

It was an undertaking from which timid men would
have shrunk with fear, and which honorable men would
have contemplated with horror. It was absolutely known,
Thursday evening, that the people of Florida, and Louisiana, had chosen Democratic electors. Therefore, the will of
the people must be disregarded. The result determined by
the constitutional methods at the polls must be reversed. In
Louisiana the machinery, provided.by an alien and wholly
irresponsible government might be abused for this unholy
purpose. The election law, enacted in defiance of the State
Constitution to enable a few scoundrels to continue their
corrupt and detestable rule, prescribed certain methods
by which the people might be disfranchised. Unless these
were strictly observed the Returning Board, as will be seen
hereafter, could not *legally* reject a single vote which had

been returned by the election officers. However, the Returning Board was composed of desperate men who would scruple at nothing, provided, they were protected, and assured of adequate rewards.

In Florida the situation was altogether different. The board of state canvassers was not vested with discretionary powers. Their duties, plainly prescribed by law, were simply ministerial. They could not legally do anything but canvass the returns as the county returning officers forwarded them and declare the result. A majority of the board of canvassers were republicans. They were known to be weak men, but were supposed to be fairly honest.

It was of the utmost importance to the conspirators that they should have the countenance and apparent support of the President of the United States. They knew the weight the name of General Grant would have with the Republican masses and the encouragement and confidence it would give to the men in Florida, South Carolina, and Louisiana upon whose active and unscrupulous coöperation the success of their scheme depended.

The President was in Philadelphia attending the closing ceremonies of the great exhibition which had been held in commemoration of the centennial anniversary of the Declaration of Independence. The Secretary of War was also in Philadelphia. There was no doubt of his readiness to coöperate in any undertaking to maintain his party in power. His political training had fitted him for desperate enterprises of this kind. He had the confidence of General Grant and exerted a potent influence with him. Mr. George W. Childs has discovered to us the fact that " an eminent Republican senator " and other " leading republicans" were early at his office to meet General Grant the morning after the election, and the unanimity with which they, "notwithstanding the returns" insisted that Hayes was elected. Grant, Mr. Childs asserts did not agree to this, but contented himself with merely expressing a negative opinion. Undoubtedly this expression of General Grant's opinion was quickly communicated to the chairman of the National Republican Committee in New York. It is certain that on the following day there was great perturbation manifested by the Republican managers gathered at the Fifth Avenue Hotel. It was deemed of the utmost importance that George F. Edmunds, Zachariah Chandler, Chester A. Arthur, and Alonzo B. Cornell should have safe means of communicating with the President and the Secretary of War in Philadelphia.

It would have attracted attention and excited suspicion if a meeting between the party managers and the President and the Secretary of War had taken place at this time either in Philadelphia or New York. It would not do to use the wires of any telegraph company, because, a tell-tale record might be left behind. Moreover, it would not be safe to trust unknown telegraphers. How was the difficulty to be overcome? George F. Edmunds had long been the confidential adviser of Jay Gould. He knew that a private wire connected Gould's house with Philadelphia. It would be easy to connect that wire with one running into the Continental Hotel where the President and the Secretary of War could meet. This was done and the necessary preliminaries arranged for a confidential talk between the conspirators gathered at Jay Gould's house in New York and the President and Secretary of War in Philadelphia.

The first and most important thing was to secure the fullest possible coöperation of the President. In this work Senator Edmunds was an invaluable agent. After Senator Conkling probably no other man could have exerted more influence with the President. The situation was carefully and ingeniously explained and the utmost stress was laid upon the conditions of affairs in Florida, Louisiana, and South Carolina. The imminent danger not only of an outbreak was dwelt upon, but it was doubtless insisted that the lives of the Republican canvassers would not be safe unless an overwhelming force of Federal troops were present to awe the turbulent populace and restrain daring Democratic leaders. It was urged that gentlemen of high political standing and eminent personal respectability ought to be invited to go to the capitals of the different states to secure a fair count of the votes. It is not to be wondered at that the President under these circumstances should have accorded all that was asked by his party friends. The responses from the President were satisfactory and that very night the following orders were issued.*

"PHILADELPHIA, Nov. 9, 1876, 10:40 P. M.
To Gen. W. T. Sherman,
Washington, D. C.

Order four companies of soldiers to Tallahassee, Fla., at once. Take them from the nearest points, not from Louisiana or Mississippi, and direct that they be moved with as little delay as possible.

J. D. CAMERON, *Secretary of War.*"

"PHILADELPHIA, Nov. 9, 1876, 11 P. M.
To Gen. W. T. Sherman,
Washington, D. C.

In addition to the four companies ordered to Tallahassee, order all troops in Florida to the same point, and if you haven't more than the companies named, draw from Alabama and South Carolina. Advise me of receipt of this and your action.

J. D. CAMERON, *Secretary of War.*"

"PHILADELPHIA, Nov. 9, 1876, 11:15 P. M.
To Gen. W. T. Sherman,
Washington, D. C.

Telegraph General Ruger to proceed at once to Tallahassee, Fla.,

* Ex. Doc. No. 30, H. R. 44th Cong. 2d Sess. pp. 22, 23.

and upon his arrival there to communicate with Gov. Stearns. Say to him to leave affairs in South Carolina in hands of an entirely discreet and reliable officer.

J. D. CAMERON, Secretary of War."

These orders were obeyed and the Secretary of War was informed of their execution. The next day the President telegraphed Gen. Sherman as follows: *

" PHILADELPHIA, Nov. 10, 1876.

[Received at Washington, Nov. 10, 1876, 2:16 P. M.]

To Gen. W. T. Sherman,

Washington, D. C.

Instruct Gen. Augur in Louisiana and Gen. Ruger in Florida to be vigilant with the force at their command to preserve peace and good order, and to see that the proper and legal boards of canvassers are unmolested in the performance of their duties. Should there be any grounds of suspicion of fraudulent counting on either side, it should be reported and denounced at once. No man worthy of the office of President would be willing to hold the office if counted in, placed there by fraud; either party can afford to be disappointed in the result, but the country cannot afford to have the result tainted by the suspicion of illegal or false returns.

U. S. GRANT."

This order to Gen. Sherman was intended for the public and was given forthwith to the press. The President was evidently anxious to satisfy the public that he would not be a party to "fraudulent counting." He concluded that he had not expressed exactly his idea and therefore sent from the Centennial Grounds the following dispatch to Gen. Sherman:

" PHILA., Nov. 10, 1876

[Received at Washington, Nov. 10, '76, 2:12 P. M.]

To Gen. W. T. Sherman,

Washington, D. C.

Send all the troops to General Augur he may deem necessary to ensure entire quiet and a peaceable count of the ballots actually cast.

* Ex. Doc. No. 30, 44th Cong. 2d Sess. p. 24.

They may be taken from South Carolina unless there is reason to expect an outbreak there. The presence of citizens from other states, I understand, is requested in Louisiana, *to see that the board of canvassers make a fair count of the votes actually cast.* It is to be hoped that representatives and fair men of both parties will go.

U. S. GRANT."

The Federal troops in South Carolina * had, two weeks before the November election, been increased by ordering thither every available man on the Atlantic seaboard from Fort Monroe northward—making in all thirty-three companies stationed in different parts of that state. Ten of these companies, with two from Atlanta, Georgia, with Gen. Ruger in command, were sent to Florida, under orders to act in conjunction with Governor Stearns. Three full regiments had already been ordered to New Orleans before the last dispatch to General Sherman was sent by the President.† The two telegrams of the President of November 10, to General Sherman were not in accordance with the arrangement made the preceding night over Jay Gould's private wire. Their language shows that Grant was endeavoring to guard against some apprehended excess of zeal. Their tone is confirmatory of Mr. Child's statement about Grant's belief in Tilden's election. The commanding generals were directed, first: " to see that the proper and legal boards of canvassers are unmolested in the performance of their duties." Second: " should there be any grounds of suspicion of fraudulent counting, on either side, it should be reported and denounced at once." The first direction could be carried out easily enough.

There was no danger whatever of the " boards of can-

---

* Ex. Doc. No. 30, H. R. 44th Cong. 2d Sess. pp. 17, 18, 19, 20, 21, 22.

† Ibid, p. 27.

vassers " being molested in the performance of their duties. General Sheridan,* who was ordered to New Orleans, arrived there on the 15th and reported on the 16th that there was " very little excitement" and " no appearance of any trouble." It was of course entirely within the scope of executive authority to have instructed General Augur in Louisiana and General Ruger in Florida, in the event of an outbreak, to coöperate with the local authorities " to preserve peace and good order." No other use of the Federal troops was justifiable, and in strict compliance with law even that could not be ordered until the† governors of the respective states had reported that they were unable to preserve the peace and protect all classes of citizens against domestic violence, unlawful combinations or conspiracies.

But how were the commanding generals to discover whether there were "any grounds of suspicion of fraudulent counting on either side," and to whom were they to report and denounce it? The counting was to be done by the Canvassing Boards. In Louisiana the canvassers were without exception republicans, and in Florida only one was a democrat. How could the commanding generals ascertain whether there were any "grounds of suspicion of fraudulent counting" unless they had been directed to supervise the reception, as well as the canvass-

* Ex. Doc. No. 30, H. R. 44th Cong. 2nd Sess. p. 41.
† The only dispatch asking for troops came from Governor Stearns of Florida, on November 9th, and was as follows: " We shall need an army to protect us. Our special train, leaving here last night for the Chattahoochee to dispatch couriers to verify and secure intact the returns from western counties, was ku-kluxed a few miles west of here, and the train thrown from the track, which was torn up and blocked in several places. Give us quickly all the protection possible." This dispatch was sent to Philadelphia to the President by Geo. W. Childs, who also informed him of the consultation to be held that night over Jay Gould's private wire. The statement about special train being ku-kluxed was a lie. There were no obstructions on the track. It was merely an ordinary accident on a Florida railroad which was in bad condition at that time. *Mis. Doc. No. 42,* 44th *Cong.* 2d *Sess. p.* 435-6.

ing, of the returns? But this would have cast suspicion upon the integrity of the Returning Boards. Was this not the object of the President's semi-military orders? "A fair count of the votes actually cast," was precisely what the conspirators did not want. Fair and honest returns of the "votes actually cast" would have made Samuel J. Tilden the next President of the United States. Before the President's remarkable dispatches were sent to General Sherman the polls had been closed two whole days and the returns "of the votes actually cast," save from remote counties and parishes, in Florida and Louisiana, were in Tallahassee and New Orleans. There was, therefore, no possibility of "fraudulent counting" unless it was done by the Returning Boards.

The direction to report and denounce at once "grounds of suspicion of fraudulent counting on either side" did not embarrass the visiting statesmen. They were determined to interpret to suit themselves the President's instructions. The further declaration that "no man worthy of the office of President would be willing to hold the office if counted in, placed there by fraud" was without other meaning to average politicians than high sounding words intended to deceive the public and cloak evil designs.

The intention was to use the machinery of the Returning Boards to return as elected the Republican electors of Florida, Louisiana, and South Carolina, regardless "of the votes actually cast." No fear was entertained of this not being done in Louisiana and South Carolina. The character of the Republican officials in those states was known. They could be depended upon, if properly "protected" and adequately "encouraged." The "encouragement" was *en route* and the action of the President and Secretary of War left no doubt as to their coöperation by the use of the army. In Florida the conditions were less favorable. There were doubts as to the powers of the Returning Board as well as to the dependence to be placed in the members thereof.* But the troops were on hand, and so was W. E. Chandler. The sinews of war were coming.

The Secretary of War telegraphed personally to Governor Stearns informing him that "a sufficient number of troops have been ordered to Tallahassee to give you the aid desired."† This language was, of course, deliberately used. It is important, because it shows that the troops were sent to "aid" and not because there was need of "protection." At the same time, Zach. Chandler had telegraphed to Stearns† that W. E. Chandler was "on the way to aid." The reception of these telegrams of Nov. 8th and 9th to Stearns and those of the President to Gen. Sherman of Nov. 10th, were interpreted in Florida as they were meant to be, and the managers at Tallahassee sent dispatches to every quarter of the state on the 10th, two days after the election, like this‡— "The national ticket depends on Florida. Save every vote to swell our majority." Three days later, on the arrival of W. E. Chandler, telegrams were

---

* W. E. Chandler telegraphed to Zach. Chandler from Tallahassee, Nov. 13th, as follows:—"Florida swarming with prominent democrats. Send some Republican lawyers and eminent men. Send Jones to E. A. Rollins, Phila. Have Arthur William warm men acting cold." According to Chandler's account of his cipher to the Potter committee,(*page* 471, *H. R. Mis. Doc. No.* 31, 45th *Cong.* 3d *Sess.*) "Send Jones to E. A. Rollins, Phila," meant send $2,000 to Centennial Bank, Phila., so I can draw for it. "Have Arthur William warm men acting cold," meant, have Arthur (C. A.) send republicans, men acting with democrats. (*H. R. Mis. Doc. No.* 42, 44th *Cong.* 2d *Sess. p.* 439.

Again Nov. 15, he telegraphed to the same. "Florida needs eminent counsel and help more than Louisiana. Can you send Robinson as well as Jones, Doctors plenty here." He wanted "Robinson" $3,000, and "Jones" $2,000, making $5,000. "Doctors plenty," danger great here. *H. R. Mis. Doc. No.* 42, 44th *Cong.* 2d *Sess. p.* 439, *and H. R. Mis. Doc. No.* 31, 45th *Cong.* 3d *Sess. p.* 470.

† Miss. Doc. No. 42 H. R. 44th Cong. 2d Sess. p. 436.

‡ Ibid, p. 437.

sent to local Republican managers, telling them that the
*"state was close, and you must make effort to render
every possible assistance," and that "funds from Washington"* would be on hand to meet every requirement. The
replies † from subordinates in various localities in many '
instances demanded the assistance of Federal troops, and
Stearns issued his orders on Gen. Ruger who was directed
by the Secretary of War to obey.

---

* Miss. Doc. No. 42, H. R. 44th Cong. 2d Sess. p. 436.
† Ibid, p. 437.

CHAPTER IV.

W. E. Chandler reaches Florida and reports the situation to Hayes:
He calls for men who can speak authoratively for Hayes: Telegrams
to Zach. Chandler calling for men and money: The efforts of Chandler to show a majority for Hayes on the face of the county returns : The fraud by which this was accomplished : The two Baker
county returns: The disadvantage the democrats labored under:
What the cipher dispatches between the conspirators disclose: The
carpet-bag rogues afraid of treachery: What Chandler wanted
with Mathews: The work Noyes did.

ON Saturday, November 11th, Mr. Chandler arrived in
Tallahassee. He found the situation, as he reported in
cipher to the private secretary of Hayes, favorable. Evidently by that time Hayes was informed of what was going
on and no longer "heartily deprecated" the dispatches
coming from the national committee. He had been communicated with and his private secretary had Chandler's
cipher. Notwithstanding W. E. Chandler found the situation favorable he felt the need of the presence of gentlemen
from Ohio—personal friends of Mr. Hayes—who could, if
necessary, speak for him. Accordingly, he telegraphed, in
cipher, to Hayes' private secretary* to "send Stanley

"Tallahassee, Fla., Nov. 13, 1876.
* To A. E. LEE, Columbus, Ohio.
   William S. Mathews and others of high character; rainy.
                              W. E. CHANDLER."
   Chandler was also in communication with another of Hayes' intimate
confidential friends in Cincinnati. The following dispatches from this
person to Chandler have survived, but Chandler's to him are missing:

Mathews and others of high character." Stanley Mathews, Edward F. Noyes, Ex-Governor, and John Little, Attorney-General of Ohio, were in New Orleans, or on their way thither, in company with John Sherman, and James A. Garfield. The request of Mr. Chandler was promptly communicated to New Orleans and in response E. F. Noyes accompanied by John A. Kasson, of Iowa, and Lew Wallace, of Indiana, started forthwith for Tallahassee.

In the meantime Thomas J. Brady, Second Assistant Postmaster General, carrying $2,000, sent by Zach. Chandler, and accompanied by H. Clay Hopkins, Wm. T. Henderson, Z. L. Tidball, B. H. Camp, and Alfred Morton, Special Agents of the Post-office Department,* had arrived at Tallahassee. The gentlemen from Ohio arrived Monday the 20th. William H. Robertson, Francis C. Barlow, and D. G. Rollins, of New York came about the same time. E. W. Maxwell, and Peyton, detectives, of the Department of Justice, followed in the wake of Brady and the contingent of the Post-office Department.

"Cincinnati, Ohio, Nov. 18th, 1876.
To W. E. CHANDLER, Tallahassee, Fla.
    What is the situation? Rumors are afloat that we are in danger and that the attention should be turned to Florida instead of Louisiana.
L. C. WEIR."
"Cincinnati, Ohio, Nov. 19, 1876.
To W. E. CHANDLER, Tallahassee, Fla.
    Dispatch received. Attorney-General Little of this state left here Saturday morning to assist you. Others will go if you think them needed."   L. C. WEIR."
    Edward F. Noyes was also in cipher communication with Weir as the following dispatch shows:
"Cincinnati, Ohio, Nov. 19, 1876.
HON. EDWARD F. NOYES, Tallahassee, Fla.
    1 Scared 2 bursting 3 try 4 me 5 &, 6 did 7 cipher 8 not 9 it 10 to 11 wit 12 for 13 are 14 use 15 out 16 same 18 you 19 dispatch 20 follow 21 took 22 sick 23 again 24 news 25 we 26 we 27 it 28 us 29 the 30 received.
L. C. WEIR."

    TRANSLATION.—" The cipher dispatch to me received. Scared me. Try it again. Did you follow same rule? We are bursting for news. Are we not outwitted?"
        * H. R. Mis. Doc. No. 31, 45th Cong. 3d Sess. p. 528.
5

On Saturday, November 18th, W. E. Chandler reported by telegraph to Zach. Chandler, as follows: *

"TALLAHASSEE, FLA., Nov. 18, 1876.

To Zach. Chandler,

Washington, D. C.

After full conference with all our friends now here we find the work to be done requires great and expeditious labor, in view of the shortness of time, which if well performed will, we believe, assure success. Noyes and Kasson will be here on Monday, and Robinson must go immediately to Philadelphia and then come here. Can we also have Jones again? Rainy, for not more than one-tenth of Smith's warm apples. You can imagine what the cold fellows are doing. Where is Cook?

C."

Mr. Chandler, being asked to explain this telegram by the Potter committee said—"The first part is all plain as it stands. 'Robinson must go immediately to Philadelphia and then come here,' means that I wished some money sent to Philadelphia to the Centennial Bank, where I could draw for it: I do not now recall the amount with certainty, but I think 'Robinson' means $3,000. 'Can we also have Jones again,' means, I think, 'can you also let me have $2,000 more (making $5,000.)' 'Rainy, for not more than one-tenth of Smith's warm apples' means 'it looks favorable for about twenty-five majority in the state.' 'You can imagine what the cold fellows are doing,' means 'you can imagine what the democrats are about.' 'Where is Cook'? is an inquiry for William A. Cook who I had requested by telegraph should be sent down."*

* See H. R. Mis. Doc. No. 31, 45th Cong. 3d Sess. p. 471.

Previous to this dispatch of Nov. 18th, Chandler had telegraphed for $2,000* and on the 13th had been notified† that it was on the way. He was, also, informed from Washington that the news from Louisiana was favorable. And at a later date he requested Zach. Chandler to send him $3,000‡ more which was promptly done. In all he received from the National Committee, according to his telegrams and the evidence of Thomas J. Brady, $15,000. How much he carried with him, and received from other sources does not appear.

The hope and expectation of Chandler at this time was that the county returns would show on their face a small majority for the Hayes electors. The first efforts were directed to the accomplishment of this much to be desired result. It was for this purpose that the local Republican managers were telegraphed to "save every vote." It would have simplified the job of counting the state for Hayes if the county returns had on their face shown a small majority. They all knew that the state canvassing board had, under

---

* H. R. Mis. Doc. No. 42, 44th Cong. 2d Sess. p. 438. — "Florida swarming with prominent democrats. Send some Republican lawyers and eminent men. Send Jones to E. A. Rollins, Philadelphia. Have Arthur William warm men acting cold."

† H. R. Mis. Doc. No. 42, 44th Cong. 2d Sess. p. 438. Zach. Chandler to W. E. Chandler.—"Dispatch received. Jones gone to Phila. Harny all along the line—Sea safe cotton high stiffen oranges. Men coming." The translation is as follows: $2,000 sent to Centennial National Bank, Phila. Serene all along the line—Outlook favorable, Louisiana all right. Stiffen the Florida fellows, Arthur has sent the men you asked for."

‡ H. R. Mis. Doc. No. 42, 44th Cong. 2d Sess. p. 439-40. W. E. Chandler to Zach. Chandler. — "William Robinson in small cherries probably shall not need him. Apples about twenty but to be ready for any emergency." Answer. — "Gen. Robinson goes to-night; cotton very high; very rainy." Translation.—"Send $3,000 in large bills, probably shall not need it. Majority about twenty. But be ready for any emergency — i. e., want the money to use if necessary. The $3,000 goes to-night; Louisiana certain, everything going well." The dates of these dispatches were Nov. 27 and 28, and at that date Chandler knew what the Returning Board in Louisiana was going to do, although it did not complete its work till eight days later — Dec. 6th.

the law, simply the authority to perform the ministerial duty of canvassing and compiling the returns of the election sent to them by the county officers. The Supreme Court of the state, had, in the case of* Bloxham vs. the State Canvassers, given a judicial construction of the law and defined their powers. The court held that "The object of the law was to ascertain the number of votes cast, and determine therefrom, and certify the result of the election." In doing this it was the "duty of the state canvassers to determine whether the papers received from them purporting to be returns were, in fact, such, and were genuine, intelligible, and substantially authenticated by law." The county returns standing these tests they must be accepted and the results determined therefrom.

If the returns from the county officers showed on their face a majority for the Hayes electors no one knew better than Mr. Chandler the advantage he would have. Failing in this his objective point was to have the Board of Canvassers reject enough returns, because of pretended irregularities by the county canvassers, and on account of frauds claimed to have been practised at the polling places, to give the Hayes electors a majority. In the preparation for both schemes the state officers and local politicians rendered efficient service. They were shrewd, unscrupulous, active, capable of any villainy, and the presence of government detectives, and an overwhelming force of troops assured them of present absolute protection. Their only concern was to achieve success for their state ticket, as well as for the Hayes electors. The successful counting in of the former was a *sina qua non* with them. The latter was only important to them, because it assured the protection of the former. All their schemes of plunder depended

* 13 Fla. 733—777.

upon the continuance of the carpet-bag rule in the state. Immunity for past, present, and future rascality could only be secured by the success of their state ticket. A great scheme of land and railroad speculation which had been worked up by Frank Sherwin,* and C. D. Willard, in conjunction with W. H. Gleason, Lieutenant-Governor, L. G. Dennis and other state officers, and officials, could only be made successful by the maintenance in power of the latter. The active agents † in the manipulation of returns from the counties were F. C. Humphreys, elector at large, Dennis Eagan, chairman of the state committee, L. G. Dennis, senator from Alachua county, J. W. Howell, deputy clerk of the circuit court of Baker county, Joseph Bowes, of Leon county, James Bell, of Jefferson county, Moses J. Taylor, clerk of Jefferson county, and Manuel Govin, of Monroe county. Dennis had as his tools in Alachua county two creatures, Thomas H. Vance and Richard H. Black. The county judge, W. K. Cessna, was another pliant scoundrel. Howell made use of E. W. Driggers, county judge, and A. A. Allen, sheriff of Baker county, and Bill Green, a justice of the peace, manufactured to order, for the purpose of a fraudulent county canvass and return. Samuel B. McLin, secretary of state, and F. A. Cowgill, comptroller of public accounts, and ex-officio member of the board of state canvassers, with George H. DeLeon, the governor's secretary, were of course all important factors.

When all the returns from the county canvassers had been received by the governor and secretary of state, Mr.

* H. R. Mis. Doc. No. 31 p. 4. 45th Cong. 3d Sess. pp. 380-1 .

† See H. R. Mis. Doc. No. 31, Parts 1 and 2, 45th Cong., 3d Sess., pp. 447, 499, 155, 171, 492, 493, 494, 169, 129, 130, 151, 154, 94, 99, 129, 152, 153, 126, 11, 47, 12, 16, 33, 14, 17, 18, 25, 19, 105, 55, 56, 107, 127, 141. Also Senate Report. No. 611, 44th Cong., 2nd Sess., pp. 356-364, 151, 154, 416, 425, 175, 178, 201, 202.

Chandler and his coadjutors discovered to their surprise that on their face they showed a majority of 91 votes for the Tilden electors. The footings were, for the Tilden electors, 24,441, and for the Hayes electors, 24,350, votes.*

This was a result which the conspirators had not calculated upon. They had made the most desperate exertions to insure just the opposite result. With a majority on the face of the returns for the Hayes electors, and their state ticket, their task would have been a comparatively easy one. They could have taken their stand thereon, and insisted that, by the law of the state, and in accordance with the decision of the Supreme Court, in the case of Bloxham vs. the State Canvassers,† the county returns were final and the canvassing board must merely perform the ministerial duty of tabulating the votes and declare the result. The democrats would have had to insist upon the canvassers going behind the returns and here the advantage would of course be with the republicans, because they had a majority of the board, and, once judicial power was assumed, they could exercise it to accomplish whatever was deemed necessary.

But this scheme was upset unless in some way the result on the face of the county returns could be changed. And Mr. Chandler knew that there must be plausible, and apparently legal ground, prepared for this change. In looking over the returns it was discovered that the one from Baker county, which had been received, was made by Coxe, county clerk, Dorman, justice of the peace, and that Driggers, the county judge, had not joined therein. The law‡ required the canvass of the precinct returns to be made not

---

* H. R. Mis. Doc. No. 31, Part 2, 45th Cong. 3d Sess. p. 54.
† Fla. R. p. 54.
‡ H. R. Mis. Doc., No. 31, Part 2, 45th Cong., 3d Sess., pp. 11, 47.

later than six days after the election, by the county clerk, the county judge, and a justice of the peace. In the absence of, or refusal of, the county clerk, or county judge, to act, the sheriff must be substituted. Here then was the opportunity. J. W. Howell,* who was deputy clerk of Baker county, was communicated with by Governor Stearns, and he promptly undertook to remedy the disaster. Driggers was dispatched forthwith to Tallahassee to procure a commission of justice of the peace for Bill Green, Dorman, who had acted with Coxe, county clerk, being the only justice of the peace in the county. Driggers went to Tallahassee, saw the governor, and secretary of state, and came back with the commission for Bill Green in his pocket.† But, unfortunately, he had previously given notice to Coxe, county clerk, and Dorman, justice of the peace, to meet with him on the 13th for the purpose of canvassing the returns.† On the appointed day they were present, at the clerk's office, but Driggers was not there. They hunted him up and he refused point blank to join with them in the canvass. Then the sheriff, who under the law, could only act in the absence, or upon the refusal of the clerk, or county judge, was asked to join, but he, too, by the direction of Driggers, refused to take part.‡ After waiting till nearly evening, and neither the county judge nor sheriff appearing, Coxe and Dorman again canvassed the precinct returns, and set out in their return to the secretary of state, and governor, all the facts connected with the refusal of the county judge and sheriff to join in the canvass.

That night* Howell let Driggers, Allen, and Green, into the clerk's office where they perfunctorily looked over the

* H. R. Mis. Doc. No. 31, Part 2, 45th Cong. 3d Sess. p. 33.
† Ibid. p. 16.
‡ Ibid. p. 12.

precinct returns and then adjourned to the house of one Canova, where they signed a return which had been prepared for them, including the votes of but two precincts, out of the four, in the county — omitting those of Darbyville and Johnsville, which gave the Tilden electors 149, and the Hayes electors only 11 votes. The two precincts returned gave the Hayes electors 130 votes, and the Tilden electors 89 votes, and by this process a Democratic majority in the county of 95 was converted into a Republican majority of 41 votes. At the same time by holding the return made by Driggers, county judge, Allen, sheriff, and Green justice of the peace, to be the only one complying with the law, the state canvassers could convert the majority on the face of the returns from 91 for the Tilden electors, into 35 majority for the Hayes electors.

There was not a scintilla of evidence * to show even the suspicion of wrong of any kind at the polls in the precincts of Darbyville and Johnsville. Driggers admitted this when examined by the Potter committee. He claimed to know that some illegal votes were counted at Darbyville. He did not know exactly how many, but thought there were four or five. As to Johnsville he knew nothing, but had been informed that there had been some irregularities at that polling place. Allen,† the sheriff, testified that Driggers told him that " they (the republicans) were beat in the state; that something must be done," and that " he proposed to have a canvass by himself." Allen asked him how he could get any one to act with him and Driggers replied he " had got it all right," that he " had a commission for Bill Green, as a justice of the peace." Allen also testified that they had "no evidence at all " in regard to the Johnsville precinct —

* H. R. Mis. Doc., No. 31, Part 2, 45th Cong., 3d Sess., pp. 18, 19, 25, 33.
† Ibid. p. 18.

they merely "believed that there was some intimidation there — that there was one party prevented from voting." In regard to this " there was only his (Driggers') statement." As to the Johnsville precinct he testified that there was "not a particle of evidence " that " we believed that there were some illegal votes cast there." The returns, so far as he knew, from these two precincts "appeared to be regular."

During the time, intervening between the arrival of W. E. Chandler and his associates, and the beginning of the canvass by the state canvassers, preparations were made for the contest. A number of democrats from the North arrived, at different times, and in connection with the local managers, took whatever steps they could to defeat the plans of their opponents. They were at a great disadvantage, because they did not know what the conspirators intended to do. They knew that on the face of the returns from all the counties, the Tilden electors, and the Democratic state ticket, had a small majority. They knew, also, that there had been a return from Baker county made by Driggers, Allen, and Green, but they did not know that the votes of two precincts — Darbyville and Johnsville — had been omitted. Their only legal and safe ground was to stand on the returns and combat the assumption, by the canvassers, of judicial powers — to insist that they could not go behind the county returns. It was impossible for them to know what returns the republicans intended to attack or what evidence they had manufactured in support of their contemplated attacks. The only thing they could do was to discover Republican frauds and irregularities and gather the best evidence thereof they could.

The evidence,* since brought to light, proves that W.

* H. R. Mis. Doc. No. 31, 45th Cong. 3d Sess. pp. 468 to 476, 477 to 495, 525, 1000 to 1493.

E. Chandler was satisfied immediately on his arrival in Tallahassee that he could depend absolutely on the Republican members of the canvassing board. His plan of operations was somewhat altered, after he discovered that the face of the returns gave the Tilden electors a majority, but he congratulated himself on the way this was offset by the Driggers return from Baker county. He knew perfectly well, however, that it would not do to stand on this return because, it was irregular, in that the sheriff had no authority, under the law, to join in the canvass except on account of the absence, or refusal, of the county judge, or county clerk, to act. It could not be safely claimed that the county clerk was absent, or had refused to join with Driggers, in his canvass. One thing Mr. Chandler always insists upon knowing — the weakness of his own case. He is too good a lawyer to be caught napping in this respect. He knew also, beyond question, of the performances of Dennis' tools in Alachua county, and of Bowes' in Leon county, and Bell's in Jefferson county. He accordingly looked for irregularities in other counties where the democrats had large majorities and prepared to have rejected the entire votes of certain counties, and of particular precincts in others.

Another advantage the Republican conspirators had was their exact knowledge of what was going on in Louisiana and South Carolina. Chandler had arranged ciphers with Kellogg and Chamberlain, that present paragon of political morality and civil service reform, whereby they kept each other informed from day to day of what was transpiring in their respective localities. But few of the Republican cipher dispatches were preserved. By an arrangement with the telegraph companies they were enabled to withdraw the ones considered most damaging.* When the Western

* H. R. Mis. Doc. 31, Part 4. 45th Cong. 3d Sess. pp. 57, 60, 63.

Union Telegraph Company produced the dispatches in obedience to subpœnas of the Senate and House of Representatives in January, 1877, the president of the company caused them to be delivered to the Senate Committee on Privileges and Elections. Senator Morton was chairman of this committee, and an employé of the Senate allowed Postmaster-General Tyner to abstract his telegrams to Zach. Chandler.* The same employé abstracted all the Democratic dispatches and those sent and received by the republicans were returned to the telegraph company and immediately destroyed. A few of the Republican cipher telegrams, however, were saved.† They show that W. E.

---

* H. R. Mis. Doc. 31, Part 4. 45th Cong. 3d Sess. p. 331,

†
                                " Tallahassee, Fla., Nov. 13, 1876.
(1) To S. B. PACKARD, New Orleans ;
      Has Kellogg my letter. Must know positively about Cotton.
                                       W. E. CHANDLER."

                               " New Orleans, Nov. 13, 1876.
(2) EVERETT CHASE, care of Gov. Stearns, Tallahassee, Fla.
      Just received your letter. Think cotton high ! how there ?
                                         KELLOGG."

                               " Tallahasse, Fla., Nov. 16, 1876.
(3) Gov. WM. P. KELLOGG, New Orleans.
      Warm and rainy in Florida. Pay no attention to cold reports. Telegrams here say cotton low and fever spreading. W. E. CHANDLER."

                               " New Orleans, Nov. 16, 1876.
(4) EVERETT CHASE, care Gov. Stearns, Tallahassee, Fla.
      Doctors plenty. Cotton high sure you be easy. KELLOGG."

                               " New Orleans, Nov. 15, 1876.
(5) To EVERETT CHASE, care Gov. Stearns, Tallahassee, Fla.
      Confident cotton high : only keep it firm there. KELLOGG."

                               " Tallahassee, Nov. 26, 1876.
(6) To Gov. WM. P. KELLOGG, New Orleans.
      Cold reports here: Doctors scarce : Cotton fever spreading : Rainy here. Answer. W. E. CHANDLER."

      These dispatches are translated as follows :

      1. Has Kellogg my letter (with cipher). Must know positively about the situation in Louisiana.

      2. Everett Chase. — The name of W. E. Chandler for Telegraphic purposes in Florida. Think Louisiana safe. How about Florida.

Chandler while on his way to Florida wrote to Wm. Pitt Kellogg and enclosed a cipher code to enable them to communicate with each other. Inasmuch as it was absolutely necessary for the republicans to count in the Presidential electors of Florida, Louisiana, and South Carolina, the importance of this inter-communication will be readily perceived. It was necessary to satisfy the members of the Returning Boards in the respective states that the conspiracy was going to be successful. If one of the three states should happen to go for Tilden the jig would be up. He required only one electoral vote. The Returning Board rascals were willing to do anything that was required of them, provided, they knew that there would be no slip between the cup and the lip. If there was danger of a slip they did not propose to take any chances.

Another important fact is disclosed by these dispatches—they show that from the moment Chandler arrived in Florida he knew that the board of state canvassers would do whatever they were told to do provided men known to be authorized to speak for Hayes gave the proper assurances. Those from Kellogg beginning Nov. 13th, prove that before the Louisiana Returning Board met, and with the knowledge that the Democratic majority approx-

---

3. Very favorable outlook in Florida. Pay no attention to Democratic reports. Telegrams here say Louisiana uncertain.

4. Returning Board all right. Louisiana absolutely sure. You may rest easy.

5. Confident about Louisiana: only keep Florida all right.

6. Democratic reports here say Returning Board uncertain and that Louisiana will be for them. All right here.

Zach. Chandler kept W. E. Chandler informed about the situation in South Carolina.

"Washington, Dec. 5, 1876.

To W. E. CHANDLER, Tallahassee, Fla.
   South Carolina cotton high absolutely.   Z. CHANDLER."
   TRANSLATION.—South Carolina absolutely safe.

imated 8,000 votes, he had no doubt of the final result. The Returning Board did not meet to begin the canvass of the votes till Nov. 17th, and yet on the 16th Kellogg telegraphed to Chandler that the Returning Board was all right and Louisiana absolutely sure. Likewise Zach. Chandler in Washington was daily advised and in turn sent the favorable news from one to the other of the different sets of visiting statesmen. All the indicia of conspiracy are made plain by these few cipher dispatches which have come down to us by a lucky chance.

The members of the Returning Boards and all the subordinate politicians of the three states whose nineteen electoral votes were needed to give Hayes one majority realized that it was a stupendous undertaking—that the margin was narrow, and the danger of failure, and consequently the risks, very great. Moreover, they were naturally suspicious. They had an intuitive fear of Hayes. They knew that the local Democratic leaders were far more anxious to get possession of the State governments than they were for the success of the national ticket. Undoubtedly they would prefer the Federal government to be turned over to the national democracy, but if they had a chance to trade for one it would always be their State government they would insist upon. In such a contingency as this the "carpet-bag and scallawag" politicians honestly believed they would have to cut and run. They knew perfectly well that they were liable to prosecutions for divers evil deeds, and that, if justice was meted out to them, their future abiding places, for years to come, would be within the walls of the penitentiaries.

On the other hand it was plain to them that the temptation to trade on the part of prominent Republican leaders was great. The success of the national ticket meant every-

thing to them—the loss of the state governments in three
southern states and the sacrifice of a few carpet-baggers
and scallawags would not matter much.   The sheet anchor
of hope to the local rascals was their knowledge, and the
certainty that they could make their peace any time, before
the work was finished, by disposing thereof to the democrats.   They were at no pains to conceal their fears, their
suspicions, and to make known their determination to un-
load, the instant they discovered a disposition to sell them
out.   They kept close watch on the Republican as well as
upon the Democratic visitors.   Their influence over the negroes was complete.   They knew their value as eves-
droppers, spies, and detectives.   Darkeys watched and listened about the quarters of republicans and democrats, and
reported everything they saw, or heard, to their carpet-bag
and scallawag friends.

The Republican visiting statesmen knew of these fears
and suspicions and hence, they were constant and emphatic,
not only in their own professions of esteem and confidence,
but dwelt often and earnestly on the fact that Mr. Hayes was
the devoted friend of southern white and black republicans.
They made skilful use of Hayes' declaration the day after
the election when believing he was defeated he said :* " I
don't care for myself.   The party, yes, and the country,
too, can stand it ; but I care for the poor colored men of
the South."   This was the acme of unselfishness!   The
man that uttered these words, who thought not of himself
in the hour, as he supposed, of defeat, but of "the poor
colored men" would never desert, or suffer to be deserted a
southern white or black man, who had been faithful through
times that had tried the faith of the truest and tested the

---

* Interview with Mr. Hayes published Nov. 9, 1876. N. Y. *Sun*,
Nov. 9, 1876.

courage of the bravest! There was no lack of fine talk on the part of Mr. Hayes' friends in Florida. It was for this protesting and pledging that Chandler wanted Stanley Mathews and others close to Hayes sent to Tallahassee. He got Noyes who unquestionably was not a laggard in the work assigned him. Chandler's purpose was doubtless a double one—first to have all doubting Thomases convinced, and, second, to have Hayes irrevocably pledged to an ultra southern policy.

CHAPTER V.

The canvass of the county returns: Chandler outwitted the Democratic visitors: The Baker county return again: Hamilton, Jackson, Manatee, and Monroe counties: The votes therefrom unjustly excluded by the State canvassers: The Republican frauds in Alachua county: The confession of Dennis: The disgraceful conduct of ex-Governor Noyes: The frauds in Leon and Jefferson counties: The confessions of Bowes and Bell: The plans of Chandler nearly defeated by Barlow: The conduct of Barlow considered: Cowgill's scruples overcome.

THE canvass of the county returns began at Tallahassee on the 27th of November with the understanding that all the returns should be first read alphabetically by counties and then taken up for objections, protests, and contests. Baker county was reached early. The democrats were completely surprised by the reading of the Driggers return. They knew that a canvass had been made by Driggers, Allen, and Green. They should have promptly demanded the production of the Coxe and Dorman return, of which they had a certified copy in their hands. They contented themselves with announcing that this certified copy would "show a change of votes of over one-half." They announced their purpose of contesting the one read and asked time "because, some of the proofs will have to be prepared." Mr. McLin suavely assured than they would "extend all the liberality we can."* It was not till after recess,

* Senáte Report, No. 611, p. 423.

late in the evening that the Democratic counsel demanded the production and reading of the other and true return from Baker county. Chandler was prompt and adroit in interposing dilatory talk without offering any objection. After a good deal of parleying and much discussion of other matters the true Baker return was finally read, but in the meantime Chandler had made his first point, by having the associated press telegraph to every quarter that the Hayes electors had a majority on the face of the returns. The production and reading of the Driggers return from Baker county, and the delay in bringing out the true one from that county, made it appear on the face of the returns that the republicans had a majority when in reality the democrats had a majority of ninety-one votes.

It was not the purpose of Chandler to insist upon the actual canvassing of the Driggers return from Baker county. He wanted a pretext for the Returning Board assuming judicial functions. He knew very well that one of the necessary powers of the state canvassers was to decide upon the regularity and truthfulness of the returns before them — that such a power was the inevitable concomitant of the power to canvass returns. He knew that the precinct returns would be before the board and that there was no evidence whatever to invalidate those of the Darbyville and Johnsville polls. He knew that the power to discriminate, in this particular, was altogether different from judicial authority — but he did not mean that the canvassers should draw this distinction. He knew his case, and he knew the canvassers, and was the master of both.

The counties* giving Democratic majorities which were

* Senate Report No. 611, 44th Cong. 2nd Sess. pp. 151—4, 356—'64, 416—'25, 201—2. Also H. R. Mis. Doc. No. 31, Part 2, 45th Cong. 3d Sess. pp. 1 to 171.

6

selected for attack were Hamilton, Jackson, Manatee, and Monroe. At poll No. 2 in Jasper precinct, Hamilton county, there were 320 votes for the Tilden and 189 for the Hayes electors. The ground of objection to receiving the vote was the affidavits of two Republican inspectors, who conducted the election, that they had absented themselves at different times during the day from the polls. There was no pretence of fraud or illegal voting. The state canvassers threw out the vote of this poll. Campbellton precinct, Jackson county gave 291 votes for the Tilden and 77 for the Hayes electors. The inspectors went to dinner after locking the ballot-box in a secure place and left the key with "the Republican inspector who certified to the returns and testified that there was no fraud or wrong about the election." This precinct was rejected by the state canvassers. Friendship precinct, Jackson county, gave 145 Democratic, and 44 Republican votes, and, because, the colored inspectors left the church, where the election was held, to go to a neighboring house for lights and paper, and there completed their return, it was cast out.

The entire vote of Manatee county — 262 for the Tilden, and 26 for the Hayes electors, was rejected on the ground that there had been no registration, when the fact was, that Governor Stearns would not appoint a county clerk in order that there might not be a registration of voters in this strong Democratic county. The proper officers had held the election and administered an oath to every voter as follows : — " You do solemnly swear that you are twenty-one years of age, and that you are a citizen of the United States, and have resided in this state for one year and in this county six months next preceding this election and that you have not voted at this election and are not disqualified to vote by the judgment of any court."

There was no allegation of fraud or pretence that the election was not fairly and honestly conducted. And yet on the ground of no registration, for which the governor was himself responsible, the entire vote was thrown out.

Precinct No. 3, Key West, Monroe county, is the white quarter and therein reside the bulk of the white voters of the place. The vote polled at this precinct were for the Tilden electors 401, and for the Hayes electors 59. On the ground that the election officers did not complete their returns on the day of the election, but without any charge of wrong-doing or fraud this precinct was rejected by the state canvassers. The proof submitted in support of the fairness of the election at this poll, and the honesty of the return made by the officers, was overwhelming. The ballots were counted after the poll closed the night of the election and the result announced. The certificate was partly made out when a bottle of ink was spilt on it and, therefore, a new one had to be made. Thereupon, this work was postponed till the next morning. At that time the ballots were recounted and, saving one more ballot found for the republicans, the result tallied exactly with the announcement the night before.

The evidence submitted to the state canvassers in regard to poll No. 2, Jasper precinct, Hamilton county, consisted of affidavits made by the two Republican inspectors and S. L. Taylor, deputy United States marshal. They proved only that the Republican officers of the election were careless but imputed no wrong-doing by anybody. There was no accusation of intimidation and no allegation that the votes returned were not actually cast.

The evidence about Cambellton precinct, Jackson county, was collected by M. C. Cooper, deputy U. S. marshal, Z. L. Tidball, and Wm. T. Henderson, post-office inspectors who went to Jackson county, accompanied by a detachment of thirty United States soldiers, commanded by three commissioned officers. They pretended to have found 112 negroes who swore that they voted the Republican ticket at Campbellton precinct. They could have easily obtained twice as many to have sworn to the same effect. The troops would march to a church or house and the negroes were collected in squads and their names written down by Tidball. The effect of the display of soldiers on the ignorant blacks may readily be imagined.

The ballot-box, during the adjournment for dinner, was proved by Republican witnesses to have been perfectly protected in a room to one door of which the Republican inspector had the key and at the only other door a Republican supervisor was stationed. The Republican inspector testified that the election was fair and honest, and that the ballots were counted and the return made in the presence of United States supervisors and others, and that there was no opportunity for fraud. It was conclusively shown that many negroes voted, of their free will, the Democratic ticket.

The failure * to register the voters of Manatee county, which was the pretext for rejecting the whole vote of that county, was the result of the refusal of Governor Stearns to appoint a registration officer. There can be no doubt that this was deliberate, and for the purpose of laying the foundation for rejecting the vote of this Democratic county, if the necessity therefor arose after the election. There was no irregularity alleged to have occurred on the day of the election, and no pretence that any republican was prevented from voting. The only evidence the state canvassers had was the affidavit of James D. Green, deputy-collector of the port of Manatee, which was supported by certificates, as to

* Senate Report No. 611 44th Cong. 2nd Sess. p. 356.

character, from L. G. Dennis, W. H. Gleason, F. N. Wicker, Joseph Bowes, John Varnum, and others of like repute.

The evidence * upon which the state canvassers acted in rejecting poll No. 3, Key West, Monroe county, was manufactured by F. N. Wicker, collector of customs, Key West, and Manuel Govin, postmaster at Jacksonville. It was completely rebutted by the evidence of unimpeached and unimpeachable witnesses. It was shown that the Republican vote was the largest ever cast at this poll.

The Returning Board ignored entirely the gross frauds perpetrated by Republican election officers in other counties notwithstanding the proof thereof was conclusive. Note the following instances :

L. G. Dennis was the Republican boss of Alachua county. His influence with, and control over, the negroes was practically unlimited. He appears to have had a repugnance to committing perjury himself, but in every other respect he was unscrupulous. He would suborn perjury and encourage and countenance every description of political rascality. Two of his negro tools, Richard H. Black and Thomas H. Vance were respectively, clerk and inspector, of the election held at Archer precinct, box 2, Alachua county. Dennis† related to the Potter committee what transpired at his home on the night of the election. Black and Vance " brought with them a blank for the returns of the election *already signed and sealed*, but as to which the figures remained to be filled in." They had procured the Democratic inspector, who could not read or write, to affix his mark to the blank return. ‡ " They were asked by Dennis

---

* H. R. Mis. Doc. No. 35, 44th Cong. 2d Sess. pp. 92—94.
† H. R. Mis. Doc. No. 31, 45th Cong. 3d Sess. pp. 477, 483, 534.
‡ Ibid, p. 11.

what was the vote at the precinct where they had attended, and they informed him that it was 178 Republican and 141 Democratic; and they had so announced it at the polls. At that he expressed great indignation, and declared that the business had not been properly managed or no such result could have been reached. They expressed contrition and their willingness to correct any error that had occurred in the returns. He accordingly furnished them with an upper room, and with a printed list of the voters of the county, and from that printed list they proceeded to add 219 names to the poll list, and as many votes to the Republican candidates. This brought the vote up to a total of 397 Republican and 141 Democratic, and their return was filled up to correspond with this result. This fraudulent return was then forwarded to the county canvassers, and embraced in their return to the state canvassers, notwithstanding one of the inspectors at that poll made affidavit that the return was false and forged. The visiting statesmen allotted to ex-Governor Noyes the task of maintaining the truth and fairness of this return before the state canvassers."

The democrats attacked the return on account of the 219 votes added. Dennis had exerted himself to the utmost to bolster the false return from Archer No. 2 with affidavits. His coadjutors were W. K. Cessna, county judge, Josiah T. Wells, ex-member of Congress and canditate for state senator from the thirteenth district, J. A. Barnes, register of U. S. Land office, Gainesville, Fla., David Brown, U. S. deputy marshall, and Joseph Bowes, of Leon county. Dennis procured Green R. Moore,* one of the Democratic inspectors, to sign an affidavit corroborating the statements of Black and Vance by paying him therefor $100. Wells secured a like affidavit from Floyd Dukes†

* H. R. Mis. Doc. No. 35. 44th Cong. 2d Sess. p. 193.
† Ibid, p. 197.

for $25. The state canvassers counted the return made by Black and Vance with its 219 fraudulent votes added.

But when ex-Governor E. H. Noyes, of Ohio, to whom was assigned the defence of the Alachua fraud before the state canvassers, wanted Dennis to give his testimony, he was given to understand that Dennis did not propose to do any swearing. The following is the testimony of Dennis on this point.*

Q. "Did Mr. Noyes ask you to become a witness yourself in regard to that precinct?" A. "Yes sir."

Q. "Were you a witness or had you made an affidavit with reference to box No. 2 of Archer precinct, which affidavit was to be used before the Returning Board?" A. "No, Sir; I never made any statement whatever for that purpose."

Q. "State the conversation which took place between you and Mr. Noyes in regard to your appearing as a witness before the Returning Board in reference to box No. 2 at Archer precinct?" A. "He did express that desire several times. I do not know that he ever spoke of it but once as though he intended to put me on the stand, and then I advised him not to do it."

Q. "What did you say to him and what did he say to you?" A. "I do not recollect the exact words, but I think he said in a familiar sort of a way that he should put me on the stand that day. I suggested to him that I should be a detriment to his case if he did, and that I thought he had better not do it."

Q. "Can you repeat the exact words which you used in reference to your being a detriment to his case?" A. "I cannot, but I made it strong. I may have said that unless he was ready to abandon his case, he had better not put

* H. R. Mis. Doc. No. 35, 45th Cong. 3d Sess. p. 478.

me on the stand. I may have made it as strong as that. I wanted to give him to understand that I did not want to go on the stand to make any statement under oath. I cannot repeat the exact words; but it was said with sufficient force to have the desired effect."

Q. "Did Governor Noyes after you told him in some form of words that it would be inconvenient to his case to put you on the stand, ever refer to that refusal on your part to go on the stand in any form of words?" A. "I think he jocosely said one day that I was not very forward about swearing, or something of that kind."

Q. "Wasn't it something like this: 'you talk well enough, Dennis, but you don't swear?'" A. "Something to that effect."

The ex-Governor and the confidential friend of Hayes joking with the man who had gotten up the evidence to support his case because he would not do any swearing himself! It was indeed a strange thing to jest about. It gave the distinguished representative of Hayes who was in Florida, in the language of the President "to see a fair count of the ballots actually cast," no concern that the man who knew the most about the returns from Archer precinct was not only unwilling to be a witness, but who told him plainly that he would have to abandon his case if he was put on the witness stand! And that "visiting statesman," after this, not only advocated the counting of the return from Archer precinct, but joked with Dennis about his reluctance to perjure himself!

Joseph Bowes* who was an inspector at precinct number 13, Leon county, "procured a lot of small Republican tickets to be printed in very fine type, and on thin paper.

---

* H. R. Mis. Doc. No. 31, Part 2. 45th Cong. 3d Sess. pp. 79, 94-7. 129, 152, 153.

These tickets, spoken of in Florida as "little jokers," he had printed at the official Republican printing office. Before the election he showed them to McLin, and stated his purpose of using them. The plan was to fold them up inside the ballots that were voted, and have them surreptitiously cast, or otherwise to smuggle them into the ballot boxes, which their small size easily admitted of. McLin advised Bowes not to use them. After the election Bowes stated that he had managed to smuggle seventy-three of them into the boxes in his precinct, and he told McLin, after the state had been awarded to the democrats, and it was known Drew was to be governor, that he was in a scrape on this account, and that he had to clear out for stuffing the boxes. It was claimed, because these ballots were found loose in the box and not folded inside the other tickets that they had been regularly cast; but it would have been very easy to have produced that effect, either by some other manner of stuffing the box than the one originally proposed, or by shaking the box after they were deposited and thus scattering them, and that circumstance is of no weight against Bowes' own admissions, and against the evidence of the persons receiving the ballots, that not one of these small ballots was voted.*

The evidence establishing this fraud of ballot box stuffing was before the Returning Board but the return for precinct No. 13, Leon county, was accepted.

James Bell,† county judge of Jefferson county, and clerk of the election board for Waukenah precinct No. 7, Jefferson county, stole a bundle of one hundred Democratic tickets, which the inspectors had tied up as they were counting the ballots, and substituted therefor 100 Republican

* H. R. Mis. Doc. No. 31, 45th Cong. 3d Sess. p. 11.
† Ibid, p. 99, 126, 130.

tickets. Bell confessed this crime to McLin and fled the state to avoid prosecution. The fact of the stuffing the ballot box at Waukenah precinct No. 7, was proven before the Returning Board and yet the return was accepted and counted.

Moses J. Taylor* clerk of the circuit court, Jefferson county, was inspector of poll No. 1, Monticello precinct. In counting the ballots they were separated first into lots— Democratic ballots, in one pile, and Republican, in another. When the return was made only five Democratic votes were credited. Taylor undoubtedly stole all but five of the Democratic ballots and substituted therefor Republican ones. Ten Democratic voters, residents of this precinct, whose votes were not counted, made affidavit that they had voted. William Scott who was United States supervisor for this precinct testified that Taylor admitted that more than five democrats had voted.

It was further proved that the registration† of Jefferson county was fraudulent and that it was made in the interest of the republicans and to facilitate frauds by Moses J. Taylor, the county clerk. The state canvassers accepted and counted the returns from Jefferson county.

The nicely laid and thoroughly executed plans of W. E. Chandler came very near being undone by the scrupulousness of one of the Republican visiting statesmen. The conduct of Francis C. Barlow, ex-Attorney-General of New York, who went to Florida at the request of President Grant "to witness a fair count of the ballots actually cast," does not deserve undiscriminating commendation. He appears to have considered that it was his duty to render whatever service he could to the Republican side, but to re-

---

* H. R. Mis. Doc. No. 31, 45th Cong. 3d Sess. p. 11.

† H. R. Mis. Doc. No. 35, 44th Cong. 2d Sess. pp. 146-7-8.

frain from absolute conclusions in regard to the result which ought to be reached by the canvassers until all the evidence was in.   His participation in the work of preparation, his undertaking to supervise, and assist in, the getting up of evidence to sustain the returns from certain Republican precincts, was not inconsistent with his intention to be fair and impartial.   He was not then acquainted, either with the character of the men with whom he was dealing, or advised that they had committed and aided in the commission of gross frauds.   He was an intense partisan and sincerely desired the election of Hayes.   His bias was in favor of Florida republicans and his prejudice strong against their Democratic opponents.   That he should have hesitated to come to a conclusion adverse to his own feelings was natural, and that he did become convinced that a fair and discriminating canvass of "the ballots actually cast" entitled the Tilden electors to the certificate of election by the board of canvassers, was deserving of the approval of honorable men.   There can be no doubt as to the sincerity and honesty of Mr. Barlow's purpose.   His character, established by an honorable career both before and since that period, is sufficient warrant for this conclusion.

It is, nevertheless, evident that Mr. Barlow lacked, in some degree, moral courage. He had an exalted idea of the position he occupied in Florida.   He had been personally invited to go there by the President of the United States, who had published to the world his desire, " that representatives and fair men of both parties," should go " to see that the board of canvassers make a fair count of the ballots actually cast."   He, also, believed that the President was sincere when he declared that " no man worthy of the office of President would be willing to hold the office if counted in, placed there by fraud."   Hence, as Mr. Chandler testified, before the Potter Committee,* Mr. Barlow said to him soon after his arrival at Tallahassee that he was there " by the request of the President" and " to see that there was a fair count, and that nothing wrong was done on either side:" and that he also said, " that Governor Hayes would not take the Presidency if there was any fraud in connection with the count: that if he thought there was any danger of his being counted in by fraudulent methods some elector chosen as a Republican would vote for Tilden at Governor Hayes request." Mr. Chandler characterized these declarations by Mr. Barlow, as " some such stuff as that in connection with this intimation to me that he was not there merely as counsel." Mr. Chandler did not believe that the President meant that his declarations should be accepted literally by " visiting statesmen." But on the other hand Mr. Barlow, doubtless, thought that the President was sincere in the expressions already quoted as well as in the one with which he closed his famous dispatch of November 10, 1876, to General Sherman—to wit—: " Either party can afford to be disappointed in the result, but the country cannot afford to have the result tainted by the suspicion of illegal or false returns."

It is clear from all the evidence in existence that Mr. Barlow did not intend to deceive his Republican associates or to practise treachery in his relations to Florida republicans. Dennis† soon discovered that Barlow was not the kind of a lawyer he wanted to assist him in the preparation and advocacy of the Alachua case. He wanted a man without conscientious scruples and, therefore, he demanded that Barlow should be retired and Noyes assigned to the duty of getting up evidence in support of, and defending the

* H. R. Mis. Doc. No. 31.   45th Cong. 3d Sess. p. 1398.
† Ibid, p. 478.

returns from Archer precinct No. 2, Alachua county. Mr. Chandler as he admits ceased to have entire confidence in Barlow from the time he talked " stuff" as to Hayes not accepting the Presidency if he was not entirely satisfied about the methods by which he obtained it. Unquestionably Chandler had a truer appreciation of Mr. Hayes character than Barlow had, and understood better the intent of the President's "glittering generalities," but he was exceedingly careful not to break with the man who thought otherwise. He knew that Barlow was a man of " many idiosyncrasies,"* and feared that he might persist in his " lofty purposes " if not adroitly and prudently managed. Chandler did not want his adversaries to have the benefit of the moral effect of the open desertion of one of "the representatives and fair men" who had come to Florida at the request of the President "to see that the board of canvassers made a fair count of the ballots actually cast." Therefore, he humored Mr. Barlow and endeavored to commit him in every possible way during the progress and at the conclusion of the public hearing of the Returning Board. He preserved carefully the originals of papers prepared by Barlow, and induced him to put in writing a summary of facts claimed to have been established to be read to the board.† And, even, when he discovered that Barlow was privately advising one of the canvassers to apply the same principles to contested Democratic returns which he applied to disputed Republican votes, Mr. Chandler made no row — did not suffer his anger to get the better of his discretion.

Mr. Barlow's idea of the legal powers of the Returning Board was erroneous, as the prior and subsequent decisions,

* H. R. Mis. Doc. No. 31. 45th Cong. 3d Sess. p. 1398. — Testimony of W. E. Chandler.

† Testimony of W. E. Chandler, Ibid p. 1398.

of the supreme court of the state demonstrate. He acted upon the assumption that the board could exercise judicial powers and determine the legality of the votes returned outside the certificates of the county canvassing boards. In this view of the election law creating the board of state canvassers, Mr. Barlow was undoubtedly mistaken. The extent of the power of the board to inquire was as to the character of the returns made by the county canvassers. The language of the decision of the supreme court, unanimously rendered in the case ex-rel. Drew vs. The State Canvassers, is as follows :

"All of the acts which this board can do under the statute must be based upon the returns; and while in some cases the officers composing the board may, like all ministerial officers of similar character, exclude what purports to be a return for irregularity, still everything they are authorized to do is limited to what is sanctioned by authentic and true returns before them. Their first act and determination must be such as appears from and is shown by the returns from the several counties to be correct. They have no general power to issue subpoenas, to summon parties, to compel the attendance of witnesses, to grant a trial by jury, or to do any act, but determine and declare who has been elected as shown by the returns. They are authorized to enter no judgment, and their power is limited by the express words of the statute, which gives them being, to the signing of a certificate containing the whole number of votes *given* for each person for each office, and therein declaring the result as shown by the returns. This certificate thus signed is not a judicial judgment, and the determination and declaration which they make is not a judicial declaration, that is, determination of a right after notice,

* H. R. Mis. Doc. No. 31, Part 2. 45th Cong. 3d Sess. p. 67.

according to the general law of the land as to the rights of parties, but it is a declaration of a conclusion limited and restricted by the letter of the statute. Such limited declaration and determination by a board of state canvassers has been declared by a large majority of the courts to be a ministerial function, power and duty, as distinct from a judicial power and jurisdiction. Indeed, with the exception of the courts in Louisiana, and perhaps another state, no judicial sanction can be found for the view that these officers are judicial in their character or that they have any discretion, either executive, legislative, or judicial, which is not bound and fixed by the returns before them."

As to the specific powers of the board under the statute the supreme court held that:

"While the general powers of the board are thus limited to and by the returns, still as to these returns the statute provides that, 'if any returns shall be shown or shall appear to be so irregular, false, or fraudulent that the board shall be unable to determine the true vote for any officer or member, they shall so certify and shall not include such return in their determination and declaration, and the secretary of state shall preserve and file in his office all such returns, together with such other documents and papers as may have been received by him or by said board of canvassers.' The words *true vote* here indicate the vote *actually cast*, as distinct from the *legal* vote. This follows, *first*, from the clear general duty of the canvassers, which is to ascertain and certify the "*votes given*" for each person for each office, and, *second*, because to determine whether a vote cast is a legal vote is beyond the power of this board. As to the words "irregular, false, and fraudulent" in this connection, their definition is not required by the questions raised by the pleadings in this case."

Mr. Barlow, proceeding upon the hypothesis that the Returning Board was vested with judicial powers, took an active part in the preparation of the Republican side of the case, but when it was completed—the evidence all in, and reviewed, he became satisfied that, by applying the same tests to Republican testimony, and weighing with the same care the objections to Republican votes, that the Republican counsel insisted must be applied to Democratic evidence, and exercised in respect to contested Democratic returns, the result of the purging would be a majority for the Tilden electors. He endeavored to impress this upon Dr. Cowgill, one of the state canvassers whom he believed to be an honest man. There was nothing improper in this, but it was not bold and manly, or corresponding to the exalted notion he had of his mission. The proper course would have been to go before the board and to have summed up the case as an impartial *amicus curia*. This would have been the effective way of executing the trust which he believed had been entrusted to him—"to see a fair count of the ballots actually cast."

And yet, with the light he had, it must be acknowledged, by fair-minded men, that he did not lack courage of a certain kind. He wanted to do right and he sought to convert to his way of thinking the one of the Republican canvassers whom he regarded as honorable and upright. There is no evidence to show that he surreptitiously went about this. Dr. Cowgill came to his room unsolicited and began talking upon the subject of the canvassing as he had repeatedly done before. Whether Cowgill was honest in seeking this interview with Barlow cannot be determined. Neither can it be determined whether he was honest in the doubts he expressed at that interview as to the course he should pursue in dealing with the questions before the board. Barlow swears that Cowgill said to him, after they had discussed all the points, "I agree with you: I cannot conscientiously vote the other way: I cannot conscientiously vote to give the state to the Hayes electors." Dr. Cowgill was at all times accessible to the Republican members of the Potter committee, and to the defenders of the transactions of their friends in Florida, and he could have been brought before the committee to contradict Mr. Barlow. He was not asked to come. He never intimated in any way that he had been misrepresented.

There is some evidence * which goes to show that Stearns and other Florida republicans were suspicious of Cowgill. They had him watched. Stearns was promptly informed that Cowgill was in Barlow's room and he hastened to Chandler's room with the intelligence. With his usual decisiveness Chandler insisted that Stearns should go direct to Barlow's room and ascertain what was going on. He went and to his surprise was admitted and told by Barlow the views he had been trying to impress on Cowgill. Stearns † expressed neither surprise nor anger, but he went away with Cowgill, but whither is not known to the public. After that Cowgill and Barlow did not meet. It is fair to presume that if Cowgill had any scruples as to counting in the Hayes electors, as he declared to Barlow he had, means were found after he left with Stearns to overcome them. He came to Washington immediately after the inauguration of Hayes and was for a time confident of a proper recognition of his services. The office he was tendered did not accord with his estimate of his deserts and he returned to Florida and has ever since maintained discreet silence.

* H. R. Mis. Doc. No. 31. 45th Cong. 3d Sess. p. 1397–8–9.
† Ibid, p. 1390.

7

CHAPTER VI.

The supreme court decided that the county returns must be accepted
by the state canvassers: The mandate of the court obeyed as to
the state ticket: The trick by which the returns for electors were
made to show a majority for Hayes: The Baker county return
twice rejected accepted by the canvassers: McLin and Dennis tell
on the visiting statesmen: Noyes, the particular friend of Hayes:
The promises he made: The rewards McLin and Dennis received:
Hayes' personal endorsement of Dennis: How the subordinate
rogues were paid for their services: The price of visiting statesmen.

THE supreme court of the state upon an application for a
mandamus to compel the state canvassers to recanvass the
votes for Governor issued the same, and in granting it, the
judges, a majority of whom were Republican, held that "the
duty and power of the board of state canvassers was
confined exclusively to the compiling of such returns of any
election as should come to their hands from the county
canvassing boards, and upon computation of the aggregate
vote, as shown by such returns, to ascertain who had received the highest number of votes for any office, and to
certify the result and declare therefrom who was elected to
any office." *

The mandate of the court to the board of state canvassers commanding them to reassemble, on or before the
27th day of December, 1876, and canvass the returns for
the votes cast for candidates for Governor was issued on the

* Fla. Report, 59.

23d of December, 1876. The board met and in accordance with the decision and mandate of the supreme court recanvassed and awarded a certificate of election to Geo. F. Drew the Democratic candidate. Here it was their duty to stop. They were not directed to recanvass the votes for Presidential electors, nevertheless the two Republican canvassers, being a majority, did so, and by accepting the Driggers return from Baker county which they had not done in recanvassing the votes for governor, and which they had rejected in their first canvass,* they made it appear that by the face of the returns the Hayes electors had a majority of all the votes. The counting of the electoral votes by the two Houses of Congress was yet to occur, and hence they resorted to this trick, and a second time violated their oaths of office, in order that it might not appear by the recanvass of the votes for governor that the Tilden electors *a fortiori* had a majority on the face of the returns and therefore in accordance with the decision of the supreme court ought to have been declared elected.

The state canvassers unquestionably had the power to determine which of the returns from Baker county was the true return. They twice decided unanimously that the Driggers return was false and accepted the one which embraced the four precinct returns. They did this in the original canvass and they adhered to that ruling in the recanvass of the votes for governor. But the two Republican members against the protest of their Democratic colleague insisted upon recanvassing the votes for electors and then they reversed themselves and adopted the Driggers return from Baker county.

* H. R. Mis. Doc. No. 31, Part 2, 45th Cong. 3d Sess. pp. 107, 127, 141.

It has been clearly proved * that the action of the Republican members of the board of state canvassers was influenced by the pledges, promises, and assurances made and given by the Republican visiting statesmen : that McLin and Cowgill expected, claimed, and in the case of the former received partial, rewards for their services. The subordinate agents in the frauds, perjuries, forgeries, ballot-box stuffing, and subornation of perjury whereby a plausible case was made for McLin and Cowgill to act upon, were also exerting themselves upon assurances of protection and reward.

L. G. Dennis ** testified before the Potter committee that the impression prevailed that the visiting statesmen "cared only to take care of Hayes." " Somebody had intimated that Mr. Hayes was in his politics favorable to the Greeley movement; that he had some such idea as that." This impression was strengthened by the conduct of Francis C. Barlow who had originally been assigned the duty of defending the Alachua returns. From some remarks of Barlow and his intimacy with some of the New York Democratic lawyers, which had been reported by the negro spies, Dennis and his carpet-bag friends concluded that treachery to the state ticket was meant. Thereupon he held, as he expressed it,† "a carpet-baggers' indignation meeting " and he led a committee to Governor Noyes' room to serve notice of their determination. ‡" We had determined," said Dennis, " that the state belonged to Tilden and Drew or to Hayes and Stearns; that it did not belong to a Republican president and a Democratic governor; that it could not be fixed

* H. R. Mis. Doc. No. 31, Part 2. 45th Cong. 3d Sess. pp. 478, 100, 98, 499, 482, 854.
** H. R. Mis. Doc. No. 31. 45th Cong. 3d Sess. p. 478.
† Ibid, 478.
‡ Ibid, 478—9.

that way." Their going to Noyes was both natural and significant.

They knew he was the personal representative of Hayes. They wanted to serve notice that the job which had been undertaken could not be accomplished if there was any doubt about Hayes standing by them. They would not have gone to Noyes on this occasion, however, if they had not known that he was there as the especial representative of Hayes. He had before this visit been making promises and giving assurances — hence the significance of their calling on him at that time for something definite, emphatic, and unequivocal. They got what they demanded. Dennis says — " Mr. Barlow did not present the case to the board as was first intended." Dennis was a shrewd judge of character and knew instinctively that Barlow was not the man to have charge of the Alachua case; that he would get at the truth and that would be the end of that case as well as of the whole Republican case.

In regard to Noyes' assurances Dennis testified * that " he often spoke of Mr. Hayes, and referred to him as his intimate friend, and gave us assurances of Mr. Hayes' fidelity to the Republican cause, and of his especial desire to take care of Southern republicans." When asked if Noyes was generally regarded by the people there as the personal representative of Hayes, Dennis answered—*" We regarded him as such. I cannot state now by what means we arrived at that conclusion, but he was regarded by the people there as the special representative of Mr. Hayes. It was generally understood that he was there at the request of Hayes."

Samuel B. McLin,† secretary of state, and ex-officio mem-

* H. R. Mis. Doc. No. 31. 45th Cong. 3d Sess. p. 478.
† H. R. Mis. Doc. No. 31 Part 2. 45th Cong. 3d Sess. pp. 98. 99.

ber of the Returning Board, testified that—"looking back now to that time (of the canvass), I feel that there was a combination of influences that must have operated most powerfully in blinding my judgment and swaying my action." What the "combination of influences" were he in part disclosed. "I was shown numerous telegrams addressed to Governor Stearns and others from the trusted leaders of the Republican party in the North, insisting that the salvation of the country depended upon the vote of Florida being cast for Hayes. These telegrams also gave assurances of the forthcoming of money and troops if necessary in securing the victory for Mr. Hayes. Following these telegrams trusted Northern republicans, party leaders, and personal friends of Mr. Hayes arrived in Florida as rapidly as the railroads could bring them. I was surrounded by these men, who were ardent republicans, and especially by friends of Governor Hayes. One gentleman particularly, Governor Noyes, of Ohio, was understood to represent him and speak with the authority of a warm personal friend, commissioned with power to act in his behalf. These men referred to the general destruction of the country should Mr. Tilden be elected; the intense anxiety of the Republican party of the North and their full sympathy with us. I cannot say how far my action may have been influenced by the intense excitement that prevailed around me, or how far my partisan zeal may have led me into error—neither can I say how far my course was influenced by the promises made by Governor Noyes, that if Mr. Hayes became President I should be rewarded. Certainly their influences must have had a strong control over my judgement and actions."

Q. "Now, Sir, state to the committee, if you please, what promises these visiting statesmen from the North made to the Republican leaders and the Returning Board, if the state should go for Mr. Hayes?"   A. "Well, General Wallace told me on several occasions that if Mr. Hayes should be elected that the members of the Returning Board should be taken care of, and no doubt about that : that Governor Noyes represented Mr. Hayes and spoke for him and was in favor of it.*   Then on one occasion, William E. Chandler came to me and stated that he didn't like to say it to me, but he would say it to me, and he spoke for General Wallace also, that if the state went and was canvassed for Mr. Hayes that the members of the Returning Board—at least he referred to a majority of the board—Dr. Cowgill and myself would be well taken care of, and there would be no doubt of it ; he said he was authorized to say that."

McLin further testified that Dr. Cowgill told him that in March, 1877 he was in Washington and saw Hayes frequently—† "that he was received very kindly by the President, and given free admission to the White House at all times, and that he had expressed himself as being under great obligations to him and me in the canvass and that he felt not only under political obligations but personal obligations that he would certainly pay at an early day."

McLin was appointed Justice of the Supreme Court of New Mexico ad interim and failed of confirmation because Senator Conover, of Florida opposed it.   He was promised another office but, after waiting several months and not receiving it, he published to the world his account of the Florida count which concluded as follows—"whatever may be the opinion of men as to my motives, I give them facts and leave my motives to a higher tribunal."

Dr. Cowgill was promised by Hayes an auditorship of the Treasury department, but was given the position of

* H. R. Mis. Doc. No. 31, Part 2, 45th Cong. 3d Sess. pp. 100, 101.
† Ibid, p. 118.

special agent in the internal revenue service, which he declined.

L. G. Dennis came to Washington immediately after the inauguration of Hayes and was introduced to him by Gen. Lew Wallace. He was graciously received and informed that he had been mentioned by Mr. Noyes and Mr. Chandler, and that he "was one of the few men whom this administration could afford to take care of."* He saw Hayes frequently afterwards and received from him at different times the two following cards:

** " SEC'Y SHERMAN: I particularly desire that Mr. L. G. Dennis, of Fla. shall be appointed to a good place, and I think he is well fitted for it.

R. B. HAYES."

† "EXECUTIVE MANSION,
Washington, April 6, 1877.

DEAR SIR: I am reliably assured that L. G. Dennis, of Fla. would make a capital special agent of the Treasury.

I especially desire that his claims may have your favorable attention.

R. B. HAYES.

Hon. JOHN SHERMAN, Etc., etc."

Governor Noyes also wrote the following letter to John Sherman:‡

" *Cincinnati*, *Ohio*, April 10, 1877.

DEAR SIR: I am informed that Hon. L. G. Dennis, of Florida, and at present a state senator, is an applicant for a position as auditor in the Treasury department.

---

* H. R. Mis. Doc. No. 31, 45th Cong. 3d Sess. p. 554.
** Ibid, p. 555.
† Ibid, p. 558.
‡ Ibid, p. 486.

I can only say of Mr. Dennis that I formed his acquaintance while the Florida contest was going on, and found him a very active, intelligent, and influential republican.

He has been ostracised with other republicans of that state, and is deserving of consideration. I respectfully · commend him to your favor.

I am, very respectfully, your obedient servant,

EDWARD F. NOYES.

HON. JOHN SHERMAN,
Secretary of the Treasury."

The result was the appointment of Dennis to a sinecure in the supervising architects office at $7 per day. He remained about Washington for a month without being assigned to any duty and then was given a leave of absence and went to Massachusetts where he remained three months. He came back and drew three months pay— $630. Then he was given a position to rove about North Carolina, South Carolina, and Florida ostensibly to examine the records of United States courts and find forfeited recognizances. The real object was to send him to Florida under protection and with pay to prepare for trial several cases pending against him in the criminal courts of that state. He remained there until the resolution appointing the Potter committee passed the House of Representatives when he was ordered to North Carolina on the edge of the Dismal Swamp.* He didn't care to go into hiding and came by way of Norfolk, Va. to Washington. His pay was $7 a day and expenses. He thought he had not been rewarded according to his deserts and a statement he had previously prepared was about this time published

* H. R. Mis. Doc. No. 31, 45th Cong. 3d Sess. p. 557.

and he was dropped, having in the meantime been transferred to the internal revenue service.

* F. C. Humphreys who was first elector at large on the Florida Republican ticket was appointed collector of customs at Pensacola, April 2, 1877, and held the office till July 7, 1882—a period of five years, three months and five days at an annual salary of $1,000 and fees and commissions.

Dennis Eagan, chairman of the Repulican state committee, Florida, was appointed collector of internal revenue, at Jacksonville, March 7, 1877, and held office till October 1, 1884—a period of seven years, seven months and twenty-four days, at an annual salary of $2,875.

M. L. Stearns who was Governor of Florida at the time of the election, candidate for re-election, and who was counted in at the first canvass of the votes by the state canvassers, but ousted by the decision of the supreme court, was appointed commissioner of the Hot Springs, Arkansas commission at a salary of $10 per day, March 30, 1877, and continued till Dec. 16, 1878—drawing $6,260 expenses.

J. M. Howell, who was deputy clerk, of Baker county, and directed and assisted the county judge, E. W. Driggers in getting up the fraudulent return from that county, whereby by omitting the votes of two precincts it was made to appear that the Hayes Electors had on the face of the county returns a majority of 35, was appointed collector of customs, at Fernandina, April 12, 1878, and held the office till June 9, 1882—a period of four years, one month and twenty-eight days, at an annual salary of $500 and fees and commissions.

* Records of Appointment Division of Treasury Dept. Authority for what follows in regard to appointments of Florida conspirators.

Richard H. Black, colored, who was clerk of Archer precinct, No. 2, Alachua county, and at the direction of L. G. Dennis assisted Thomas H. Vance, inspector, in adding 219 fraudulent Republican votes to the return from that precinct and swore to every affidavit the visiting statesmen dictated through Dennis and other agents, was appointed night inspector in the Philadelphia custom house May 2. 1877 and has held the place ever since and was still holding it July 1, 1885, at a salary of $3 per day or $1,095 a year, during a period of 8 years and 2 months=$8,903.

Thomas H. Vance, who was inspector of Archer precinct No. 2, Alachua county, and assisted Rich. H. Black in the preparation of the false return and the fraudulent addition of 219 votes for the Republican national and state ticket and did all the swearing that was required of him, was appointed a clerk in the office of the auditor of the Treasury for the Post-office department, July 1, 1877, and was continued there until he was discharged, June 30, 1885 — a period of eight years at a salary of $1,200 per annum.

Joseph Bowes, who had printed "little jokers," tickets one inch and a half long, and one inch wide, containing the Republican national and state tickets, and stuffed the ballot-box at precinct No. 13, Leon county, he being one of the election officers, to the number of 74 of these "jokers," and who was about generally over the state helping to manufacture affidavits for use before the Returning Board, doing a great deal of swearing himself, was appointed a clerk of class 3 in the division of public moneys, secretary's office, Treasury department, June 1, 1877, salary $1,600 per annum. Having to flee the State of Florida to escape punishment for his crimes he found an asylum in the Treasury department at Washington on the recommendation of Edward F. Noyes, W. E. Chandler, M. L. Stearns, and Aaron A. Sargeant, which sheltered him till he resigned March 3, 1885 — a period of seven years and nine months, during which time he drew pay to the amount of $12,400.

W. K. Cessna, who was county judge of Alachua county and with full knowledge of the false return from Archer precinct No. 2 included it in the canvass of the county returns, and assisted L. G. Dennis to procure Green R. Moore to make for $100 an affidavit false in substance and inferences in regard to the vote at said precinct, was appointed a postmaster at Gainesville, Fla., by President Hayes at a salary of $1,100 per annum, and held the same from December 10, 1878, to May 22, 1882 — a period of 4 years — drawing $4,400.

Lewis A. Barnes, who assisted L. G. Dennis in the manufacture of evidence to sustain before the Returning Board the frauds of Alachua county was register of the U. S. land office, Gainesville, Florida, July 1, 1879, Salary $500, fees and commission of 1% on all moneys received.

James Bell, county judge of Jefferson county and inspector of election at Waukeenah precinct No. 7, who stole, while the ballots were being counted, 100 Democratic tickets and substituted therefor 100 Republican tickets and made several false affidavits, was appointed a clerk in the general land office, Washington, D. C., March 27, 1877, salary $1,200 per annum. On May 31, 1883, was appointed special agent: has received to July 1, 1885, $9,900.

Moses J. Taylor, clerk of Jefferson county, and inspector of poll No. 1, Monticello precinct, and who stole all but 5 of the Democratic tickets and substituted therefor Republican ones, was made a clerk in the general land office, Washington, D. C., April 7, 1877, salary $1,200 per annum. Still in office — has received $9,900 to July 7, 1885.

Frank N. Wicker, who with the assistance of Manuel Govin, postmaster at Jacksonville, manufactured the evidence about alleged irregularity in making the return frôm precinct No. 3, Key West, Monroe county, and which the state canvassers rejected thereby depriving the democrats of 401 votes, was at the time of the election Collector of the port of Key West, salary $500 per annum and fees. He was retained until May 15, 1885.

John Varnum, adjutant-general state militia, assisted in the manufacture of affidavits, appointed March 1, 1877, receiver of U. S. land office, Gainesville, Fla., salary $500, fees, and commission of 1% on all moneys received. Held office till July 1, 1879 — held office 1 year and 3 months.

Manuel Govin, postmaster at Jacksonville, Fla., the assistant of Wicker in affidavit-making at Key West, was made consul to Leghorn, Italy, November 30, 1877; salary $1,500 per annum and fees.

William M. Artrell, an affidavit-maker for Wicker, Key West, Monroe county, was an inspector in the custom house at a salary of $3 per day. He has been continued in this employment.

M. Martin, acting-chairman Republican state committee of Florida, and one of the most active of the conspirators, was made surveyor-general of Florida, February 25, 1881, just before Hayes went out of office, salary $2,000 per annum.

Geo. H. DeLeon, who was secretary to Governor Stearns, and, by reason of this confidential position, familiar with all that transpired before the election, during the canvass by the state canvassers, who received and opened the governor's mail and telegrams, was appointed a clerk in the second auditor's office at Washington, May 25, 1877, at a salary of $1,200 per annum, and promoted to $1,600 in 1882.

He resigned March 30, 1885, to take effect on the 20th of April.

. Geo. D. Mills, telegrapher at Tallahassee and one of the clerks of the state canvassers, with knowledge of all that was done as well as of a great deal of the telegraphing done by visiting statesmen, was appointed a clerk in the pension office at a salary of $1,200 per annum, March 1, 1877, and is still in office: has received to July 1, 1885, $9,900.

Thomas J. Brady, who followed on the heels of William E. Chandler to Florida, in charge of the post-office inspectors, ordered thither by James N. Tyner, postmaster-general, and carrying money to Chandler, was second assistant postmaster-general and in charge of all mail service. He was continued in office and protected by Hayes notwithstanding the most serious charges were repeatedly made against him in connection with the star route mail contracts. It was during the Hayes administration that the gigantic star route frauds were perpetrated which resulted in a loss to the government, according to the statement of Attorney-General Benj. H. Brewster to the Bar Association meeting at Saratoga in 1882, of more than $4,000,000. The facts and evidence in support thereof which secured the removal of Brady in 1881, by Attorney-General MacVeagh and Postmaster-General James, and enabled an investigation to be made that resulted in the complete exposure of the star route villainy, was made known to the Hayes administration in 1880. Sufficient evidence to have put honest men on inquiry was made public at a much earlier date, but Brady was protected.

H. Clay Hopkins, agent of the postal stamp division stationed at New York City, was one of those who accompanied Brady to Florida and was absent from his official duties one month. His salary was $2,500 per annum.

Wm. T. Henderson, post-office inspector, salary $1,600 per annum and $5 per diem for travelling expenses while on the business of the department, together with free transportation, accompanied Brady to Florida, travelled on post-office inspector's pass, and charged up $5 a day for travelling expenses. With United States troops to impress negroes went to Jackson county, accompanied by Z. L. Tilball, post-office inspector, and M. C. Cooper, deputy United States marshal to collect negro affidavits. Henderson is still in the service as post-office inspector.

Z. L. Tilball, post-office inspector, salary $1,600 per annum, $5 per diem travelling expenses while absent from Washington on business of the department, and free transportation, accompanied Brady to Florida, travelled on post-office inspector's pass and drew his per diem as if on official business, was with Henderson in Jackson county collecting affidavits from negroes. — Remained in post-office department as inspector till July 18, 1882, when he was appointed United States marshal for the Territory of Arizona. His successor was appointed July 8, 1885.

B. H. Camp, post-office inspector, salary $1,600 per annum, $5 per diem travelling expenses while absent from post on business of the department, and free transportation, accompanied Brady to Florida : travelled on post-office inspector's pass and drew per diem as if on department business. His real business in Florida was to assist the subordinates of Stearns in working up evidence to sustain Republican frauds.

Alfred Morton, post-office inspector, salary $1,600, per annum, $5 per diem travelling expenses, and free transportation. Accompanied Brady to Florida, and assisted James

Bell in the manufacture of evidence to sustain the frauds in Jefferson county—ballot-box stuffing.

E. W. Maxwell, detective attached to the department of justice, salary $5 per diem, and actual travelling expenses; went to Florida but according to W. E. Chandler rendered no service—was a "drone"—*i. e.* a dead beat, nevertheless drew pay and expenses.

Edward H. Noyes, of Ohio, the particular personal friend of R. B. Hayes, the man who nominated him at Cincinnati, and his especial representative in Florida, was appointed envoy extraordinary and minister plenipotentiary to France and commissioned July 1, 1877—holding till March 21, 1881, a period of three years, eight months and twenty days, salary $17,500 per annum, = $65,138.86.

John A. Kasson, of Iowa, accompanied Noyes to Florida and rendered himself useful as voucher and sponsor for Hayes, was commissioned envoy extraordinary and minister plenipotentiary to Austria, June 11, 1877 and remained till April 26, 1882—a period of four years, ten months and fifteen days, salary $12,000 per annum, = $58,500.

Lew Wallace, soldier, author, statesman, accompanied Noyes to Florida, and according to the testimony of Dennis and McLin pledged Hayes generally and giving Noyes as reference, was appointed Governor of New Mexico, salary only $2,600 per annnm. Reward not being adequate was made minister resident to Turkey, July 13, 1882, where he remained and drew pay till June 1, 1885.

William E. Chandler, who came to the rescue on the morning of Wednesday, Nov. 8, 1876 and re-encouraged the demoralized National committee, conceived the plan of counting Hayes in, organized the conspirators, and left the same day for Florida to execute a part of the hazardous undertaking, and did his work thoroughly well, became disgusted with the fraudulent administration when it abandoned Packard in Louisiana, and Chamberlain in South Carolina, and not being promptly rewarded for his services attacked Hayes and proved that by deserting the Louisiana and South Carolina carpet-baggers he thereby acknowledged to the world that he had not been elected President.

Francis C. Barlow, the one "visiting statesman" who was troubled with a conscience and endeavored to fulfil the duties to which he had been invited by the President of the United States in accordance with sentiments expressed by the chief executive of the nation, was not rewarded with any office but was bitterly assailed for his alleged betrayal of his party.

CHAPTER VII.

Preparation for frauds: The state census of 1875 the basis of fraudulent registration: Republican managers determined to prevent a
fair election: The bad characters who were selected for supervisors
of registration: The registration frauds in New Orleans and in
the parishes demonstrated by official statistics: Depriving democrats of the right to vote: Registration of negroes facilitated:
The election was fair, free, and peaceable: The proof of this conclusive: The election law analyzed: What was required in report-
ing intimidation or violence: Laws conferring such great power
on returning officers must be strictly construed.

PRIOR to the election of 1876 in Louisiana very elaborate
preparations were made for stupendous frauds by the *de
facto* governor, William Pitt Kellogg and his characterless
subordinates. The entire election machinery was absolutely
controlled by the governor. How Kellogg was made *de
facto* governor will be told in succeeding chapters wherein the remarkable story of Louisiana politics from 1868
to 1876 will be related. To maintain themselves in
power the carpet-bag and scalaway rogues who were enabled, by the reconstruction act, to seize the state, enacted
in 1870 registration and election laws. These enactments
were designed to place the machinery of election in the
hands of a few men. Among other things provided for was
a quadrennial census which was intended to be the foundation for a dishonest registration of the voters.

In 1875 a state census was taken which was the basis
for the registration of 1876. This census made the negro

population appear to be 45,695 more than the white population, and the negro voters to be 104,192, while the white
voters were only 84,167.* The census of the United
States for 1880 shows that the excess of negro population
in Louisiana over white was 26,364, and that the white
males of twenty-one years of age and over, exceeded the
negro males, of the voting age and upwards, by 1,513.
The census of 1870 showed an excess of white males of
voting age of 153 over male negroes of like age. Therefore, it was an impossibility to honestly show in 1875 a
majority of 20,025 colored voters in Louisiana. The state
registrar of voters was Michael Hahn and his chief clerk
was James P. McArdle. D. J. M. A. Jewett was secretary
of the Republican committee on canvassing and registration, and he and McArdle ran the state registrar's office.
They converted it into a partisan political machine. The
supervisors of registration, appointed by Kellogg, were all
unscrupulous men and most of them Federal office holders.

It was the deliberate purpose of the Republican leaders
to prevent legal elections from being held in certain parishes
where they could not control the negro vote. Jewett stated †
that it was their intention to invalidate the election in the
parishes of De Soto, Ouachita, Grant, Morehouse, East and
West Feliciana, and East Baton Rouge. All the circumstances show that it was the scheme of the Republican leaders
in New Orleans to prevent, if possible, the holding of a legal
election in those parishes. There was some difference among
them as to the best method of accomplishing this result.
† Jewett, B. P. Blanchard, and the more reckless leaders,
advocated the bold plan of refusing to appoint supervisors
of registration on the ground that it was impossible to

---

* Senate Report No. 701 vol. 3, 44th Cong. 2nd Sess. pp. 2634-5.
† H. R. Mis. Doc. No. 31, 45th Cong. 3d Sess. p. 1441.

have a fair, free, and full registration, and that any election
which might be held would be a farce. But Kellogg preferred a more devious course.   The evidence is ample and
conclusive that he selected men for supervisors of registration, or accepted those recommended to him, who he
thought would accomplish the same result in another way.
They were to go to the parishes and if they could not manage to have the bulk of the Republican negro votes cast
at a few polls they were to leave the parishes before com-
pleting the registration, alleging danger to their lives and
general intimidation, violence, and turbulence.

* D. A. Ward, a resident of New Orleans, was made
supervisor of registration for Grant parish.   He returned
to New Orleans before he had completed his work, alleging
as an excuse for leaving that he was going after ballot-
boxes, the furnishing of which was the business of the
. sheriff of the parish.   In New Orleans he told E. A. Burke
that it was not the intention of his party leaders to have an
election held in Grant and several other parishes.   Subsequently, upon Burke remonstrating with Kellogg, he issued
an order to Ward to return to the parish.   Several days
later Burke met Ward who showed him the governor's
order but said it was a sham — that Jewett and Blanchard
told him to stay; that he had no money to pay expenses
and the committee would not give him any.   He did
not go back.   The democrats and republicans in Grant
parish mutually agreed that the election should be held
under the direction of an United States supervisor of elections.   But the absence of the supervisor of registration
was subsequently held by the Returning Board to have invalidated the election.

* H. R. Mis. Doc. No. 34 Part 2, 44th Cong. 2nd Sess. p. 443.

* James E. Anderson, a clerk in the New Orleans Customs House, was made supervisor of the parish of East Feliciana. He was especially interested in Charles E. Nash, a colored man, who was a candidate for Congress in the Sixth District which included the Felicianas. He went to the parish and began the registration but found a disagreement between the negro and white Republican leaders. The latter did not want an election held, and the former wanted an election but insisted that the white republicans should not run the party. The white republicans told Anderson to leave the parish and, finding that he still remained, they, as he subsequently testified, attempted to assassinate him. He returned to New Orleans. His presence there was the subject of complaint by the democrats to Kellogg. Anderson swore, subsequently, that Kellogg told him to return and have the negroes massed and voted at certain polls in wards where they could be controlled, and to have riots and disturbances at the polls where the bulk of Democratic votes were cast, so they could be rejected by the Returning Board. He returned to East Feliciana but made no effort to carry out the plan suggested.

† George L. Smith, a native of New Hampshire, settled in Shreveport, Louisiana, after the war, and became an active " carpet-bag " politician. He was a member of the legislature in 1870 and 1872, and was proprietor of *The Southwestern Telegram*, a journal supported by the state printing bestowed upon it by the governor, under the printing law. He was a member of the Forty-third Congress from the Fourth Congressional District, and in 1876 was a candidate for re-election. He conducted the canvass in the re-

* H. R. Mis. Doc. No. 31, 45th Cong. 3d Sess. pp. 5, 6, 7, 8.

† Ibid p. 1450 and H. R. Mis. Doc. No. 34 part 6, 44th Cong. 2nd Ses. p. 208.

gion about Shreveport and received from Kellogg commissions, signed in blank, for the supervisors of registration for the parishes composing his district. He made three of his partisans, C. L. Ferguson, T. H. Hutton, and John T. Morrow, supervisors of the parishes of De Soto, Bossier, and Webster. Ward, supervisor of Grant parish, although a resident of New Orleans, was under Smith's direction, his clerk, W. P. Guynes being an appointee of Smith. Ferguson and Morrow were not residents of De Soto and Webster parishes but lived in Shreveport or near that place.

* F. A. Clover, supervisor of the parish of East Baton Rouge, was not a qualified elector of Louisiana, having recently removed there from Mississippi. His first occupation in New Orleans was that of "roper-in" for a snake show. He had been a member of the Mississippi legislature and upon the overthrow of the "carpet-bag" government in that state sought refuge in Louisiana. He proved a fit instrument for the work assigned him in East Baton Rouge.

* The supervisors for the parishes of Morehouse and Richland, F. M. Grant and J. F. Kelley, resided there. M. J. Grady, supervisor of Ouachita parish, was a deputy collector of internal revenue. James E. Scott, supervisor of Claiborne parish, was a clerk in the New Orleans Post-office, and R. B. Edgeworth, supervisor of the parish of Plaquimine was an inspector in the Custom House, New Orleans. B. F. Woodruff, supervisor of Rapides parish, was also a clerk in the New Orleans Post-office. A. W. Cornog, supervisor of Red River parish, was borne on the rolls of the New Orleans Custom House. Phillip Joseph, supervisor of Madison parish, was a fugitive from Alabama,

* H. R. Mis. Doc. No. 34 Part 2, 44th Cong. 2nd Sess. p. 1049.

and had been indicted in New Orleans for burglary and house-breaking. The supervisor of St. Tammany parish, Victor Guadias, was a resident of New Orleans. A. W. Kenchen and J. A. Veasey, supervisors of Livingston and La Fayette parishes, were under indictment for murder. H. F. Brennan, corporal of police, was assistant supervisor of the first ward, New Orleans. A. J. Brim, Custom House officer, was assistant supervisor of the second ward, and Pat. Creagh, Inspector in the Custom House, was assistant supervisor of the third ward. R. C. Howard, J. G. Pulchler, W. J. Moore, Thomas Levie, H. C. Bartlett, T. H. Rowan, P. J. Malloney, assistant supervisors of the fourth, sixth, seventh, eighth, ninth, tenth, and fourteenth wards, were all borne on the pay roll of the Custom House. L. C. Backers, assistant supervisor of the eleventh ward, was a police officer, and W. F. Loan, chief of police, was the assistant supervisor of the fifteenth ward.

* A determined effort was made to increase the registration of negro voters in the city of New Orleans and to prevent a full registration of the whites. Every facility was given to negroes to register, while well-known white citizens were annoyed in every possible way. The registration offices were not kept open the full number of hours required by law. The democrats were required to form in line and await their turns to register. The assistant supervisors would consume at least fifteen minutes in registering well-known white men,† while negroes could slip into the offices and get their certificates in a few moments. Negroes were sent to the places of registry the night before to form a long line and keep white men away.

The census of 1870 showed that the white population

---

* H. R. Mis. Doc. No. 34 Part 2, 44th Cong. 2nd Sess. p. 1020.

† Ibid. p. 478. Testimony of Prof. Chaille.

of New Orleans parish was 140,923 and the negro 50,456. In 1880 the white population was 158,367, and the negro 57,617. The state census,* made for political purposes in 1875, placed the negro population of New Orleans at 57,647, and the white at 145,721. When the registration was completed in New Orleans 57,647 negro population yielded 23,495 voters, and 145,721 whites yielded only 34,913 voters. This vast difference cannot be accounted for on any other theory than fraudulent registration of colored voters. The total foreign born population of New Orleans, according to the state census of 1875, was 43,712. The number of naturalized foreigners was given as 14,984, and the number of foreigners, over 21 years of age, not naturalized, as 5,266. These statistics will not stand any test applied to them. Deducting the foreign population, 43,712 — allowing it to be white — from the total white population, 145,721, leaves 102,009 native whites. Adding to the 14,928 naturalized foreigners the 5,266 unnaturalized, over 21 years of age, and there would be 20,250, over 21 years old, from a total of 43,712 foreigners. This is absurd. The mining population of California in 1849-50 scarcely yielded so great a proportion of males over twenty-one years of age. Again, accepting the 14,984 naturalized foreign voters, as correct, from a total of 43,712 foreign population, and add 23,495 negro voters registered and we have 38,479 negro and foreign white voters. But the state census of 1875 gives the total number of persons entitled to vote in New Orleans as 44,392 — leaving the native white population of 102,009 to supply 5,913 voters! It is, therefore, evident that the statistics of foreign males, twenty-one years old and over, and of the naturalized foreign voters,

* H. R. Mis. Doc. No. 34, Part 2, 44th Cong. 2d Sess. pp. 494-5.

are thrown in, as figures and words in cryptography, to deceive.

But the state census of 1875 states that of the 57,647 negroes in New Orleans there is an excess of 7,210 females over males. Deducting this excess of females and there remains only 21,614 males! And yet in 1876 23,495 negro voters were registered! It certainly is unnecessary to bring forward another fact to demonstrate the fraudulent character of the negro registration in New Orleans.

But not satisfied with a registration of 23,495 negro voters from a total male population of 21,614 in 1875, and only 34,913 white voters from a total population of 145,721 in 1875, the Republican managers proceeded secretly to strike off the registration lists the names of 7,738 white voters.* They, with the coöperation of United States Marshal Pitkin, and the employés of the Post-office, sent out about 30,000 circulars with instructions to the letter-carriers to return all not personally delivered to those to whom addressed. Some eleven thousand were so returned, and, thereupon, warrants were sworn out, a few days before the election, against these 11,000 citizens. In the mean-time the registration books were secretly taken to the Custom House and the assistant supervisors marshalled there and directed to strike off the registry lists the names of those against whom warrants had been issued. One United States commissioner, who had issued a large number of warrants, published the names and a great number of gentlemen, finding theirs among the rest, hastened to the commissioner's office, and being well-known citizens, were promptly discharged. By this means, and by the strenuous efforts of Major E. A. Burke, chairman of the Democratic

* H. R. Mis. Doc., No. 34, Part 2, 44th Cong., 2d Sess., pp. 1031-'32-'33.

campaign committee, quite a large number got their names restored to the registry lists, but a total of 7,738 white men were deprived of the right to vote. On the other hand the democrats only succeeded in having 3,368 names of fraudulently-registered colored men stricken from the registration lists. Professor Chaille,* an eminent authority on vital statistics, and a careful student of those of New Orleans, and Louisiana, gives as his judgment, after a careful examination of all the available data, that an honest and complete registration of the voters of New Orleans in 1876 would have given about 40,584 white and 13,500 negro voters. Allowing for reasonable contingencies, absence and sickness, there ought not to have been more than 12,000 colored citizens registered.

The registration of the entire state, according to the statistics of the State registrars office in 1876, was 207,622, divided into colored, 115,268, and white, 92,354.* The state census of 1875 gave the total number of persons entitled to vote as 188,059, divided into colored, 104,192, and white 84,167. The registration, therefore, showed an increase during one year of the negro voters of 11,076 and of 8,187 white voters — very nearly an equal percentage of increase. This is conclusive as to the effect of alleged intimidation on the registration of colored voters. Their own figures demonstrate that the negroes were at least suffered by the terrible (?) " bulldozers " to register in peace. Therefore, it must be concluded that whatever statements were made by supervisors of registration about " intimidation " preventing a full, fair, and free registration of colored voters, were absolutely untrue. But it is equally certain that, instead of negroes not being allowed to register, there

* H. R. Mis. Doc., No. 34, Part 2, 44th Cong., 2nd Sess. p. 478.
† Ibid, p. 494-'5.

must have been a very large fraudulent negro registration in the parishes outside of New Orleans. This fact is proved by the official data furnished by the census of 1870 and that of 1880. In 1870 the colored males, of twenty-one years of age and over, were 86,913, and white males of like age 87,066. The "colored" class included negroes, Chinese, and Indians. In 1880 the white males of twenty-one and over, were 108,810, and the colored males of like age, 107,979. These proportions could not have varied in 1876. The increase was very nearly the same in ten years. But how about the foreign-born males? The foreign population of Louisiana has steadily decreased since 1860. There was a loss up to 1880 of 26,829. In 1880 the native and foreign males, twenty-one years of age and over, were divided as follows — natives 81,777 — foreign 27,033=108,810. These proportions could not have varied much in 1876, because, we find that year 22,134 naturalized citizens registered. If from colored males, Chinese, Indians and foreign-born negroes are deducted, it will be found that the colored voters could not have exceeded the white electors in 1876. It is the opinion of Professor Chaille, an eminent authority, that there was a small majority of white voters in the state.*

These statistics prove two things incontrovertibly—first, that the stories about the great number of negroes being killed in Louisiana from 1870 to 1880 were altogether false; and, second, that the registration of 1876, which showed a majority of 22,314, colored voters in the state, was fraudulent. It has been demonstrated that there were at least 11,500 fraudulent negro voters registered in New Orleans. There must have been several thousand more false registrations outside the city. The supervisors were

* H. R. Mis. Doc. No. 34, Part 2, 44th Cong. 2d Sess. pp. 476 to 480.

with few exceptions men of bad character. The facility with which negroes can be falsely registered and used as "repeaters" at the polls is well known.

The election was a peaceable one throughout the state. There is not only abundant affirmative proof of this, but all attempts to prove the contrary have signally failed. There is not in all the thousands of pages * of testimony, which have been taken in regard to the election of 1876 in Louisiana, a scintilla of evidence to prove that on the day of the election there was at a single polling place in the State any riot, tumult, disturbance, or intimidation. The election officers were all republicans. The supervisors of registration were selected with a view to their reckless unscrupulousness and their entire dependence on the Republican leaders. They were not only carefully instructed in regard to the advantages which the law gave them, and how to avail themselves thereof, but they were plainly told that their political future depended entirely upon their work.† The committee on canvassing and registration issued its orders to the supervisors of every parish, and set the mark they were to obtain, and notified them that unless this result was achieved they would "not be held to have done" their "full duty in the premises." At the same time

* Senate Reports No. 701, 44th Cong., 2nd Sess., 3 vols., 3,100 pages. H. R. Mis. Doc., 44th Cong., 2nd Sess., 6 parts, 3,000 pages. H. R. Mis. Doc., No. 42, 44th Cong., 2nd Sess., 440 pages. H. R. Mis. Doc., No. 31, 5 parts, 2,116 pages.

†   HEADQUARTERS REPUBLICAN PARTY OF LOUISIANA,
    Rooms Joint Committee on Canvassing and Registration,
    MECHANICS' INSTITUTE, Sept 25, 1876.

Supervisor of Registration, Parish of Assumption, La.:

DEAR SIR: It is well known to this committee that, from examination of the census of 1875, the Republican vote in your parish is 2,200, and the Republican majority is 900.

You are expected to register and vote the full strength of the Republican party in your parish.

Your recognition by the next state administration will depend upon your doing your full duty in the premises, and you will not be held to have

they were promised "ample and generous recognition" if they deserved it. The census of 1875, prepared as the basis for the election frauds of 1876, was also made the standard by which the services of the election officers were to be judged. The deliberation and cool impudence with which these unconscionable rogues set about their infamous work cannot be paralleled in the history of political scoundrelism!

There were fifty-six parishes, exclusive of New Orleans, and nearly a thousand polling places in the state. There were seventy-four supervisors and assistant supervisors of registration, their clerks and three commissioners of election for each poll, selected by the Republican managers. And yet when the election closed and the returns came to the supervisors, and were consolidated, and made ready to be transmitted to the Returning Board, only two supervisors made, then and there, as the law required, any protests affecting the fairness and freeness of the registration, or the peaceable and honest character of the election had or held under their supervision.

In but one solitary instance throughout the entire State, and that was in the city of New Orleans, did the commissioners of election allege intimidation. This exception was at poll 2, eleventh ward, New Orleans, where A. W. Kempton* and A. M. C. Hearsey, two Custom House pensioners, after the returns were completed, refused to

---

done your full duty unless the Republican registration in your parish reaches 2,200, and the Republican vote is at least 2,100.

All local candidates and committees are directed to aid you to the utmost in obtaining the result, and every facility is, and will be, afforded you; but you must obtain the results called for herein without fail. Once obtained, your recognition will be ample and generous.

Very respectfully your obedient servant,

D. J. M. A. JEWETT,

Secretary.

* H. R. Mis. Doc. No, 34 Part 2, 44th Cong. 2nd Sess. p. 18.

sign them at the last moment, alleging that they had been intimidated.   This was a mere pretext.   The poll was surrounded all day by deputy marshals and metropolitan police, and the United States supervisor of election was present in the room.   It was simply a case of "pure cussedness" on the part of Kempton and Hearsey, who were determined to furnish a pretext for the disfranchisment of 412 respectable citizens living in the best portion of the residence quarter of the city.   There was no legal process by which these two miscreants could be compelled to do their duty.   Had the men, who were to be disfranchised, been black, an appeal could have been made to the United States court, but inasmuch as they were white gentlemen they had no remedy save to "the political court" presided over by one of Kellogg's creatures.   No attempt was ever made to justify the conduct of Kempton and Hearsey.

The assistant supervisor for the ward, one of Kellogg's police officers, refused to compile the vote of this poll, although it was his duty under the law to do so and state the facts in regard to the action of the commissioners; and the Returning Board, of course, did not count it.   The two instances where supervisors accompanied their consolidated statements of the votes of their parishes by objections, made in conformity to the law, were N. McKenny, of Caddo, and C. A. Bossier, of St. Charles.   In the one case the objections affected only the votes for justices of the peace and constables, and in the other the supervisor declined to incorporate the votes of two polls, because, where he had established one, the commissioners made two, which by law they had no right to do.

The election law * which conferred such vast authority

* For Louisiana election law and instructions to Supervisors of

upon election officers, upon the supervisors of registration, and upon the Returning Board prescribed exactly what they should do, and how they should do it. If there had been any occurrence to prevent, or tending to prevent, " a full, fair, and free registration," when they came to make up ˙ their consolidated statements of the votes from the returns to them by commissioners of election, they must note on the blank furnished them on which to compile the returns, under the head of "remarks," their statements about inter- ference with registration and must swear to the truth there- of and have three respectable citizens, qualified voters of the parish, corroborate the same under oath.

As to all occurrences on the day of the election at the polls, it was the duty of the commissioners of election to certify, under oath, and have the same corroborated under oath, by three respectable citizens, qualified voters of the voting place. When they made out their returns, which must be on the day of the election, if there had been any- thing happen which in their judgment affected "the purity and freedom" of the election, they must make a statement thereof under oath and have three citizens vouch for the truth of the same, and forward it along with their returns, the tally sheets, registration lists, all made out in duplicate, one set to the supervisor, and one to the clerk of the parish court.

The supervisor must note under the head of "remarks" on his consolidated statement, the facts in regard to any polls reported by the commissioners, and must attach thereto, "by paste, wax, or other adhesive substance," the statement of the commissioners. This consolidated state-

---

Registration issued by State Registrar of voters see H. R. Mis. Doc. No. 34, Part 2, 44th Cong. 2nd Sess. pp. 539 to 589. For elaborate analysis of same see Electoral Count—Arguments of ex-Senators Carpenter and Trumbull, pp. 263 to 299 and 301 to 341.

ment, the remarks thereon, with statements attached, must
be certified as correct by the clerk of the court, and a duplicate deposited in his office. The supervisors had no authority to reject the returns from any polls, or to refuse to
compile the same on their consolidated statements. It was
their duty to compile and to note under "remarks" the facts,
and send, attached to their statements, the evidence required
by law. They were omnipotent in all matters relating to
registration, but, that completed, their functions became
wholly ministerial and they could only report facts and evidence, in the manner prescribed, to the Returning Board
who were to pass judgment thereon.

It was further provided, by section 43 of the election
law, that the supervisors should, " after the receipt of all the
returns for the different polling places," consolidate the
same in duplicate and, after certification by the clerk of the
district court that the same were correct, according to the
duplicate returns in his possession, deposit one copy of the
consolidated statement with the said clerk, and " FORWARD
BY MAIL, *inclosed in an envelope of strong paper, or cloth,
securely sealed,*" to the Returning Board the other, with
all the returns made by the commissioners to the supervisors, tally sheets, registered lists of voters for each polling place, and the statements, if any, in regard to occurrences affecting "the purity and freedom" of the voting,
attached thereto.

The provisions to prevent tampering with the returns
were ample. Duplicates of everything went to the clerks of
the courts at the parish towns, and there the supervisors
made up, on blanks furnished for that purpose, duplicate
consolidated statements of the returns from the commissioners of election, making under the head of "remarks"
whatever statements they had to make concerning registra-

tion, and having the same verified as the law required, and also such statements as the reports of the commissioners justified concerning the character of the election at the respective polls, and attach thereto the said reports, and have the clerk certify to the correctness of all; this done, one copy of the consolidated statements must be deposited with the said clerks, who were the custodians of duplicates of the commissioners' returns, tally sheets, lists of registered voters, and the boxes containing the ballots, and the other, with duplicates of returns, tally sheets, and lists of registered voters, and statements, if any, by commissioners, properly verified, affecting "the purity and freedom" of election, must be forwarded by mail to the Returning Board.

When the law had been thus obeyed, and all formalities strictly complied with, the Returning Board, coming into possession of the original returns from every poll or voting place in the State, and for their convenience tabulated by parishes, said tabulations, or consolidated statements, having attached thereto whatever evidence there was affecting "the purity and freedom" of the voting at any polls, and whatever evidence there was concerning interference with registration, then the process of canvassing and compiling began.

In canvassing and compiling the law regulated the process in the strictest manner. It said, "they shall compile first the statements from all polls or voting places at which there shall have been a fair, free, and peaceable registration and election." How were they to know that at any poll there had not been "a fair, free, and peaceable registration and election?" The law tells how. "Whenever, from any poll or voting place, there shall be received the statement of any supervisor of registration or commissioner of election, in form as required by section twenty-six of this act, on affidavit of three or more citizens, of any riot, tumult, acts of violence, intimidation, armed disturbance, bribery, or currupt influences, which prevented, or tended to prevent, a fair, free, and peaceable vote of all qualified electors, entitled to vote at such poll or voting place, such returning officers shall not canvass, count, or compile the statements of votes from such poll or voting place until the statements from all other polls or voting places shall have been canvassed and compiled."

That is to say — all statements from polls or voting places which were not affected by " the statement of any supervisor of registration or commissioner of election in form as required by section twenty-six," must be canvassed and compiled. Of course, these words, " canvass " and " compile," have an exact, definite, legal meaning. That meaning has been determined time out of mind. " Canvass " means, in the connection here used, as the courts have invariably decided," to examine thoroughly " for errors of computation, or mistatement in figures of results, and to " compile " means to " put together." Therefore, the returning officers were first " to examine thoroughly " and " put together " the votes from all polls or voting places concerning which there had not come to them " the statement of any supervisor of registration or commissioner of election, in form as required by section twenty-six of this act."

They could take no other " statement." It must come from a *supervisor of registration or commissioner of election, in form as required by section twenty-six.* And section twenty-six " *required* " these statements to be exact and definite; in a certain " *form*," made at a certain time and place, verified by certain persons, and certified as correct by certain officers independent of the supervisors or commissioners. The supervisors could only make " statements " as to the registration and they must make these under oath, and have them corroborated by three reputable citizens, qualified voters, who must swear to their knowledge; then these statements must be made on the blank for consolidated returns, or attached thereto, with reference to the same on the blank. The clerk of the court must certify thereto and an *exact* duplicate must be filed with him.

The commissioners of election must make their statements affecting the voting at the polls, they must have them corroborated by three respectable witnesses, qualified voters, they must be sworn to, and in duplicate, and must be forwarded along with their returns, one with their duplicate returns, tally lists, lists of registered voters, and the ballot-boxes, to the clerk of the court, and one to the supervisor of registration for their parish, with duplicate of returns, tally lists, and lists of registered voters. The supervisor must forward these attached to his consolidated statement in an envelope of strong paper, or cloth, securely sealed, *by mail* to the returning officers, and deposit a duplicate of his statement with the clerk of the court, both having first been certified to by the clerk.

Having "examined thoroughly" and "put together" the votes from all polls or voting places unaffected by "the statement of any supervisor of registration or commissioner of election in form as required by section twenty-six," the returning officers had fulfilled their functions so far as these polls or voting places were concerned. And, moreover, the law required them to proceed *by polls*, and not *by parishes.* "They shall compile first the statements from all polls or voting places at which there shall have been a fair, free, and peaceable registration and election." There was no discretion — the law was mandatory. They were vested with extraordinary powers and the law-makers prescribed in positive terms not only their duties but the manner in which they should exercise them.

The votes from all polls or voting places at which there was a fair, free, peaceable registration and election, having been ‾passed upon and put together, the law says, " the returning officers *shall then* proceed to investigate the statements of riot, tumult, acts of violence, intimidation, armed disturbance, bribery, or corrupt influences at any such poll or voting place : and if from the evidence of *such statement...*" that is, the statement of any supervisor of registration or commissioner of election, in form as required by section twenty-six — " they shall be convinced that such riot, tumult, acts of violence, intimidation, armed disturbance, bribery, or corrupt influences did not materially interfere with the purity and freedom of the election at such poll or voting place, or did not prevent a sufficient number of qualified voters thereat from registering or voting to materially change the result of the election, then and not otherwise, said returning officers shall canvass and compile the vote of such poll or voting place with those previously canvassed and compiled : but if said returning officers shall not be fully satisfied thereof, it shall be their duty to examine further testimony in regard thereto, and to this end they shall have power to send for persons and papers. If, after such examination, the said returning officers shall be convinced that said riot, tumult, acts of violence, intimidation, armed disturbance, bribery, or corrupt influences did materially interfere with the purity and freedom of the election at such poll or voting place, or did prevent a sufficient number of the qualified electors thereat from registering and voting to materially change the result of the election, then the said returning officers shall not canvass or compile the statement of the votes of such poll or voting place, but shall exclude it from their returns: *Provided*, that any person interested in said election by reason of being a candidate for office shall be allowed a hearing before said returning officers upon making application within the time allowed for the forwarding of the returns of said election."

It will be observed that throughout, section 3 of the election law, conferring judicial power upon the returning officers, is strikingly exact and specific in the language used. In the proviso, even, giving candidates a chance for a hearing it requires that they shall make application "within the time allowed for the forwarding of the returns of said election." This language is important, because, it proves that all the proceedings by the commissioners of election and the supervisors were to be open and public. For this reason, among others, duplicates of everything had to be filed with the clerk of the court at the parish town, so that all men might be informed of what had been done. How else could they know certainly what had transpired and make "application within the time allowed for the forwarding of the returns?"

The election of all local officers depended upon the action taken by the returning officers. The candidates learning from the clerk of the court, from duplicates on file with him, that returns from certain polls or voting places were impeached for certain causes, could have a hearing before the returning officers, provided, they made their application in due season. It must be made "within the time allowed for the forwarding of the returns." How long was this time? Section 43 of the election law says, "*within twenty-four hours* after the receipt of all the returns from the different polling places," the supervisors of registration were "to consolidate such returns" and forward them by mail. Therefore, within the "*twenty-four hours* after the receipt of all the returns from the different polling places " the application to the returning officers must be made for a hearing. Bearing these provisions of the election law in mind let us see what happened.

CHAPTER VIII.

A gain of 2500 votes in New Orleans by means of registration frauds made the republicans hopeful of the state: Provision made beforehand for the Returning Board villainy: The Republican visiting statesmen: How they prated about the forms of law and encouraged their violation: The monument they left behind: The manufacture of affidavits in the custom house: The modus operandi: The supervisors of registration did not make their returns according to law: They brought them to New Orleans to be doctored: Evidence of intimidation had to be supplied by means of perjury and forgery: The part played by visiting statesmen: The Sherman letter: The evidence concerning it: The use made of the New Orleans Post-office: The mails tampered with: What was done in the postmaster's private office: A statement by one of the principal actors: Falsification of records.

THE Republican managers, as they have testified themselves,[*] were confident for one week after the election on 7th of November 1876, that their plans had worked successfully, and that they would have on the face of the returns a majority of all the votes cast. They had made a gain of 2,500 votes in New Orleans over the vote of 1874, and they did not doubt that they had made corresponding gains in other localities. As the returns came in their views seemed to be corroborated and they were correspondingly jubilant. They assured their northern friends that they had carried the state.

---

[*] See Jewett's testimony, H. R. Mis. Doc. No. 31, 45th Cong. 3d Sess. p. 1441.

D. J. M. A. Jewett, testified before the Potter committee, that it was not until the 12th or 13th of November
that they were satisfied the returns would be against
them. This is not improbable. Their success in increasing the negro registration in New Orleans, and in
voting a large number of those fraudulently registered,
gave them ground of hope for the success of like tactics outside the city. They knew that they had registered fully 20,000 more negro voters than there were qualified negro electors in the state, and they did not doubt that
this fraudulent registration would enable them to secure
large majorities — increases in proportion to the gain in
New Orleans — in certain negro wards in different parishes.
Hence their confidence.

But they nevertheless had provided against contingencies by instructing* their supervisors of registration
to disobey the law, and, instead of forwarding their
returns *by mail* to the returning officers, to bring them
in person to New Orleans. As they came in the supervisors did not deposit the returns with the returning
officers but carried them to the Custom House. Some of
them had obeyed the law and forwarded their returns by
mail but the registered packages containing the same were
stopped in the New Orleans Post-office and either retained
there, or turned over to the Republican managers. Only
seventeen supervisors of registration obeyed the law and
forwarded their returns by mail.

On November 12 and 13 the " visiting statesmen," who
had been invited by the President of the United States to
be present "in Louisiana, to see that the board of canvassers make a fair count of the votes actually cast," began

---

* See Jewett's testimony, H. R. Mis. Doc. No. 31, 45th Cong. 3d
Sess. p. 1460.

to arrive in New Orleans.* The Democratic visitors arrived about the same time and they addressed a communication to Stanley Mathews, James A. Garfield, John A. Logan, William D. Kelley, John A. Kasson, William M. Evarts, E. W. Stoughton, John A. Dix, and others, stating that it was understood that they were there at the request of the President " to see that the board of canvassers make a fair count of the votes actually cast," and inviting a conference " in order that such influence as we possess may be exerted in behalf of such a canvass of the votes actually cast as by its fairness and impartiality shall command the respect and acquiescence of the American people of all parties."

This invitation was replied to by Republican visitors, † on the 16th, John Sherman signing first, captiously declining to coöperate, " to influence " the judicial action of the Returning Board. They declared that they could not " concur in your proposition for a conference " on the basis of reducing " to the mere clerical duty of counting ' the votes actually cast ' in distinction from votes legally cast and returned, irrespective of the question whether they are fraudulently and violently cast, or otherwise vitiated." They further stated that " it is, in our judgment, vital to the preservation of constitutional liberty that the habit of obedience to the forms of law should be sedulously inculcated and cultivated, and that the result to extra-constitutional modes of redress, for even actual grievances, should be avoided and condemned as revolutionary, disorganizing, and tending to disorder and anarchy."

* Sherman Report; Senate, Ex. Doc. No. 2, 44th Cong. 2d Sess. p. 31.
    † Ibid, p. 32.

The " forms of law " for the guidance of election officers
and supervisors of registration in making their returns, and
for the returning officers in canvassing and compiling the
same have been pointed out.   Let us see how the Republican visiting statesmen "sedulously inculcated and cultivated " obedience thereto.   In only one single instance
had the commissioners of election alleged intimidation and
that was not an allegation that the voters had been intimidated.   There was not from a single polling place in the
state a statement "in form as required by section twenty-
six."   Not one of the supervisors of registration had "in
form as required by section twenty-six " made objections to
the registration of voters for a single voting place.   Two of
them had, at the time and place designated by law, noted
on their consolidated statements informalities and irregularities affecting returns from two polls, but not alleging intimidation, or acts of violence.   Four supervisors had assumed "judicial powers," which the law conferred alone
upon the returning officers, and had rejected — refused to
compile — the commissioners' returns from twelve polling
places ; and three assistant supervisors for wards of New
Orleans had likewise illegally declined to consolidate returns from three polls.   Did one of these gentlemen who
thought it so " vital to the preservation of constitutional
liberty that the habit of obedience to the forms of law
should be sedulously inculcated and cultivated " insist that
the returning officers rebuke the unlawful action of these
four supervisors and three assistant supervisors ?   Did they *

---

* James A. Garfield testified as follows : " We very soon organized by
electing Senator Sherman as chairman. * * * One of the first consultations
we had was to determine on a course of procedure and the first thing
was that a committee should be appointed of our number to examine the
laws of Louisiana touching the whole questions of elections, and of the
Returning Board. * * * * There was a careful examination of the laws to
find precisely what they were both in their letter and in their scope, so far
as we could discover."—*H. R. Mis. Doc. No.* 31, 45th *Cong.* 3d *Sess. p.* 790.

advise the returning officers that "the forms of law" pre-
scribing the method of canvassing and compiling "first the
statements from all polls or polling places at which there
shall have been a fair, free, and peaceable registration
and election" should be observed? Did they insist that
the only legal method the returning officers had of determining that "a fair, free, and peaceable registration and
election" had not been had at any poll or voting place,
was to ascertain whether "the statement of any supervisor
of registration or commissioner of election, in form as required by section twenty-six" had been received? Did they
maintain that "the forms of law" required these statements
of supervisors of registration and of commissioners of election to be filed in duplicate with the clerks of courts in their
respective parishes and other duplicates certified by these
clerks to be "forwarded by mail" to the returning officers?

What monument "more enduring than brass" did these
gentleman leave behind them to attest their belief that it
was so "vital to the preservation of constitutional liberty
that the habit of obedience to the forms of law should be
sedulously inculcated and cultivated, and that the resort to
extra-constitutional modes of redress, for even actual
grievances, should be avoided as revolutionary, disorganizing, and tending to disorder and anarchy?" They left
behind them a monument which it is devoutly to be hoped
will prove "a beacon light and warning" to succeeding
generations. The labor was vast and they subdivided it.
John Sherman headed a committee of five that attended
the open sessions of the Returning Board to give countenance to those eminent and impartial jurists (?) J. Madison
Wells, Thomas C. Anderson, Louis M. Kenner, and G.
Cassannave who were to preserve "the purity and freedom"
of elections in Louisiana! James A. Garfield, Courtlandt

Parker, and other distinguished sticklers for the "habit
of obedience to the forms of law," were established in the
Custom House * to supervise the manufacture *there* of affidavits which were to supply the place of the "statement of
any supervisor of registration or commissioner of election,
in form as required by section twenty-six" of the election
law. Still other eminent gentlemen, aided on extraordinary
occasions by John Sherman and Stanley Mathews, coöperated with Kellogg, Packard, and other cogging, cozening

* "I occupied a room in the Custom House, in the corner of the building. I do not know now whose room it was. It was a room that was not
very much used. I think it was one of the private offices, perhaps of the
collector himself."
　　Q. "What did you do?" A. "I took all those papers, commencing
with the protest, and read them very carefully, and made a careful brief of
their contents, giving the summary of each witness in my own way as I
would if I were a lawyer in the case; and, when I had completed that, I
felt a good deal of anxiety to see the men who had testified, if I could. I
confess that I felt a good deal of surprise and astonishment at the revelations contained in those documents, and that I went there not a little ap-
prehensive that there must be a good deal of lying on both sides, in the
papers connected with the election. I made inquiry and found that a considerable number of those witnesses were in the city. I made out a list of
perhaps one-half or three-fourths of the names of the witnesses whose testimony I had examined, and I inquired for them and procured interviews
with them. I sat down with them and asked them to tell me in their own
way the story of their relations to the election. I cannot name all the witnesses whom I so conversed with, but some of them I remember very distinctly. One, a Mrs. Amy Mitchell, a young woman whose husband had
been killed during the progress of registration or election . . . I draughted
some inquiries to draw out more fully from some of the witnesses the testimony which they had given rather in brief and some of the interrogatories
which subsequently were appended to the testimony of those witnesses,
were of my draughting." *Jas. A. Garfield, Ibid, p.* 791.
　　Amy Mitchell, examined July 20, 1878.
　　Q. "You made an affidavit which purports to have been sworn to on
the 30th of Nov., 1876. Do you remember taking an oath?" A. "I remember of making an affidavit here that people made me make."
　　Q. "Who made you make it?" A. "They just pushed me up to
make it. I don't know his name. Men that were here when I was making
it pushed me up to make it. I don't know who they were who pushed me
up."
　　　*　　　*　　　*　　　*　　　*　　　*　　　*
　　Q. "Where was it made?" A. "It was made in the Custom
House."
　　　*　　　*　　　*　　　*　　　*　　　*　　　*
　　Q. "Do you know who wrote it?" A. "No, sir; I don't know who
wrote. Somebody I never saw — one of them clerks down there."

carpet-bag knaves, to pledge " recognition " to the covetous, the doubtful, the suspicious, and to promise " protection " to others who hesitated to become " swift witnesses " through a wholesome fear of the law.*

The counsel selected by Kellogg and Packard to direct the preparation of " evidence "(?) to supply the place of that which the supervisors of registration and commissioners of election had failed to furnish were Dibble, Gorham,

Q. " Did you know him at the time?" A. " No, sir; I didn't ever see him before."

* * * * * * *

Q. " You have heard me read this affidavit. Was it taken down here as you gave it to the man who questioned you about these things?" A. " No, sir; I didn't say but a little bit of it, and that little bit I didn't know, and I was told to say that little bit I did say."

Q. " State whether or not you said anything to them beyond the fact that your husband had been killed?" A. " That I said: I didn't know it."

Q. " Did you state to them you did not know who killed him?" A. " Yes, sir; I told them I didn't know who had killed him."

The killing of Mitchell was charged in the affidavit upon some of the most prominent democrats in the parish of West Feliciana and Amy Mitchell was made to identify them and to swear that she saw the killing, and give exactly the talk that occured at the time of the killing. *Ibid, Part 2, pp. 471, 473.*

Hon. Wm. D. Kelley, " visiting statesman."—Q. " You have spoken of some affidavits being redraughted, who did that work?" A. " My impression is that Gen. Harry White redraughted one or two, and I have a vague impression *that Mr. Courtlandt Parker, finding that some of the affidavits were insensible,* sought to see whether the parties had meant to express anything and finding that they had redraughted the affidavits." *Ibid-p, 724.*

* Q. " You know Dr. Darrall, who used to be a Member of Congress from Louisiana?" A. " Yes."

Q. " Do you recollect putting your arm across his shoulder and saying to him ' now, Darrall, see that these fellows stand firm?'" A. " I do not remember it, but I should probably have done that if I thought that they needed any strengthening." *Jas. A. Garfield's testimony, Ibid, p. 797.*

" I am not positive which of the parties present asked me to bring Anderson and D. A. Weber to the collector's rooms where the statesmen and state leaders were convened, but I do know that Mr. Sherman was alleged and believed to be the special representative of Mr. Hayes and was spokesman of the visiting statesmen in their dealings with the Democratic visitors, and that his words and assurances were considered authoritative, and more influential than any other leader; and my recollection is he requested me to go for my brother and Anderson." *Testimony of E. L. Weber, Ibid, p. 591.*

Hardy, Harris, Morey, Campbell, Blanchard, and Jewett. A small army of clerks was gathered in the Custom House and the " affidavit mill" began to grind out, " the proof of violence, intimidation, and armed disturbance." The manner in which this manufacture of " proof" was conducted has been fully described by witnesses who signed the affidavits and by persons who were employed as clerks.*
Negroes by the scores were marshalled to the Custom House under the guard of deputy marshals. Campbell and Morey, Harris and Hardy, Jewett and Blanchard, had direction of the preperation of affidavits for the stories of " outrages " which they were chiefly responsible for, while George L. Smith and O. H. Brewster looked after the details of similar occurrences in the regions of Shreveport

---

* Thos. H. Nolan, a clerk employed in the Custom House to get up intimidation affidavits testified as follows—" we would say that he ' knew' of so and so instead of saying he (the witness) heard " . . . " I found very few who did know of their own personal knowledge those things; but in taking affidavits it would not be of any use to take an affidavit of that kind, that is, say, a hearsay affidavit. I did not suppose it would amount to anything." Some witnesses testified that Garfield, Hale, Sherman, and Stoughton were in the Custom House frequently and manifested great interest in the operations of the "affidavit mill." Garfield made up a synopsis of evidence for Sherman's report from notes he took from the affidavits in Custom House—*see H. R. Mis. Doc., No.* 31, *part* 3, 45th *Cong.,* 3d *Sess., p.* 582.—Also Ibid, p. 471 where Amy Mitchell describes how she was made to lie about the killing of her husband. Also p. 306, testimony of Andrew Duncan, colored, as to how negroes were made to swear to falsehoods. Also the following by R. B. Edgeworth supervisor of registration for parish of Plaquemine.
Q. " Were you where they were making affidavits for use before the Returning Board?" A. " Yes, I was there quite often."
Q. " Tell us what you saw in regard to their preparation ?" A. " Well I saw them making the affidavits."
Q. " Were the persons who made the affidavits mostly colored?" A. " All colored."
Q. " Who collected the information that went into the affidavits, the person who drew the paper?" A. " The person who drew up the paper asked them some questions and made the affidavit in a general way to suit his own fancy more than anything else I should judge."
Q. " When he got done with it did he go over it with them?" A. " No, sir; it was passed over to Hugh J. Campbell, a judge there, and signed and taken away."
Q. " And that the affidavits never were read over to them?" A. " I never heard them read over while I was there." *Ibid, p.* 1077.

and Monroe. There were stereotyped forms of questions to be put to the negroes. " Do you remember the killing of Logwood, or Dinkgrave, or the whipping of Jim. Stewart, or the shooting of Ben. James ?" as the case might be. If the affiant did not answer " yes, sah," some one standing by would insist that he did remember and " coach " him. The clerks wrote away with little regard to who was talking. The forms filled up, the affiants were mustered before a commissioner, or a judge, and sworn by the dozen.

The supervisors were more important witnesses. As they came to New Orleans they sought the state registrar's office to have their accounts approved. There they fell into the hands of Jewett, or McArdle, or Blanchard. The first questions put to them were, " where are your returns ?" " Did any of your commissioners of election protest ?" " Have you made a protest ?"* All but seventeen of the fifty-seven supervisors had obeyed the instructions of Jewett's committee on canvassing and registration to bring their returns to New Orleans, and very few of the sixty obedient ones had been thoughtless enough to deposit their papers with the returning officers. Not one of the commissioners of election had reported anything wrong at their polls, and most of them had certified under oath that " fair, free, and peaceable elections" had been held under their auspices. There was no way of remedying these unfortunate oversights on the part of the commissioners. But the supervisors could, if they were willing to commit perjury, make affidavits as to intimidation, acts of violence, disturbances and killings, whippings and shootings.

By law their statements had to be made at the parish town, sworn to before the clerk of the court, noted on their consolidated statements of returns and attached thereto, and

* H. R. Mis. Doc., No. 31, 45th Cong., 3d Sess., p. 1453.

duplicates deposited with said clerk. These "forms of law" could not be complied with. Fifty-seven of the sixty, it must be said to their credit, did not commit the crime of falsifying their records. Only three " interpolated " on their consolidated statements, above the jurats, under the head of "remarks," statements affecting certain polls in their parishes.* They were Ferguson, for De Soto, Hutton, for Bossier, and Clover, for East Baton Rouge. It is known that three, Kelley, for Richland, Grady, for Ouachita, and Grant, for Morehouse, were reluctant to comply with the demands of their masters, and that it required much "persuasion " on the part of Kellogg to induce them to do the requisite swearing. Two, Anderson, for East Feliciana, and Weber, for West Feliciana, refused positively to make protests until they had exacted stipulated terms therefor.

† Jewett states that he was informed and believed that Grant and Grady had interviews with the "visiting statesmen " before they signed and swore to the statements respecting their parishes.   ‡ Anderson testified that he in connection with Weber had received in writing from John Sherman the assurance that they should be " provided for as soon after the fourth of March as may be practicable, and in such a manner as will enable you both to leave Louisiana should you deem it necessary." A copy of a letter, alleged by Anderson to have been written by Sherman, was submitted to the Potter committee. Before ad-

* As to interpolations on consolidated statements by Ferguson, Hutton, and Clover, see testimony of Jewett, H. R. Mis. Doc., No. 31, 45th Cong., 3d Sess., pp. 14, 51.—Also H, R. Mis. Doc., No. 34, part 1, 44th Cong., 2d Sess., p. 65. As to Kelley see H. R. Mis. Doc., No. 31, part 3, 45th Cong., 3d Sess., pp. 172, 173, 174. As to Grady and Grant see same Mis. Doc., No. 31, p. 1453 and Jewett's statement in Appendix.

† See Jewett's Statement in Appendix.

‡ H. R. Mis. Doc. No. 31, 44th Cong. 3d Sess. pp. 9, 10. Also testimony of J. Hale Sypher, p. 753.

mitting it in evidence, Mr. Sherman was called, * and on being shown the copy, testified that he had " no recollection of ever writing such a letter:" that he did not believe he had written such a letter; but he further swore: "at the same time there are things in this letter that I would have written to these or any other men who were engaged in the performance of what I believed to be their duty, if I had been asked."

The letter was brief. It acknowledged the receipt of a note from Weber and Anderson, and stated that "neither Mr. Hayes, myself, the gentlemen who accompany me, nor the country at large can ever forget the obligation under which you will have placed us should you stand firm in the position you have taken." Mr. Sherman did not specify what the " things " were in this letter which he would have written had he been asked. The admission of an " obligation " im-

---

* H. R. Mis. Doc. No. 31, 45th Cong. 3d Sess. pp. 16, 17. See also p. 753, testimony of J. Hale Sypher, ex-member of Congress from La. and a prominent carpet-bag politician of that State. Ibid, p. 753.

Q. " Did you know D. A. Weber, supervisor of registration in the Parish of West Feliciana?" A. "I did."

Q. " Did you know him pretty well?" A. " Very well."

Q. " Did he have any conversation with you in respect to his action as supervisor of registration?" A. " On one occasion."

Q. "Where was that conversation?" A. "At the entrance to the Custom House, on Canal street, where he met me. He inquired of me in about this language: 'Can I take the promises of gentlemen who are here to provide for me in case I am driven out of my parish?' Said I: 'Whom do you mean?' He mentioned Mr. Mathews and Mr. Sherman, especially. I remarked to him, ' These gentlemen stand very close to the President-elect. They are his intimate personal and political friends, and I think you can trust any promises they make to you.' That was the substance of the conversation."

Q. " Did you have any further talk with D. A. Weber on that subject during that visit of yours to New Orleans?" A. " Yes, sir. On the next day, or the second day after our meeting he met me again on the street and exhibited a letter to me, which I read and returned to him."

Q. "By whom did the letter purport to be signed?" A. "It seemed to have been signed by John Sherman."

Q. " Had you ever had occasion to see any of Mr. Sherman's writing before that?" A. " Yes, sir; I had seen some little of it."

Q. " So far as you could judge from what you did know, did you or not assume it to be his?" A. " I presumed it was his at the time I read the letter."

10

plies the moral responsibility to discharge it. If Mr. Sherman "would have written" the second sentence of the letter admitting an "obligation" which neither Mr. Hayes, nor himself, nor the gentlemen who accompanied him, nor the country at large could "ever forget," then it would seem reasonable to assume that he "would have written" also the concluding sentence of that letter, which was as follows: "From a long and intimate acquaintance with Gov. Hayes, I am justified in assuming responsibility for promises made, and will guarantee that you shall be provided for as soon after the 4th of March as may be practicable, and in such manner as will enable you both to leave Louisiana should you deem it necessary."*

Anderson's reputation for truth and veracity was bad. There was some other evidence to show that there was a letter like the purport of the copy of the one produced by Anderson. Ex-Representative Sypher testified that D. A. Weber showed him one which purported to be signed by John Sherman in November, 1876, and it agreed, according to his recollection with the copy Anderson claimed to have made. E. L. Weber testified that his brother, D. A. Weber, showed him a letter signed by John Sherman which agreed with the copy Anderson had. Several other witnesses testified that at the time the visiting

---

* The following is the text of the alleged letter to Weber and Anderson:

"NEW ORLEANS, November 20, 1876.

"*Gentlemen:* Your note of even date has just been received. Neither Mr. Hayes, myself, the gentlemen who accompany me, nor the country at large can ever forget the obligation under which you will have placed us should you stand firm in the position you have taken. From a long and intimate acquaintance with Gov. Hayes, I am justified in assuming responsibility for promises made, and will guarantee that you shall be provided for as soon after the 4th of March as may be practicable, and in such manner as will enable you both to leave Louisiana should you deem it necessary.   "Very truly yours,

"JOHN SHERMAN.

"MESSRS. D. A. WEBER AND JAMES E. ANDERSON."

statesmen were in New Orleans he claimed to have a document in his pocket which would "fix" him "all right" at the proper time. Dr. C. B. Darrall, ex-member of Congress from Louisiana, testified that until it was discovered that Anderson had permitted his documents to be seen by Democratic leaders, he had considerable influence with the administration, and that if he, Darrall, could have controlled Anderson, he could have secured the collectorship of New Orleans.*

However, waving all questions about the authenticity of the alleged letter from Sherman, it would be interesting to know from Mr. Sherman, what were the "things" in this letter that he would have written to Anderson and Weber if they had "asked" them. Unfortunately, Mr. Sherman did not volunteer to state them, and the committee failed to ask him to do so.†

Weber was killed in March, 1877. Mr. Hayes and Stanley Mathews recognized that "the country at large" was under "obligations" to Anderson, and the latter exerted himself to secure in some measure the discharge thereof, and the President did appoint him consul to Funchal — which Anderson refused to accept as an equivalent for services rendered. The correspondence

---

* Q. "You expected to get into office on the fears of the Administration, or of some of its members or attachés, of the publication of these documents?" A. "That was one of the means."

Q. "Do you not believe that you failed because copies of these papers had got out, and because it was not quite certain that your appointment would heal the sore? In your own mind, and between God and your own conscience, was that not the case?" A. "In my own opinion, either myself or some other party — Mr. Packard or some one suggested by Mr. Anderson — would have been appointed, but for the fact that it was known that copies of those documents were in the possession of other parties and that they were virtually public property."—*Darrall's Testimony*.

† Two months later Mr. Sherman, July 24, 1878, at Atlantic City reaffirmed his testimony given in Washington and was still more positive about the writing of the letter, but he did not say then that he would not have written some of the "things" in it if he "had been asked."

between Anderson and Mathews * on the subject of the former's appointment to a suitable place is very curious and not at all creditable to the latter.   Anderson had obtained from C. E. Nash, a colored member of Congress, and a candidate for reelection from the district including the parish of East Feliciana, an agreement to the effect that Nash was to secure for him the position of naval officer at New Orleans on condition that Anderson was to "suppress evidence showing that the said parish of East Feliciana was fairly carried by the Democratic party at the election held Nov. 7, 1876, thereby electing the entire Democratic state ticket and congressmen."   Mr. Mathews had accepted from Anderson the custody of this agreement, and was undoubtedly quite anxious to have him

---

* Mr. Mathews was placed in a very embarrassing dilemma by the Potter investigation. The correspondence betwen himself and Jas. E. Anderson, the testimony of Anderson and that of Dr. C. B. Darrall, and Darrall's letters, left him in a very bad light.   Instead of coming before the Potter Committee and making some explanation he refused to obey the summons of the committee, falling back on his senatorial privilege, and asking to be investigated by a Senate committee.   He was evidently afraid of being cross-examined by Gen. Butler who was exceedingly anxious to bring out all the facts in relation to the bargain by which Packard was abandoned in return for counting in Hayes.   Hon. Henry Waterson, a nephew of Mr. Mathews, and in the enjoyment of close personal relation's made this explanation of his conduct, in an interview published in the New York *Sun*, June 21, 1878: " The head and front of Mathews' offending was his effort to save his party friends from a scandalous exposure, knowledge of which had reached him.   No one pretends that he participated in the Louisiana frauds.   He was in New Orleans but a few days. His subsequent operations against Packard were open and above board. I happen to know that his vote to seat Kellogg in the Senate was given at the urgency of the President himself, and, as I believe, against Mathews' own better judgment as well as against his inclination.   He thought Anderson, in the first place, a meritorious poor devil, and tried to help him. After he had committed himself he discovered his mistake, and then tried to get him and *the dangerous knowledge in his possession* out of the country. Meanwhile Anderson was trading on his information, and when he had exhausted the patience of the administration, and such patronage as he could obtain by a double process of blackmailing, he dropped on Mathews."

" You think, then, that Mathews is innocent?"

" I am sure of it.   With him, all is lost save honor, and his only way to save that is to keep his mouth shut, refusing alike to perjure himself or peach upon his friends."

given some good place in order to keep him quiet and prevent the exposure of damaging facts in connection with the Louisiana election. Anderson was undoubtedly a " terror " to the fraudulent administration and had he been a more reasonable man, and less impetuous, he would have, in due time, been " taken care of" in a handsome way.*

George L. Smith, candidate for Congress in the fourth district, managed the preparation of affidavits for supervisors of registration of some of the parishes in his district. He had conferences with them at Shreveport, La. immediately after the election and accompanied them to New Orleans. It required some little time after arriving in New Orleans to ascertain exactly what was necessary to be done in the parishes of De Soto, Webster, and Bossier, to accomplish the result desired. It was not till November 24, that the conspirators met in the private office of the postmaster of New Orleans to decide upon and do the things necessary to be done to get rid of certain Democratic polls in those parishes.

The gathering was at night.† Those present were Geo. L. Smith, D. D. Smith, cashier of the Post-office, C. L. Ferguson, supervisor of De Soto, T. H. Hutton, supervisor of Bossier, John T. Morrow, supervisor of Webster, Fred. E. Heath, candidate for House of Representatives from Webster, Sam'l Gardner, citizen of Webster, D. J. M. A. Jewett, and one or two others whose names have not been recalled. D. D. Smith unlocked the Post-office vault and took therefrom the returns of De Soto, Bossier, Caddo, and Webster. Those from Caddo,

---

* See note to page 147.

† H. R. Mis. Doc: No. 31, 45th Cong. 3d Sess. p. 1442. Also Jewett's statement in Appendix.

Webster, and Bossier had been brought either by Geo. L. Smith or the supervisors of those parishes and given to the postmaster for safe keeping until such time as they had been "fixed" for the Returning Board. The return from De Soto had come by registered mail, but it was nevertheless in the vault of the Post-office at New Orleans subject to the control of Smith and Ferguson. Jewett testified that the De Soto returns were opened and examined by Smith and himself and that it was found* "not possible to create a Republican majority except by throwing out polls 1, 3, 5, 7 and 8. These were selected for protest and Ferguson was asked for facts. I draughted a process based on such facts as he had knowledge of either personally or from information received or as were suggested by Geo. L. Smith, or by the well-known conditions of the parish. This, Ferguson copied and was directed to take the same before F. A. Woolfly for administration of the oath. It was suggested by me, that of course, it was not possible to attach this protest and various affidavits in hand affecting the same parish (taken before Commissioner Levisee) to the consolidated statement of votes, this having come forward by mail and there being a disagreement of dates, but they should be handed or sent in. Notwithstanding, the unbounded stupidity of somebody rolled them up, put in the original package, which restored apparently to its original condition, went forward by carrier to the board Nov. 25.

"The returns of Bossier were handed by Capt. Hutton, the supervisor, to Geo. L. Smith for safe-keeping upon his (Hutton's) arrival in the city and were by Smith placed in the vault of the Post-office. T. H. Hutton had on Nov. 13 (the day that he started from Bellevue for New Orleans)

* See Jewett's statement in Appendix.

sworn to his consolidated statement of votes (popularly known as the returns) before Geo. B. Abercrombie, clerk of court, and had deposited a copy as required by law at the date named, and when the returns were examined by me in the Post-office this document bore, in the space for remarks, a protest of the Atkin's Landing box (No. 1) and no other. In my presence in the private office of the Post-office the supervisor interpolated in the same space under the protest noted above and above the jurat, a second protest affecting the Red Land box (No. 3). There is no question in my mind but that the protest and exclusion of this box was an afterthought which first took shape at this time, Nov. 24.

"John W. Morrow, supervisor of registration, (for Webster parish) forwarded his returns by mail to New Orleans as I now believe. If I am mistaken herein he had deposited them with Geo. L. Smith for safe-keeping. On the night of Nov. 24, I saw them taken out of the Post-office vault. At this time they were unrolled and examined. Those present took the view that it would be highly convenient to get rid of about 250 votes in this parish. An affidavit made in Meriden, La., Nov. 20, by W. L. Franks was at hand affecting poll No. 1. Sam'l Gardner, then present, made another affecting poll 5, (Meriden). I draughted a protest for Morrow on this occasion based on facts stated in the affidavits and by Fred. E. Heath and John W. Morrow. This protest Morrow copied, or it was copied for him by F. E. Heath, and he signed in the clerk's office U. S. Court the following day. This protest and these two affidavits were forwarded to the board with his returns."

F. A. Clover, * supervisor of East Baton Rouge, arrived

* For the facts about Clover and his conduct as supervisor of regis-

in New Orleans on the 12th of November. He had previously made out his consolidated statement of returns from commissioners of election, excluding therefrom the votes of polls 1, 5, 6, 7, 8, 9, and 13 (1, 3, 4, 5, 6, 7, 11, Sherman report) and swore to the same before the clerk of the district court at Baton Rouge on Nov. 11. He had received no statements from the commissioners of election for polls 1, 5, 6, 7, 8, 9, and 13 impeaching in any way the character of the elections held thereat. He assumed, contrary to law, the power to exclude the votes cast at these polls, on the ground that the returns made to him by the commissioners were irregular. These votes were for the Hayes electors 150 and for the Tilden electors 1,136. The majority for the Tilden electors in the parish, including those rejected by Clover, was 612; by omitting the votes cast at the polls, the returns whereof he rejected, the majority for the Hayes electors was made to be 374.

Clover doubtless thought he had done his work thoroughly and that there was no necessity for making any statement in regard to the registration of the parish, or of obtaining statements from the commissioners of election about intimidation, acts of violence or disturbances affecting the vote at any of the polls. But when he reached New Orleans on the 12th it was deemed advisable to fortify his proceedings with some affidavits and to supply his omission to make a statement about the rejected polls on his consolidated statement of votes. To do this required time and, therefore, he retained possession of the returns until November 23d. In the meantime he interpolated on his consolidated statement above the jurat made at Baton

<hr/>

tration for East Baton Rouge, see H. R. Mis. Doc. No. 34, part 1, 44th Cong. 2d Ses. pp. 65, 67, 68. Also testimony of Jewett H. R. Mis. Doc. No. 31, 45th Cong. 3d Sess. p. 1446 and Jewett's statement in Appendix.

Rouge, Nov. 11th, the reasons for refusing to compile the returns from the seven polling places. This was a falsification of a public record.

All the affidavits deemed necessary to enable the Returning Board to reject the votes cast at the seven polls on the ground of intimidation, which was not the reason assigned by the supervisor for his action, were not obtained until the 22nd. Clover handed in his returns with affidavits Nov. 23d and when they were opened on the 24th the original consolidated statement was not exhibited but in its place one certified to be a correct copy by Charles S. Abell, secretary of the Returning Board.* This fact and the incident, related hereafter, connected with the opening of the package from De Soto parish settles beyond controversy the fact that the Returning Board and their subordinates were privy to the tampering with the returns.

* See Sherman Report, Senate Ex. Doc. No. 2, 44th Cong. 2d Sess. p. 258.

CHAPTER IX.

The Returning Board not in a hurry to begin canvassing: Why the
vacancy in the Board was not filled: The characters of Wells, Anderson, and the two mulatoes: Time consumed to allow the affidavit mill to begin grinding: The farce of inviting northern democrats to witness the opening of returns: The tampering with
returns: Stoughton's clerical error: Returns held back to be falsified: The Eliza Pinkston case examined: A set up job: Her story
gotten up for the occasion: It was rehearsed in the Custom House:
The character of Pinkston: She offered to retract and expose those
who had used her: She was unworthy of belief: Three efforts to
count out the Tilden electors before the work was done: How
Kellogg improved affidavits: Testimony of Kelly, Supervisor of
Richland Parish: The counting out finally accomplished:

THE law required the returning officers to meet in New
Orleans "within ten days after the closing of the election
to canvass and compile the statements of the votes made
by the commissioners of election," and to continue in session until "such returns have been compiled." The returning
officers required by law were "five persons, to be elected
by the Senate from all political parties." The Senate in
pretended compliance with this provision of the law had
originally elected four republicans and one democrat.

The one democrat having resigned, the important question
to be settled was whether the remaining four members were
compelled to fill the vacancy thus created. The law said
"in case of any vacancy, by death, resignation, or otherwise, by either of the board, then the vacancy *shall be filled*

by the residue of the returning officers." If the vacancy was filled by a democrat his presence in executive sessions of the board would be dangerous. Therefore, it was determined not to fill the vacancy. Wells gave the reason therefor as follows : " We had a republican on the board and he resigned, and then a Democratic legislature filled the vacancy with a democrat, and that democrat resigned. Speaking individually, I don't think you have any claim, therefore, to representation; that you forfeited it by resignation."* The fact that a democrat had resigned relieved the remaining Republican members from the mandatory requirements of the law, was a novel idea.

The four republicans who constituted the board were J. Madison Wells, Thomas C. Anderson, Louis M. Kenner, and G. Cassannave, colored. Wells † was an historic character.   In his early life he was a ruffian and bully.   Few more desperate men ever lived and none more treacherous. His conduct while governor of the state under the constitution of 1864 was infamous politically and thoroughly dishonest officially. His misdeeds were so flagrant that Gen. Phil. Sheridan was compelled in 1867 to remove him under the power vested in him as commander of the district by the reconstruction acts. He was, and is yet, notoriously a defaulter to the state in a large amount. Tom. Anderson's ‡ " character for honesty was equally bad ; he had earned

* Sherman's Report, p. 75-76.

† For character of Wells see H. R. Mis. Doc. No. 34, Part 2 44th Cong. 2d Sess. pp. 506, 508, 509. Also testimony of Jack Wharton, H. R. Mis. Doc. No. 31, 45th Cong. 3d Sess. pp. 1424 to 1429.   Also testimony of J. H. Maddox, H. R. Mis. Doc. No. 42, 44th Cong. 2d Sess. pp. 143 to 163, 178 to 183.   Also testimony of Duncan F. Kenner same Mis. Doc. pp. 376 to 387.   Also testimony of Wm. Ward, colored, H. R. Mis. Doc. No. 34, Part 2, 44th Cong. 2d Sess. pp. 482, 483.   Also same Doc. pp. 353, 360, 363, 507, 803, 810, 982, 987, 997, 1004, 1008, 1015.   Also H. R. Mis. Doc. No. 42, 44th Cong. 2d Sess. pp. 40 to 49, 191 to 245.

‡ H. R. Mis. Doc., No. 34, part 2, 44th Cong., 2d Sess., pp. 589 to 594.

it in part by aiding, while he was a senator, to put up a fraudulent job on the State, and taking the iniquitous proceeds to himself. Of the two mulatoes, one was indicted for larceny, and, after admitting his guilt, was allowed to escape punishment, and *promptly* taken into the board. The other was too ignorant to know his duty, but his testimony showed such indifference to the obligations of an oath that he was deemed as safe for the carpet baggers as either of his colleagues."

These four worthies, who were eulogized as possessors of every virtue * by John Sherman and his colleagues in their report to the President, should have begun their labors on November 17th, but beyond a secret conference to agree upon the plans best calculated to enable them to accomplish their purpose of counting out the Democratic candidates, nothing was done on that day. Time was needed for their confederates to get up affidavits and manipulate returns. The next day, being Saturday, they met again and adopted a resolution reciting that † "distinguished gentlemen of national reputation from other states, some at the request of the President of the United States, and some at the request of the National executive committee of the Democratic party, are present in this city with a view to witness the proceedings of this board in canvassing and compiling the returns of the recent election in this state for Presidential electors," and inviting five from each of the two bodies named to be present at the meetings of the board.

Sunday intervened, and the first meeting of the Returning Board for open business was Monday, November 20th. "There were present from " the distinguished

* Senate Ex. Doc., No. 2, 44th Cong., 2d Sess., p. 6.
† Ibid, p. 35.

RULES FOR A PURPOSE.

gentlemen of national reputation,[*] John Sherman, E. W. Stoughton, James A. Garfield, Courtlandt Parker, J. M. Tuttle, John M. Palmer, Lyman Trumbull, William Bigler, Geo. W. Smith, and Peter H. Watson. The rules which were to govern the board were announced. They provided among other things, that the board would first take up, canvass and compile returns from the *parishes* where no objection is made to the canvassing and compiling of the votes cast at any polling place in such parish or parishes." This was a violation of the law which required the returning officers to proceed by *polls* and not by *parishes* in canvassing returns. It was also provided that "the distinguished gentlemen of National reputation" to the number of ten might be present and see the returns *opened* but not to see them canvassed and compiled. Attorneys representing candidates, or candidates themselves, could only be present when the board desired to hear evidence, and then could only submit motions in writing, and all interrogatories to witnesses must be in writing and submitted to opponents twenty-four hours for cross interrogatories.

These rules were for a purpose other than that which appeared on their face. The returning officers had no objection to five democrats, from a distance, entirely unfamiliar with the election law and the minutia of election proceedings in Louisiana, being present to witness the opening of returns. But they shut out the local lawyers and politicians on the Democratic side because their presence might be inconvenient. However, it happened that on November 25, the returns from De Soto parish were brought in before the visitors when Mr. Burke and Mr. McGloin, two of the Democratic counsel, happened to be present looking after some papers in the cases of parishes laid aside for contests.

[*] Senate Ex. Doc., No. 2, 44th Cong., 2d Sess., p. 39.

The announcement was made with some emphasis that the returns from De Soto had come by mail. It had been remarked by the Democratic visitors that very few had been forwarded by mail, and it was a subject of complaint that so many returns from the parishes had not been received.

Anderson, who opened the returns and did the reading, was, therefore, quite emphatic in stating that this particular package was by mail. He opened it and read " consolidated statement of votes of the parish of De Soto " — pause — and then — " with any quantity of affidavits attached." Mr. Burke wanted to know when the package was mailed, and Anderson replied that it was mailed at Mansfield, Louisiana, and was received on the 18th. " What is the date of the first affidavit ?" asked Burke. Anderson with some hesitation replied, November 25. " How does it happen that affidavits made on the 25th were in a package mailed on the 18th ?" demanded Mr. McGloin.

There was confusion. The chief clerks, Abell and Green, hastened to make explanations. But McGloin and Burke were pressing hard and Abell had to do some "lying from the shoulder." He declared that there were two packages — one received on November 18, and another that morning : that the first contained the supervisors consolidated statement and the other affidavits. E. W. Stoughton attempted to help out of the scrape by asking — " what return is this that was received to-day ?" Mr. Abell — "the return before the board now. I also received a small package on the 18th which I presumed was a consolidated statement." Mr. Stoughton — " was the evidence you received in the package to-day ?" Mr. Abell — " yes, sir." Mr. Stoughton — "O! that settles it — merely a clerical error!" It "settled" conclusively the fact that the returns which came by registered mail had been tampered with.

The package Anderson had opened, after announcing that it came by mail, and was receipted for on the 18th, was the one from which he took the consolidated statement "with any quantity of affidavits attached." The transactions in the private office of the postmaster the night previous was the "clerical error" Mr. Stoughton made so light of.*

From beginning to end the proceedings of the board in opening the returns before the visitors were farcical. There was great pretence of fairness and frankness in asking Democratic visitors to examine returns from parishes where there was no probability of subsequent "doctoring" by the board, but the utmost care was taken to conceal the fact that returns from parishes near New Orleans were not in their possession.

For instance, Clover had sworn to his consolidated statement of the votes of the parish of East Baton Rouge on November 11. He had wantonly rejected returns from seven polls. The Democratic counsel were anxious to have the East Baton Rouge returns opened early in order that they might insist upon an order for the production of the commissioners' returns and the ballot-boxes deposited with the clerk of the court at Baton Rouge. They insisted on the third day of the board's meeting they should have notice at least of the parishes in which there were contests. The next day they asked that a day might be set for considering East Baton Rouge and that they might be informed of the nature of the evidence the supervisor had filed.

The reply was that the returns had not been examined. The fact was that they did not have them. The day after they were received, November 24, they were opened and upon the request of the Democratic counsel the promise was

* Senate Ex. Doc., No. 2., 44th Cong., 2d Sess., pp. 88, 89.

made that the returns of the commissioners and the ballot-boxes of the rejected polls should be sent for. Day after day till the 2d of December the board was reminded of this promise but failed to keep it.* The commissioners' returns and the ballot-boxes were not sent for. The board alone had power to compel their production.

† The attention of the board was time and time again called to the well-known fact that supervisors were in the city whose returns had not been delivered to the returning officers. Summary process on these persons was demanded and the production of their returns compelled, but it was mere waste of time and words. The board knew very well the purpose for which these returns were withheld and would not interfere to mar the plans of their fellow-conspirators. Notwithstanding the great urgency for dispatch of business which Wells continually insisted on, there were all sorts of delays.

But the *chef d'œuvre* of all that transpired at these open sessions of the board, before the visitors, was the production and examination of Eliza Pinkston. For dramatic effect this was a well-conceived and well-arranged episode, but it was dishonest from beginning to end. Eliza Pinkston was a low, disreputable negress — a common wretch, notorious in three states for her unchastity, and disoluteness, and lying. In 1878 she proffered through a gentleman, on whose plantation in Mississippi she was then living with a negro, to come before the Potter committee and retract what she had testified to before the Returning Board in 1876, and to make known by whom she was "coached" to tell what she did. Of course, this proposition was declined.

* Senate Ex. Doc., No. 2, 44th Cong., 2d Sess., pp. 58, 74, 91, 133.
† Ibid, p. 69, 76, 124.

On the eighth day of the board's sessions,* Nov. 28, Eliza was borne into the presence of the board and "the distinguished gentlemen of national reputation" by two stalwart men, and attended by a negro woman who ostentatiously carried restoratives. She was placed on a lounge and, after apparently recovering from the effects of her transportation from the custom house, she was sworn and examined as to her evidence and exhibited *in puris naturalis* as to her wounds. It was a shocking sight. The woman had been brutally dealt with, having wounds on the head, frightful cuts on the breasts, and a gaping gash in one of her thighs. These wounds were partially healed but were unquestionably painful. It is, however, an incontestible fact that the extreme weakness exhibited before the board was assumed, because when brought back to the custom house *she walked up one flight of stairs, exhibiting her person, and shouting and laughing at the top of her voice.*

The story she told was most improbable. It had been unskilfully constructed. She doubtless embellished greatly the one she had been coached to tell. In brief she swore that her husband had been taken from his house in the night, shot seven times, run through and through with knives, his body mutilated ; that after this the murderers cut her child's throat as she held it in her arms, and then, after shooting her twice, had violated her person more times than she could remember ; that they cut her twice with an axe, and slashed her with knives. And this was done as she averred by young white men of the neighborhood many of whom she knew well and identified. They were not, she swore, even disguised. One of them who was the most cruel, and bloodthirsty, and lustful, she claimed was a well-

---

* Senate Ex. Doc. 44th Cong. 2d Sess. p. 113.
† H. R. Mis. Doc. No. 31, 45th Cong. 3d Sess. pp. 1079, 1080, 1801.

known and highly respectable physician of the neighbor-hood in which she lived.

Is it probable that white men who could be so brutally fiendish, so utterly depraved, would have suffered the woman to live to tell the awful story of her wrongs? And, yet, she admitted that the next day the doctor, who she asserted had been the chief monster, came, when sent for by the owner of the plantation on which her husband lived, and dressed her wounds and ministered to her wants. Is it probable that, if he had been one of her assailants, the murderer of her husband and the slayer of her child, he would have come to her bedside and sought to save her life? Preposterous! The exaggerations of the story ought to have convinced the hearers it was a " set-up job."

And yet the sight of the wounds, the pretended fainting, so shocked Governor Palmer of Illinois that he expressed his horror in emphatic language which was telegraphed over the land as an unqualified condemnation of the alleged perpetrators of the outrage and an endorsement of the credibility of the woman's story. It was an unwarranted liberty taken with the governor's language. He had de-manded that the case should be thoroughly investigated, and warned the board that half-way work in the inquiry would not satisfy the country. The board would suffer but two witnesses to be examined in rebuttal. A score of reputable gentlemen were present who would have contra-dicted the essential portions of the story, but they were not allowed to testify.

It was not the truth these people were after — it was *immediate effect*, and they secured it. Pinkston lived in Ouachita parish. It gave a large Democratic majority. The board wanted a pretext for throwing out that parish and a startling, dramatic piece of evidence which would be telegraphed everywhere and go far towards justifying in the public mind all their contemplated villainy.

A Democratic committee of the House of Representatives subsequently visited the locality and carefully and thoroughly investigated Eliza Pinkston's story. It was established beyond controversy that her statement that Henry Pinkston was mutilated after beiug shot to death was untrue. It was proved that the throat of the child had not been cut and that there was no mark of violence on its body save a slight contusion on the head. It was proved that the men who she swore were the leaders and chief criminals could not possibly have been in that neighborhood on the night in question. It was proved that she had made an affidavit for use with the Returning Board in Monroe, La., before J. H. Dinkgrave, in which she charged the crime of murder and outrage on other persons : that this affidavit was sent to the Returning Board on Nov. 23d by M. J. Grady, supervisor of Ouachita parish : that it was suppressed — withdrawn and another made in New Orleans on Dec. 2, substituted for it. Not only this, but the board falsified its own record of the receipt of the returns of the parish of Ouachita. The secretary announced that they had been received Nov. 24, and yet when they were opened a letter from the supervisor was found addressed to Mr. Abell saying — " Inclosed please find affidavit of Eliza Pinkston which I received too late to file with my returns. Please see that it is brought in with the other evidence filed with my returns." *This letter was dated Nov. 23.*

The plan of bringing Eliza Pinkston to New Orleans was an afterthought. Her exhibition before the board was determined on after consultation with some other persons than those originally cognizant of her affidavit. The

Republican visiting. statesmen saw her at the custom house and heard her story rehearsed. Their surprise and amazement, their expressions of horror, their shuddering, at the sight of the woman's wounds, at hearing her story before the Returning Board were not spontaneous. They had seen the sight and heard the narrative, doubtless with variations, before. Did they believe the story ? It seems incredible.

But how heartless and cowardly of them to content themselves with converting the story to political uses and taking no steps to have the woman's wrongs righted by having the fiends in human shape brought to justice ! They were all powerful at Washington. They, a few months later, became councillors of state. If Eliza Pinkston's story was true, and they professed to believe it, a series of offences had been committed against the laws of the United States. The woman averred that the crimes were for political purposes — to intimidate negro voters — the result of a conspiracy to deprive them of their rights. This was what John Sherman and his colleagues declared the murder of Henry Pinkston and scores of other killings were — crimes against humanity, against liberty, against the laws of the United States in such cases made and provided. Then why in God's name did they not *try* to have the criminals brought to punishment ?

Can it be that they suspected that Eliza Pinkston's character, her reputation for truth and veracity, would not stand the test of judicial investigation ? A Democratic committee reported a frightful array of facts which bore heavily against the woman's character, * but that surely did not

* "The character of Eliza Pinkston, as developed before your sub-committee to the fullest extent, was such as to render her a fit instrument in the hands of designing men. She had been charged with the murder of the child of persons with whom she had but recently quarrelled. The

give Sherman, Garfield, Stoughton, and Mathews pause. It was the verdict of a partisan committee based upon the testimony of white men living in Ouachita parish, Louisiana, — bulldozers — whose recreation they insisted was whipping negroes, murdering fathers, cutting children's throats, and ravishing the bereaved mothers. Perish the thought that such a report as this could have changed the belief of the " visiting statesmen " in Eliza Pinkston's morality, veracity, and chastity !

The Returning Board stretched the opening of returns over ten days, and two more were given to so-called hearings and arguments. On December 3, they began in secret sessions to figure out a majority which would bring in the Republican presidential electors, State ticket, Congressmen, a majority of both houses of the legislature and local officers in particular parishes. It was a difficult un-

---

child died of poison. Eliza Pinkston, then known as Lizzie Finch in Morehouse parish, was arrested, and acquitted only because the main witness to the crime was too young to understand the nature of an oath. The general impression was that she was guilty. When residing in Union parish, she had shamefully beaten an old woman living with her, death ensuing in a few days after. She had abandoned one of her young children, leaving it to starve to death in a fence corner. Another she made way with shortly after its birth. She was an habitual abortionist. She was in perpetual quarrel. Her testimony had been so effectually impeached in the courts of Morehouse parish that the Republican district attorney refused to call her as a witness. Everybody who knew her considered her a desperate character. Eye-witnesses proved that she lived with her husband on very bad terms. She was about to kill him at one time when she supposed him asleep. Upon another occasion she assaulted him with an axe intending to kill him. He was in perpetual dread of harm as witnesses testified. She was ugly, vulgar, indecent, and lewd beyond the worst. In the midst of twenty men in the cotton-field she would pull up her clothes beyond her waist and turn herself around completely. And she would lie down in the field, or in the fence corner, or the open road, with any man who had a quarter to spare for the hideous entertainment. So quarrelsome, so dangerous, and so disgusting was this creature, that upon two several occasions she was driven off by express demand of the colored men and women with whom she was engaged, they stating that if she remained they would leave in a body. And this wretched creature, this miserable prostitute, has become a saint in the political calendar of the Republican party of Louisiana."

Report 156 *Part* 1 *House of Rep.* 44*th Cong.* 2*d Sess,* *Pages* 45-6.

dertaking. There had been a miscalculation in the beginning. *

The first hypothesis was that they could get rid of enough Democratic votes in what they termed the five bulldozed parishes, namely, East and West Feliciana, East Baton Rouge, Ouachita, and Morehouse. But it was soon discovered that several other parishes would have to be "purged" of a considerable number of Democratic votes. Five of the Republican electors, it was found, † ran far

---

* H. R. Mis. Doc. No. 31, 45th Cong. 3d Sess. Testimony of D. J. M. A. Jewett:
Q. "Had it been ascertained by you gentlemen that it was necessary to examine these returns from the different parishes and prepare protests to them, in order to save the Republican ticket in the State?" A. "We had about this understanding: that discounting the bulldozed parishes and some polls in other parishes in regard to which there was reasonable ground of complaint, Mr. Packard would probably come through by a very small majority; but that two, or perhaps three of the electors might be left owing to blunders made in Iberville and West Baton Rouge."
See Jewett's statement in Appendix — "That thereafter in pursuance of a conspiracy between J. M. Wells, Thos. C. Anderson, John Sherman, and Jas. A. Garfield, and others, polls were excluded in the parishes of Caldwell, Natchitoches, Richland, Catahoula, Iberia, Livingston, and Tangipahoa, with the result and for the purpose of returning as elected 5 Hayes electors who were otherwise defeated. That the consideration of this conspiracy was the absolute control of the Federal patronage within the State of Louisiana by the said Wells and Anderson; that the evidence used to effect the object of the conspiracy was manufactured without regard to actual facts and with the knowledge of the several conspirators, and that the consideration to be given to said Wells and Anderson has been delivered up to date."

† The date of this discovery was prior to November 23d, 1876 — which must have been about the time the Returning Board began to open the returns — for on that day John Sherman wrote to R. B. Hayes from Kellogg's office on official State paper — "We are now approaching the contested parishes. As to five of them, viz: Baton Rouge, East and West Feliciana, Morehouse, and Ouachita, the evidence of intimidation is so well made out on paper that no man can doubt as to the just exclusion of their vote. In these parishes alone we ought to have a majority of 7,000, but, under the law, the entire return must be excluded in all election districts where the intimidation affected or changed the result. If this is done, the result will give the Hayes electors majorities aggregating 24,111. and the Tilden electors 22,633. But in almost every parish the official returns vary somewhat from these stated majorities, and thus far slightly reduce the Republican majority. The vote of each disputed parish has thus far been laid aside, and among them are two parishes where a most foolish blunder (some think worse) was made in omitting from the Republican tickets the names of all the electors but the two senatorial and one district elector.

behind the rest of the ticket, and all of the electors were behind the State ticket.   They knew that they must make the electors carry them over the stream.   The "visiting statesmen" were present, with the Northern sentiment they represented, and the power of the National Administration behind them to sanction and approve the counting-in of the Hayes electors.

The returning officers had no disposition to stop half-way in their nefarious work, but they were quick to see and to take advantage of the fact that the falling behind of five of the Republican electors gave them an opportunity to count in some of their friends whom they might otherwise have felt compelled to leave out.

Kellogg insisted upon a majority in the legislature. A seat in the United States Senate was to be the price of his villainy.   But a majority in both houses of the legislature was almost a necessity.   Packard could scarcely be maintained as governor, even with Federal bayonets, if the legislative body was hostile.   The candidates for Congress were also to be taken care of.   George L. Smith, for instance, was not altogether unselfish.   It was not pure love of

---

The democrats claim this will lose us over 2,000 votes, but our friends, whose information we have generally found confirmed, say it will lose us at most 1,193 votes.   The law seems conclusive that the defective ballots cannot be counted for any electors but those named on the ticket, though it is conclusively shown that the remaining electors were omitted by reason of the mistaken idea that the district could only vote for one elector.   The whole trouble grew out of the fact that in these two parishes a candidate for district judge was not named on the ticket printed by the State committee, and he undertook to correct this by printing new tickets, which were voted in those parishes.   The result of this blunder will leave the poll so close as to render it probable that one or more of the Tilden electors would have a majority.   There are other parishes where the organized intimidation was not so general as in the parishes named, though in single election precincts it was effective.   These parishes where formal protests have been filed are Bienville, Bossier, Caldwell, Franklin, Grant, Iberia, Lincoln, Richland, and Sabine.   How far the proof in these parishes will sustain the protests we cannot judge until the evidence is read before the Returning Board."

the Republican party that induced him to be *particeps criminis* in the forgeries and perjuries concocted and perpetrated in the New Orleans Post-office on the night of the 24th of November. Then, again, there were local candidates for parish officers who wanted their share of the plunder. In thieves' parlance the "swag" must be fairly divided. The fellows who pried the doors open, bore the heat and burden of the day, did the false swearing, demanded their rights.

A new estimate of the counting-out to be done was hastily made, and the conclusion was arrived at that by throwing out certain polls in the parishes of Richland, De Soto, Webster, Livingston, Lafayette, and Natchitoches, in addition to those determined on in the Felicianas, East Baton Rouge, Ouachita and Morehouse, the requisite Republican majority could be obtained. It was, however, necessary to get up affidavits, to have, if possible, statements from supervisors of registration for these parishes. This required delay. This necessitated the holding back of returns. Hence the dilatoriness of the board, and the refusal to comply with the demands of the Democratic counsel for the production of the returns held back by supervisors.

In the case of Richland parish the supervisor, J. F. Kelley, was, with great difficulty, induced to make a statement. D. J. M. A. Jewett says of the efforts made to coerce Kelley the following: "J. F. Kelley, supervisor, brought consolidated statement to New Orleans in person: waited upon Governor Kellogg,* before delivering returns to board, and reported to him certain facts respecting registration and election. The governor then and there draughted a protest for Kelley, who having disappeared meanwhile,

---

* H. R. Mis. Doc., No. 31, part 2, 45th Cong., 3d Sess., p. 172.

Kellogg handed the draught to me with the request that I would see that Kelley signed something like that, and that he filed the same with his returns. Upon meeting Kelley the next day, he declined to sign a statement such as the governor had draughted, assigning as a reason, that he did not personally know the facts stated to be true. Mr. Kelley returned to his parish without making any protest.*

" Kelley returned to New Orleans with witnesses about November 25, when I handed Judge Campbell a substantial copy of Kellogg's draught and requested him to take charge of the matter. I think the judge afterwards told me Kelley still refused to sign. About November 30, Mr. Kelley signed an inconsequential affidavit respecting the election in Richland which was shown to me, whereupon I drew up the protest which appears with his returns and handed it to Mr. Hagin, I think for Mr. Kelley's signature. This Mr. Kelley signed 16 or 17 days after his returns were in the office of the board."

Kelley testified† that he had signed, but did not swear to, an affidavit draughted by Jewett and that subsequently, after his return from Richland parish, he made an affidavit draughted by Kellogg. On being shown the original of the affidavits he pointed out interlineations in one of them, the one draughted by Kellogg, which he was positive were made after he had sworn to it. The other one which he had signed for Jewett had a jurat attached, and he was positive that he never made the oath which it is there stated he took before Commissioner Woolfley. He testified that he persistently resisted the many efforts made by Kellogg, Jewett, and Campbell to induce him to swear to things which he did not know to be true: that he told them if they wanted

* H. R. Mis. Doc., No. 31, part 2, 45th Cong., 3d Sess., p. 1447.
† Ibid, pp. 171 to 182.

people to do that kind of swearing he could send them down from Richland. They then gave him subpœnas and sent him after them; he remained at home ten days and did not intend to return, but a deputy marshal came after him.

He further testified that he believed the election in Richland parish was fair, free, and peaceable, and knew nothing to the contrary, and would not have believed on oath the persons who reported to him otherwise: that he told Kellogg, Jewett, and Campbell he would not swear to a lie for them or the party: that Kellogg repeatedly coaxed and urged him to make an affidavit stating he had personal knowledge of acts of intimidation and told him the result of the election depended on the vote of his parish. The two affidavits purporting to be made by Kelley printed in the Sherman report are of the date of November 30. In the proceedings of the Returning Board printed in the same report, it is stated in the account of the opening of the returns of Richland parish, November 25, that there were no statements except those showing " the peaceable and quiet character of the election."

The supervisor of Livingston parish forwarded his returns by express,* addressed to " Michael Hahn, state registrar of voters, C. O. D." Hahn refused to pay the charges as did likewise the returning officers. The democrats after furnishing the trifling amount could not induce the board to send for the package. Finally Hahn consented to receipt for the package and after opening it sent it to the board. The vote for Presidential electors was Hayes 121, Tilden 769. The supervisor had failed to sign his name to the consolidated statement, but the jurat and certificate by the clerk of the court were attached, and in every other re-

* Senate Ex. Doc. No. 2, 44th Cong. 2d Sess. p. 124.

spect the returns were regular — including those from the commissioners of election. The supervisor was in New Orleans, but the board declined to issue a subpœna for him.

The law required them to canvass and compile the returns of the commissioners of election and the consolidated statement of the supervisor was merely made for their convenience. They were bound to go to the original returns from the polling places. There were no irregularities alleged — no objetions on the part of the commissioners — and none by the supervisor. The affidavits filed with the board after Nov. 28, were not only *ex parte*, but wholly hearsay statements. They could not under the law be received by the board because jurisdiction was only conferred by the statements of commissioners of election and of the supervisor " in form as required by section twenty-six." But even admitting these affidavits they proved nothing whatever affecting either the registration or the election.

The returns of Natchitoches parish* gave three Hayes electors 2,099, and five 1,558, three Tilden electors, 1,761, and five 1,558 votes. On Dec. 1 and 3 a dozen affidavits were filed with the board alleging general intimidation. There was no complaint from the commissioners of election and no statement by the supervisor. The affidavits proved not one single fact. The allegations were of the most general character — the opinions of individuals that the Republican majority ought to have been from 800 to 1,000 votes.

The supervisor of Lafayette † parish withheld his returns till the 29th of November. His consolidated state-

---

* Senate Ex. Doc. No. 2, 44th Cong. 2d Sess., pp. 62, 63, 558 to 568.
† Ibid, p. 129, 524 to 533.

ment was sworn to on the 14th and contained no reference to complaints against the peaceable character of the election held at any of the polls, and no allegations affecting the registration.   An affidavit made by the supervisor Nov. 28 with others made on that and subsequent days appear in the Sherman report.   They contain vague allegations in regard to alleged intimidation affecting the registration for polls 1 and 2, but only claim that three or four electors were induced by threats to vote the Democratic ticket, and but one of these could be induced to swear that he did vote that ticket under compulsion.

When the board came to figure exactly on the returns it was found that they would have to go further than they expected after the second estimate had been made and to throw out polls * in the parishes of Franklin, Caldwell, Vernon, Catahoula, St. Charles, St. Landry, Tangipahoa, Claiborne, and Iberia.   They finally rejected the whole vote of East Feliciana and threw out Grant parish on the ground that there was no legal election held, the supervisor, Ward, having, abandoned the parish before the day of election.   They threw out in addition sixty-nine * polls from twenty-two other parishes, and refused to include the polls which the supervisors of East Baton Rouge, Lafayette, La Fourche, and the assistant supervisors of wards two, three, and six, New Orleans, had, without warrant of law refused to compile.   In all, 13,213 Democratic electors were disfranchised and 2,415 republicans.   The highest number of votes "actually cast" for a Democratic elector was 83,817 and for a Republican elector 77,332.   Five of the Republican electors ran behind the vote of their colleagues 1,141.   The average majority for the Democratic electors was 7,116! *

* H. R. Mis. Doc. No. 34, Part 2, 44th Cong. 2d Sess. pp. 790–794.

CHAPTER X.

The counting-in finished and same day the Hayes' electors met and voted: They did not comply with the Constitution and the laws of the United States: Tom. Anderson carried the defective return of electoral votes to Washington: The President of the Senate pointed out the failure to comply with the law: Anderson opened the package and discovered defect in certificate: What passed between Anderson and the President of the Senate: A conspiracy to suppress the defective returns and manufacture new ones: How this was done: The persons who conspired: The forgery of the signatures of Levissee and Joffroin, two absent electors: Those who knew of the forgery: Kellogg warned Senator Morton: Why he gave the warning: The testimony of Anderson, Clark, Kellogg, Sheldon and Kelley reviewed and analyzed: The way Kellogg took care of Kelley: The Smith bogus return: Proceeding in joint convention: The way Morton managed the Electoral commission: A chapter of crimes.

THE Returning Board announced the result of its manipulations and certified the election Dec. 6th, the day the electors are required by law to meet and vote for President and Vice-President. The Republican electors knowing what the board was going to do were on hand and ready to perform their parts. They met, cast their votes for President, Rutherford B. Hayes; for Vice-President, William A. Wheeler. They used but a single ballot, writing thereon the names of both candidates. The Constitution of the United States requires electors to vote for candidates for President and Vice-President by *distinct* ballots. Having voted as described they proceeded to sign in triplicate a certificate of the votes cast and included in *one list* the electoral votes for President as well as those given for Vice-President. This was violation number two of the Constitution, which requires "*distinct* lists of all persons voted for as President, and of all persons voted for as Vice-President, and of the number of votes for each, which lists they shall sign and certify, and transmit sealed to the seat of government of the United States directed to the President of the Senate."

Kellogg as governor complied with the law which required him to deliver to each elector three certificates stating that they were duly chosen as electors, and annexed one of these to each of the triplicate certificates the electors had signed. Thereupon, H. Conquest Clark, the governor's private secretary, enveloped the triplicate certificates, and endorsed on the outside of each envelope a statement that it contained a list of all the votes for President and Vice-President, but the electors failed to sign these statements as the law required. Thos. C. Anderson, having been chosen to carry one of the packages to Washington, received the same on Dec. 21st. One of the others was forwarded by mail to the President of the Senate, and the other was deposited with the judge of the United States District Court.

Anderson reached Washington the evening of Dec. 24, and on Christmas morning called upon the President of the Senate, Mr. Ferry, to deliver the package whereof he was the bearer. Mr. Ferry, upon examining the superscriptions on the envelope called * Anderson's attention to the fact that the statement of the contents of the envelope endorsed thereon was not signed by the electors as the law required.

* H. R. Mis. Doc, No. 31, 45th Cong. 3d Sess. p. 539.

Anderson testified * that he suggested to Mr. Ferry to open the package and see if the endorsement was not inside. This could not have occurred, because, Mr. Ferry had just pointed out to Anderson that the law required that the sealed *envelope* must have endorsed *thereon* the certificate of the electors that it contains the returns of the electoral votes. After having had this explanation made to him it is not possible that Anderson could have asked the President of the Senate to open the package to find whether the proper endorsement was on the *inside* of the envelope.

Anderson persisted in swearing that this was all that occurred between Mr. Ferry and himself; that they did not discuss the question as to the correctness and regularity of the contents of the package. But Kellogg † admitted on cross-examination that Anderson told him, on his return to New Orleans, that Ferry had advised him to examine the law and see whether the certificate had been made in accordance therewith.

Anderson after his interview with Ferry went to his hotel, stopping on the way to buy a ticket for New Orleans. He claimed that he opened the package in his room late the afternoon of that day to see if the endorsement which the law says shall be written *on* was not *inside* of the envelope.* Of course, this statement is untrue. He opened the envelope to find whether the certificate it contained was in form as the Constitution and the laws required. He had seen, he admitted, several friends before opening the package, but could not remember what he had said to them. * It was possible, he thought, that he might have said that the certificate was not in form and he was going back to

* H. R. Mis. Doc. No. 31, 45th Cong. 3d Sess. p. 540.
‡ Ibid, p. 674.

New Orleans to have it fixed.   His memory was a blank
as to everything else and the most searching examination
could not extract other particulars.

Certain facts are, however, established.   Mr. Ferry did
not accept the package from Anderson.   He pointed out
the law to Anderson which requires the sealed envelope,
containing the electoral certificates, to have an endorsement signed by the electors that it contains the
electoral vote.   He advised Anderson to examine the law
and see what it required in regard to the certificates themselves.   After seeing " several friends," but just who he
failed to recollect, Anderson went to his room and opened
the package " to see if the endorsement was on the *inside*"
and not finding it, left that night for New Orleans carrying back the opened package.

Mr. Ferry ought to have received the package which
Mr. Anderson handed to him.   Anderson's credentials
were in due form.   Mr. Ferry had already received by mail
the duplicate in all respects, so far as the superscription indicated, of the package Anderson handed him.   Unquestionably Mr. Ferry knew that the electors who had met on
the sixth of December and voted for President and for Vice-
President and made out the return thereof were *functus
officio ;* that they could not subsequently — weeks after they
had ceased to have legal existence — correct errors, either
of omission, or of commission.   The law gave him no discretion in the premises.   The returns came to him as
the President of the Senate and he was merely the custodian
of them until the two Houses of Congress met in joint convention on the day fixed by law when they were to be
opened and counted.

There was no legal method of remedying any defect,
error, or mistake made by the electors.   In this case the so-

called Republican electors had failed, first, to comply with
the positive requirements of the Constitution in voting for
candidates for President, and for candidates for Vice-President. They had voted ballots on which were written the
names of Hayes and Wheeler, when they should have voted
separate — " distinct " — ballots, each containing the respective names of the candidates for President and Vice-
President; and, second, they had failed to make their return
of the votes cast for each candidate in "distinct lists," or
separate certificates. These failures to obey the Constitution
undoubtedly vitiated their acts.   The discovery of non-
compliance with these constitutional requirements by the
Republican Presidential electors of Louisiana, on December 25, 1876, must have created consternation among the
Republican leaders in Washington.   Without the vote of
Louisiana Hayes and Wheeler could not be counted in.
After all that had been done and risked, to lose the mighty
stake they had so desperately played for, was enough to
make them resort to still more desperate measures.   They
could scarcely hope to have the two Houses of Congress
accept a certificate of the electoral vote of a state which
was not in accordance with the precise and specific requirements of the Constitution.   A contest over the vote
of Louisiana was inevitable without this constitutional objection.   With that superadded the complication would
indeed be serious.

But what could be done ?   Manifestly but one thing —
the certificates made out in triplicate on December 6, 1876,
must be suppressed and false ones, complying with the
provisions of the Constitution, must be substituted therefor.
This unquestionably was the conspiracy concocted in
Washington on Christmas day, 1876.   In this connection
the slightest circumstances and the most trivial details

become of the greatest consequence. They are often important links in the chain of circumstantial evidence by which conspirators are convicted. Mr. Ferry advised Anderson to examine the law to see what it required. He had shown him the law in regard to the endorsement prescribed for the outside of the envelope, therefore, he did not advise him to examine the law in reference to that defect.

Anderson asked Ferry to open the package. What for? Anderson said the object was to see whether the proper endorsement was on the *inside.* But this was false. The omission Ferry had pointed out was the absence of the signatures of the electors to the endorsement on the *envelope* which the law required to be there. The endorsement was written on the envelope in due form, but the electors had not signed it. Anderson undoubtedly told the truth when he said he asked Ferry to open the package but lied when he said the object was to find whether the endorsement was on the *inside.* He asked Ferry to open the package *and ascertain whether the contents were all right— whether any other mistakes had been made.*

But Mr. Ferry was not ready to commit a crime himself. He, however, did not hesitate to suggest the commission of one by others. He advised Anderson to examine the law and see for·himself what was required. To what purpose unless he examined the certificate also? Anderson could not be made to say whom he saw in Washington after he left Ferry. He admitted that he took a carriage and drove to Senator West's house but claimed that he did not find him at home. The utmost that he could be got to say was that he saw "several friends" and that he might have mentioned that he was going back to New Orleans because the electoral certificate was defective. He admits that it was after "seeing several friends" that he opened the package containing the electoral certificate.

He reached New Orleans the morning of December 28th and went directly to see Kellogg whom he found in the executive office.* He told him " something " as to what Ferry said about the certificate not being right. This, he professed, was all he could recollect of this important interview with Kellogg. And singular enough Kellogg's recollection was not any better except he finally remembered that Anderson told him that Ferry advised him to examine the law and find out what was required in the certificates of electoral votes. But Kellogg had a distinct recollection that he sent for Clark, his private secretary, and turned the matter over to him and Anderson.** In this Anderson corroborated Kellogg so far as " the turning over " to Clark was concerned, but beyond that he was not willing to admit that he assumed any responsibility. He could not recollect that he told Clark anything in particular except that Ferry had pointed out the omission of the signatures of the electors on the envelope.** He recollected that either he or Clark took out of the envelope its contents, but he had no recollection of pointing out any defects therein.

Kellogg's recollection was almost a blank; he " really paid no attention to the matter "—he " had the whole state on his shoulders."† Clark,‡ however, had a distinct recollection that Anderson " stated that friends in Washington thought that instead of the names for President and Vice-President being on one sheet they should be on two sheets." Who these " friends in Washington " were, Clark had no personal knowledge, or any other kind, except what he obtained from the newspapers. He asked Anderson no

* H. R. Mis. Doc. No. 31, 45th Cong. 3d Sess. p. 541.
** Ibid, p. 674.   † Ibid, p. 710.   ‡ Ibid, p. 258.

questions. He was equally discreet with Kellogg. All that passed between them was this — * " Governor Kellogg said to me, ' I wish you would see General Anderson. He says there is something wrong about these certificates,' and at the governor's request I went into a room in the state building where General Anderson was sitting, and then the conversation took place." He professed not to have consulted with any one concerning the defects of the first certificates of the electoral votes, or how these defects were to be remedied in the new ones. His professions in this respect were doubtless true—" friends in Washington " had instructed Anderson and Anderson instructed Clark !

Clark went about the preparation of the new certificates without a moment's delay. They must be ready for signature the next day and the messenger must leave at 5:20 P. M. with one set, and another set must be mailed before that hour, in order to reach Washington within the time fixed by law for their reception. The time expired January 3, 1877, and, therefore, the latest train the messenger could take in New Orleans was the one leaving at 5:20 P. M. December 29th. But pressing as the time was Clark had certificates printed * from the same type from which the impressions of those used on the 6th of December were made. Having obtained his *fac simile* printed blanks — as to paper and type — Clark prepared a room on the third floor of the State House and spread out the certificates to be signed on a large table.*

There were triplicate certificates which required triplicate certification by the governor. Clark ingeniously * accounted for the way in which he obtained these certificates of the governor, without having him execute an ante-dated document and the secretary of state to

* H. R. Mis. Doc. No. 31, 45th Cong. 3d Sess. pp. 258 to 265.

countersign and affix the great seal as of December 6th, as follows: He claimed that on December 6th, he had made out in triplicate, signed, countersigned, and sealed, certificates but that Governor Kellogg objected to the *illegibility of the handwriting* of the clerk who drew them up, and, therefore, he had to have another set of governor's certificates prepared and executed in triplicate; that he had preserved the first lot and when they were needed on December 29th they were ready to hand. But strange to say when Mr. Clark came to attach the governor's certificates to the new and forged lists of electoral votes he detached from the certificate Anderson had brought back, the governor's certificate and used only two of the ones, he said, he had on hand. The reason assigned for these extra governor's certificates being on hand was the *illegibility* of the handwriting. But the two returns made on December 29, 1876, which came to Washington, one by messenger, and one by mail, had attached governor's certificates in *as legible handwriting* as that of the governor's certificate attached to the returns made December 6, 1876, which came by mail.

The late electors did not gather * in the room on the third floor of the State House where Clark had arranged the new certificates for signature. Those of them available were taken up one by one, either by Clark or Thomas S. Kelley, the colored messenger of the Executive office. Clark says he took Kellogg up to the room to sign and that he also saw Brewster,* the last one to sign, write his name. He saw none of the remaining six sign. He professed to have made no inquiry, * whatever, and to have heard none made, as to the whereabouts of A. B. Levissee and Oscar Joffroin He wrote a note to Morris

* H. R. Mis. Doc., No. 31, 45th Cong., 3d Sess. pp. 270-271.

Marks * at Donaldsonville asking him to come to the State House, but he did this without a suggestion from any one.

Kellogg insisted that he paid very little attention to the preparation or signing of the second set of certificates because he "had the whole state on his shoulders,"—his time and mind being engrossed with other things. He claimed that he made no inquiries about Levissee and Joffroin or either of them; that he heard of none being made.

Sheldon † testified that on the day Anderson returned from Washington he was at Kellogg's office and met there Kellogg, Anderson, and Clark; that the fact of the absence of Levissee and Joffroin was known to him, and he asked Kellogg if they could be got there and Kellogg replied that he had sent for them; that the next morning, when he went to the State House to sign, he asked Kellogg if Levissee and Joffroin had arrived and the reply was they had.

But Mr. Sheldon undoubtedly prevaricated. He knew that Levissee could not have come from Shreveport to New Orleans if he had been asked to come on the morning of the 28th. At that time there was no way of making the journey between Shreveport and New Orleans in less than seventy-two hours. Joffroin lived in the parish of Pointe Coupé and it was a physical impossibility to have sent for and to have brought him to New Orleans in twenty-four hours.

And yet Mr. Sheldon swore that as soon as he learned the facts from Anderson on December 28th he asked Kellogg what had been done about Levissee and Joffroin who were not in the city. Kellogg told him then they had been sent for, and the next morning Kellogg told him

* H. R. Mis. Doc. No. 31, 45th Cong. 3d Sess. p. 264.
† Ibid. p. 1274.

they had arrived.   All of the parties in New Orleans including Sheldon testified that they knew nothing of the
defects in the certificates of December 6th until Anderson
reached New Orleans on December 28th.   Anderson testified * that to the best of his recollection he did not telegraph either from Washington or on his way home.

Is it possible that Sheldon was the only person who
made inquiry about the two absentees ?   Is it possible that
he accepted as true Kellogg's statement when he knew that
it was a physical impossibility for Kellogg to have secured
their presence in the period of time that had elapsed ?
Of course not !   Sheldon was simply trying to tell a plausible story, and failed.   He knew that if he testified that he
made no inquiries about these two men, whose absence
from New Orleans had been proved, he would not be believed.

As to Kellogg, and Burch, and Joseph, and Marks,
and Brewster, and Clark, who swore they made no inquiries
about Levissee and Joffroin, but took it for granted that
they were there and signed, there can be but one conclusion — they one and all committed perjury.

What was the object of this systematic perjury ?   They
one and all knew that the names of Levissee and Joffroin
were forged to the certificates of electoral votes they signed
on the 29th of December.   Upon no other hypothesis can
this uniform professed absence of curiosity about the two
missing men be accounted for.   The sudden return of Anderson from Washington, the preparation of new certificates
of electoral votes, their being dated back twenty-three days,
the knowledge that upon the electoral vote of Louisiana
depended the result of the Presidential election, the secrecy
with which the manufacture of the ante-dated certificates

* H. R. Mis. Doc. No. 31, 45th Cong. 3d Sess. p. 540.

was conducted, the going up one by one to a room on the third floor of the State House — all these circumstances must have excited their curiosity to the highest pitch.

The utmost secrecy was to be preserved as to the rest of the world and, therefore, the greater the discussion among themselves. They would naturally want to know wherein their certificates of December 6th were defective; who advised Anderson to have the defects remedied; what was to become of the set that had been sent by mail, and of the one deposited with the judge of the District Court of the United States; these and many other inquiries must inevitably have to be made. Is it within the limit of human credulity to believe that no one remarked the absence of Levissee and Joffroin?

Anderson who had carried the first set of certificates did not take the forged set to Washington. A man named Hill,* who was a clerk in the State Auditor's office, bore the forged electoral votes to the National Capital with a sealed letter of advice from Kellogg to Zach. Chandler. Arriving in Washington, Hill called upon Chandler at the Interior Department and presented Kellogg's letter. Chandler read it and directed him to go direct to the Capitol and deliver the package containing the forged electoral votes to the President of the Senate. On reaching the Capitol and finding Mr. Ferry the latter called into the Vice-President's room John Sherman to witness the delivery and receipt of the package. Sherman then took Hill to the room of the committee of finance and there wrote a letter to Kellogg which was delivered sealed to the messenger for delivery in person.

The same train that carried Hill to Washington also bore by mail a duplicate package of the forged certificates

* H. R. Mis. Doc. No. 31, 45th Cong. 3d Sess. pp. 49 to 60.

and the same day that the messenger made his delivery the one by post was received by Mr. Ferry.* So far the conspiracy to substitute the forged certificates, regular in form as required by the Constitution and the laws of the United States, for the genuine but fatally defective ones made on Dec. 6th, had been successfully and secretly executed.

It only remained to obtain from the United States district judge in New Orleans the package which had been deposited with him on the sixth of December and substitute therefor the one containing the electoral certificate forged on the twenty-ninth of December. Application was made to the judge, Hon. E. C. Billings,† for permission to make the substitution but he declined to grant it on the ground that he was merely the custodian without authority to deliver to any one unless upon requisition from the Speaker of the House. ‡ This unexpected refusal of Judge Billings marred the plan which had been so systematically, secretly, and criminally conceived and carried out.

The forgery of the names of A. B. Levissee and Oscar Joffroin to the ante-dated certificates must have been known, as has already been demonstrated, to a number of persons. It is probable, however, that the knowledge as to the forger might have been confined to a few persons. It is demonstrable that Kellogg and Clark must have known who the guilty party was. Only one of all the persons about the State House confessed to any knowledge of the forgery and pretended to know who was the forger.

Thomas S. Kelley who was a colored messenger of the

---

* H. R. Mis. Doc. No. 31, 45th Cong. 3d Sess. p. 1382.

† Ibid, p. 1105.

‡ Curiously enough Judge Billings did not know that the Secretary of State can alone send for the package deposited with the U. S. district judge.

executive office under Kellögg, wrote* to Hon. Clarkson N. Potter on June 9, 1878, from Lake Providence, Louisiana, stating that he was " familiar with all the facts pertaining to the forgery of the certificates of the Louisiana electors." He also said that " Oscar Joffroin, another elector's name, was forged as well as Levissee's, and if I can see the certificates of the electors, I will show the forged ones. I have marks on them that will prove it beyond any doubt, and I will show you the men that forged them."

In a postscript to this letter Kelley referred to a colored man, named James D. Kennedy, employed in the sergeant-at-arms' office of the Senate, who, he said, could tell who he was. Three days before this letter was written A. B. Levissee ** had testified before the Potter committee that his name had been forged to the second set of electoral certificates: that it was a bungling piece of work : that on the 28th and 29th of December, 1876, he was at his home in Shreveport, Louisiana, having left New Orleans on the 22d or 23d of that month.

Mr. Potter immediately took steps to have Thomas S. Kelley subpœnaed to appear before a sub-committee which he was about to send to New Orleans to take testimony. But the day the deputy sergeant-at-arms of the House of Representatives, † reached Lake Providence, James D. Kennedy arrived there also and brought Kelley to Washington. Kennedy ‡ subsequently testified that he had gone to New Orleans at the request of Kellogg, who procured him a leave of absence; that he held his position, under the sergeant-at-arms of the Senate, through Kellogg's influence; that he had received a letter from Kelley, the contents of which he communicated to Kellogg; that he stopped at

* H. R. Mis. Doc. No. 31, 45th Cong. 3d Sess. p. 1446.
** Ibid, p. 129.   † Ibid. p. 568.   ‡ Ibid, pp. 1115, 1116.

Lake Providence to see Kelley and brought him direct to Washington, paying his expenses; that they arrived on July 1st, 1878.

Kelley remained in Washington and was supported until Dec. 16, 1879, by money furnished by Kellogg through John A. Walsh, a former citizen of New Orleans, who was then doing business as a banker at 916 F Street, Washington, D. C. On Dec. 16, 1879 * Kellogg had Thomas S. Kelley placed on the pay roll of the New Orleans Custom House and he drew pay at the rate of $1,000 a year until March 4, 1880, without rendering any services, and without leaving Washington. On the fourth of March, 1880, Kelley was by order of John Sherman, upon the recommendation of Kellogg,* appointed a clerk in the second auditor's office of the Treasury Department at a salary of $1,000 per annum. He was, through the influence of Kellogg, twice promoted and is now a second-class clerk receiving a salary of $1,400 a year.

During the fall of 1878, Kelley requested permission to appear before the Potter committee and testify. On the 11th of January, 1879, he was examined † and, after admitting knowledge of the forgery, declined to tell what he knew on the ground that he had been accused of the crime, and, therefore, if he admitted that he was guilty people would say he was a fool for telling, and, if he denied having committed the forgery, no one would believe him. He, however, refused to say that his answers would criminate himself and, the committee directed him to answer the questions propounded. He requested two days' delay to consult counsel and was given three days. He was re-

Records Appt. Division, U. S. Treasury Dept.
† H. R. Mis. Doc. No. 31, 45th Cong. 3d Sess. pp. 1131 to 1140 and 1144 to 1159.

called January 14th and then denied that he had forged the names of Levissee and Joffroin. He admitted that he knew who had forged the name of Joffroin, but declined to tell who was the forger. He pretended great fear of the consequences to himself, although claiming that he had no part in the crime save to witness its commission.

On being required to answer he told the following improbable story. He said he assisted Kellogg's private secretary, Clark, in arranging the room on the third floor of the State House where the certificates of electoral votes which had been prepared Dec. 28th were spread on a table, and that he attended several of the late electors to the room; that when Clark was not in this room he, Kelley, was on duty; that the afternoon of Dec. 29th he came into the room and noticed B. P. Blanchard, Kellogg's executive clerk, sitting at the table and without noticing what he was doing walked to the fire-place and took a seat; that he sat there a few moments and saw and heard nothing until Blanchard exclaimed " how is that for high ?" whereupon he got up and walked to the table and saw Blanchard with a pen in his hand, and noticed that the name of Oscar Joffroin was written on the certificates, and that the ink was not dry; that Blanchard said nothing and he asked no questions.

The cross-examination was conducted by General B. F. Butler and the result was very damaging to Kelley. His pretended unwillingness to answer the first day, and his hesitation and coquetting the second day were shown to be mere masquerading. He had asked for delay to consult counsel, but claimed he had not talked with any one. The theory of the cross-examination was that Kelley was the forger. He persistently refused to write the name of Oscar Joffroin. His penmanship was shown to be

fair but not good. The imitation of Levissee's and Joffroin's signatures were poor, as Levissee had testified.
Blanchard was a skilful penman, and one of the
shrewdest of the many expert scamps in Kellogg's employ.
He died of yellow fever several months before Kelley testified. Would he have taken a negro like Kelley into his
confidence? Jewett, who was the intimate friend of
Blanchard, and well informed about all that transpired during that period, testified that he knew of the preparation of
the second set of certificates of electoral votes on December 28th and 29th; that the absence of Levissee and Joffroin was known to himself and Blanchard; that the forgery
of their signatures was frequently the subject of conversation between Blanchard and himself; that it was their
belief, and the general conviction of those who knew of the
occurrence, that Kelley was the forger.

Whether Kelley was or was not the forger is immaterial.
He possessed knowledge which Kellogg was exceedingly
anxious to have concealed. A more parsimonious man than
Kellogg does not live. He never expended a dollar of his
own money except in cases of the direst necessity. He
maintained Kelley in Washington at very considerable
expense for eighteen months. The demands on Kellogg
during that period and for another year thereafter were
incessant. His contest with Spofford taxed to the utmost
his command of the patronage of the custom house in
New Orleans and of the departments in Washington. He
had to provide places for thirty-four * of the members of
the legislature who had supported him for the United States
Senate. That he had no real affection for Kelley is shown
by the fact that he neglected to provide for him during
more than a year, and only made provision for him when

* Senate Mis. Doc. No. 79, 46th. Cong. 2d. Sess. pp. 21 to 23.

he discoved that he was about to tell all he knew of the forgery of the certificates of the electoral votes.

Clark was trusted by Kellogg implicitly. He is an Irishman, a bright and capable man, an accomplished journalist, a stenographer, and was always serviceable to his employers. Kellogg committed to him the preparation of the second set of certificates when Anderson returned from Washington, and the dispatch, cleverness, and adroitness with which he executed his task demonstrated his capacity for such work. Kellogg provided him with a place in the Internal Revenue bureau at Washington as soon as the Packard government broke to pieces.* It is significant that Clark and all the other witnesses, who professed to have any knowledge of the preparation and signing of the forged electoral certificates, had no recollection of seeing Kelley about the State House on the 29th of December.

It is marvellous how the secret of this crime was preserved. It was known in a general way to ten or a dozen persons in New Orleans, and to several in Washington, and yet not a whisper concerning it escaped till some time after the Electoral Commission had been organized. Then the allusion to it was vague and mysterious and conveyed no information that attracted the attention of persons not cognizant of all the facts. It was a brief paragraph in a letter from New Orleans to a Cincinnati paper and was intended only to warn Kellogg and his co-conspirators that some one had knowledge of the crime. The letter was written by a man named Richardson who derived his information from D. J. M. A. Jewett. Clark saw the paragraph and sent it with a letter to Kellogg. Both Clark and Kellogg undoubtedly suspected the source from whence the hint came.

* H. R. Mis. Doc. No. 31, 45th Cong. 3d Sess. p. 264.

The paragraph attracted no attention in Democratic circles. It was not intended for that purpose. They had no suspicion that the Louisiana conspirators had neglected to comply with the forms prescribed by the Constitution and the statutes of the United States in making the return of electoral votes. They took it for granted that the visiting statesmen, who remained in New Orleans until after the meeting of the Republican electors, had looked after every detail of this kind.

The purpose originally was to suppress the first returns made by the Republican electors of Louisiana. This has been clearly shown elsewhere in this chapter. The failure to obtain from Judge Billings the certificate deposited with him shortly after the sixth of December and to substitute therefor a duplicate of the one forged December 29th probably would have compelled a change in the programme, but the paragraph in the Cincinnati paper impelled Kellogg to disclose to Senator Morton and other Republican leaders in Washington the fact that there was something wrong with the second set of returns.*

Kellogg was very guarded in giving his testimony on this point to the Potter committee. The utmost that he would admit he had said to Morton and other leading republicans was that "the second set could not be depended on." He talked very glibly about his confidence in the original certificate being all right, in spite of the fact that it did not comply with the Constitution or the statute law of the United States, and he dwelt particularly on his recognition of the fact that the dating back of the second set of certificates would have invalidated them, but, of course, the purpose of this talk was apparent. He would not admit

* H. R. Mis. Doc., No. 31, 45th Cong., 3d Sess., p. 711.

that he knew of the forgery of the signatures of Levissee and Joffroin. That would have been "giving himself away."

The admission that he mentioned to Morton and others the existence of something "crooked" in the second set of certificates convicts him of knowledge of the forgery, because, it was known to Mr. Ferry, Mr. Sherman, both the Chandlers, and other "leading friends in Washington" that the second set had been manufactured after Christmas, 1876. Therefore, there was no necessity for Kellogg to tell Morton and "other friends" about that irregularity. They knew that fact as well as he did. He could have told them but one thing — namely — that the second set of certificates could not be "depended on" because they were *forged*, and there was danger that the crime might be disclosed.

There was another incident connected with the electoral returns from Louisiana which has an important bearing in this connection. A burlesque certificate was prepared by some person or persons in New Orleans and mailed to the President of the Senate. It was endorsed in due form to the effect that the envelope contained the certificate of the electoral vote of Louisiana, but the signatures of the electors were wanting. In this respect it corresponded exactly with the package containing the first certificate of the electoral votes mailed at New Orleans on or about December 6, 1876. The package containing the burlesque certificate was received by the President January 9, 1877, just six days after the receipt of the second and forged set of certificates.

When the two Houses of Congress in joint convention reached Louisiana in the opening of the certificates of electoral votes, Mr. Ferry, as the presiding officer, first handed to the tellers "the genuine Kellogg certificate, which had come to him by mail; next the McEnery certificate, which had come to him in duplicate, one copy by mail, and the other by messenger; and next the forged Kellogg certificate, of which two copies, one by mail and the other by Hill as messenger, had reached him; and finally a certificate signed by John Smith, declaring that the vote of Louisiana had been cast for Peter Cooper." This Smith certificate was read as the others had been, but the convention unanimously ordered that it should be suppressed and no mention of it made in the record of the proceedings.

It was the first time in the history of the count of electoral votes that a burlesque certificate had been sent in. The last place one would have come from without an ulterior object was New Orleans. The situation there from the 7th of November onward was of the most grave and serious character. The democrats were fighting mad and the other side balanced between hope and uncertainty. Their future depended upon the success of the scheme to count in Hayes.

Whoever got up the burlesque certificate had an object in view other than creating a laugh in the joint convention. Whoever the author of it was he had an object in concealing his authorship, for to this day the secret has been jealously guarded. The purpose of this burlesque was, and could have been, no other than to create a diversion in the joint convention which would draw away attention from the *three* Republican electoral certificates. When it was found that one of the forged set of certificates could not be substituted for the one which had been deposited with Judge Billings, it became a certainty that the first certificate sent to the President of the Senate by mail could not be safely suppressed.

A diversion was created in the joint convention by the production and reading of the burlesque Smith certificate.

Not one of the Democratic lawyers, managers, senators, or representatives noticed that there was one certificate made by the Republican electors of Louisiana which did not comply with the constitutional requirements and that there were duplicates of another certificate from the same electors which were in proper form.

It is scarcely possible that such an apparent difference would have escaped some one of the many keen observers on the Democratic side, if there had not been an exciting interruption of the deliberate proceedings of the convention caused by the production of such an unseemly paper. As soon as this paper had been read great confusion ensued in the hall and it required several minutes to order its suppression and to strike from the record of the proceedings all reference to it. No trace of the paper was ever found after the joint convention took a recess that day. It was carried off by some one who had a reason therefor.

There was no time for inspection or examination of the certificates. All the papers went to the Electoral Commission which met immediately upon the separation of the two houses. As soon as the Commission met and the secretary began to read the papers which had come from the joint convention one of the Democratic commissioners moved that the reading be dispensed with and that the papers be printed. It was so ordered. The President of the Commission, Hon. Nathan Clifford, marked for identification the papers, beginning with the certificates as follows: The first certificate of the Kellogg electors — the one which did not comply with the constitutional requirements — was marked " No. 1, N. C.;" the Democratic certificate was marked " No. 2, N. C.;" and the forged Kellogg certificate " No. 3, N. C." With these marks on the different certificates in the large bold handwriting of Judge Clifford they went to a private printer, and not as was the invariable rule before and afterwards to the public printer.

The distinguishing marks were omitted in the printed copies. This was a remarkable oversight by the printer. He did another singular thing — instead of sending the originals with the printed copies back the next morning to the secretary of the Commission, he sent the originals to the secretary and caused two of his press-boys to distribute the printed copies among the members of the Commission and the counsel.* There is no means of proving that copies of the genuine Kellogg certificate, " No. 1, N. C," were not distributed, but if they were, it seems unaccountable that the Democratic commissioners, the Democratic lawyers, and the two hundred Democratic members of the House and Senate, should not have observed that they did not correspond with the copies of the " No. 3, N. C." — the Kellogg certificate correct in form but forged.

If printed copies of the "No. 1, N. C." certificate had been about its defective form would inevitably have been detected. Comparison with the other Republican electoral certificate — " No. 3, N. C." would certainly have been made, and the difference noted. Nothing of this kind happened and the conclusion is irresistible that two copies of the forged certificate were distributed instead of one copy of the genuine and defective and one copy of the correct in form but forged certificate.

But this was not all; when the Electoral Commission had decided, eight to seven, to count the electoral vote of Louisiana for Hayes and Wheeler, Senator Morton † was careful, in his motion, to specify the electoral votes in certificate "No. 1, N. C." the genuine but constitutionally defec-

* H. R. Miss. Doc. No. 26, 45th Cong. 3d Sess. pp. 118, 567, 568.
† Electoral Count p. 420.

tive one. Therefore, the Electoral Commission, by a partisan vote counted the electoral votes of Louisiana which were not returned as the Constitution of the United States prescribes they shall be, and this was done so far as Mr. Morton was concerned with the knowledge that the other set of Republican electoral certificates from Louisiana could " not be depended on."

* " And when, later, the record of the proceedings in Congress and of the Electoral Commission came to be made up, this formally correct but forged certificate was in fact wholly suppressed, while a second copy of the genuine but defective certificate was inserted in its place.   That is, the record declares that there was before the Congress, and by it referred to the Commission, and there considered, the Democratic certificate and the genuine but defective certificate of the Republican electors, and no others, the latter in duplicate, once by the name of No. 1, and later by the name of No. 3.   Whereas, it is altogether certain that this was not the fact, and altogether probable that the prints which were before the Electoral Commission were a print of the Democratic certificate and two prints of the forged Republican certificate, and of these alone, and that nothing whatever was considered or acted upon by the Commissioners or Congress but these, and that instead of it being a fact, as these records state, that Congress and the Commission had before them two prints of the genuine but defective, and no other Republican certificate, there was before them, and really considered by them, only two copies of the regular but forged—and of no other Republican certificate, and that neither Congress nor the Commission ever had an opportunity to or did consider the defects of the genuine certificate at all."

* H. R. Mis. Doc. No. 31, 45th Cong. 3d Sess. p. 70.

The boldness of the conception, the secrecy of the execution of the crime was only equalled by the dextrous and unscrupulous manipulation of the printed record of the proceedings in Washington. The intention was undoubtedly to conceal so far as the published record could the fact that there had been a conspiracy to manufacture a forged certificate of electoral votes by Kellogg and his coadjutors in Washington and Louisiana. Happily the investigation ordered by the House of Representatives in 1878 disclosed sufficient facts to enable the historian to trace the devious ways of the conspirators and to tell the story of one of the crimes which the perpetrators thereof fondly hoped would not be brought to light.

CHAPTER XI.

How the Republican visiting statesmen disobeyed General Grant's instructions: How they prostituted themselves: Preaching rigid adherence to "forms of law" they encouraged disregard of the same: John Sherman made Secretary of the Treasury and Almoner of the fraudulent administration: His pet bank in New York: Stanley Mathews, his services and reward therefor: James A. Garfield, his work and reward: William M. Evarts, what he did and how he was paid: E. W. Stoughton, author of the infamous report to the President made Minister to Russia: John M. Harlan made Justice of the Supreme Court of the United States for helping to get rid of Packard: Joseph R. Hawley sent on a pleasure trip to Paris: John Coburn also paid: Eugene Hale and William D. Kelley rewarded with "patronage."

THE Republican visiting statesmen did not conduct themselves in Louisiana as impartial judges commissioned " to see that the board of canvassers make a fair count of the votes actually cast." On the contrary they lent the great weight of their "national reputation" to influence and encourage the Returning Board officers to violate the spirit as well as "the forms of law" and to disregard the will of the people by refusing "to make a fair count of the votes actually cast."

Among those who thus prostituted their high calling as statesmen and lawyers were gentlemen well known to be near to, and to speak with authority for, Rutherford B. Hayes. After having obtained the Presidency by means of the frauds, perjuries, and forgeries, which these personal

representatives encouraged and promoted, Mr. Hayes rewarded these men for their services with high offices, and
bestowed upon the members of the Returning Board, upon
state officers, and party managers, and on many of the subordinate rogues, honorable and lucrative Federal offices.

John Sherman was the recognized chief of " the visiting
statesmen " in New Orleans. His name heads the signatures appended to the report, made to the President of the
United States, which attempts a defence of the illegal and
indefensible conduct of the Returning Board, and presents
in support thereof, a mass of *ex-parte* affidavits. The manufacture of these affidavits has already been noticed. The election law of Louisiana which created the Returning Board,
and vested it with extraordinary powers, was unquestionably
unconstitutional, and had been so adjudged by Senator
Edmunds * and a majority of the Senate of the United
States, in the spring of 1875, on the question of seating
Pinchback, as Senator from Louisiana, whose credentials
were based on an election by a legislative body, a majority
of whose members had been " counted in " by the Returning Board.

But waiving the question of constitutionality, it will certainly be admitted that the Returning Board could have no
legal powers save those conferred upon it by the election
law. If those powers could only be exercised in certain
contingencies, when certain forms, prescribed by the law
itself, had been strictly complied with, then, of course, the
Returning Board exceeded its authority if it exerted power
in the cases wherein it had no jurisdiction whatever.

It is an incontestible fact that John Sherman and his
associated " visiting statesmen " learned, immediately on
their arrival in New Orleans, that the Louisiana election

* See Cong. Rec. Part I, Vol. IV, p. 65.

law * required the commissioners of election to certify to
the supervisors of registration for their parishes the facts
concerning any occurrences which in their judgment had
invalidated the elections at the polling places where they
were the officers; that this certificate must be verified by
three respectable citizens, qualified voters, at that voting
place.

These certificates coming to the supervisors of registration were to be forwarded to the Returning Board, *and they
alone* gave jurisdiction to that body. The supervisors of
registration could report only such facts as related to the
registration of voters, because they had no personal knowledge of anything else.

Before the Returning Board began its sessions, on the
17th of November, it was known to the members thereof,
to the Republican managers, and to "the visiting statesmen," that in not one single instance, throughout the entire state, had the election officers entered a complaint
against the fair, free, and peaceable character of the election; that not one of the supervisors of registration had reported a single fact reflecting on the fairness, freeness, and
fullness of the registration in one of the parishes of the state.
This being so, the Returning Board was bound, legally, to
canvass and compile the votes as they had been returned by
the Commissioners of election.

And if the law — even the Louisiana election law — had
been obeyed — the Tilden electors, the Democratic state
ticket, and a large majority of the Democratic candidates
for the legislature, would have been found elected by majorities ranging from 7,000 to 10,000 votes. It was, therefore
necessary for the Returning Board wrongfully, illegally, arbitrarily, to assume jurisdiction, and, without one jot or

* H. R. Mis. Doc. No. 31. 45th Cong. 3d Sess. p. 790.

tittle of legal evidence before it, to proceed to throw out enough Democratic votes to bring in the Hayes electors, the Republican state ticket, and enough candidates for the legislature to give a majority in both Houses thereof.

To do this there must be some semblance of jurisdiction as well as some pretended evidence. The supervisors, by the express terms of the election law, were required to make up their returns "*within twenty-four hours* AFTER all returns had been received" from the commissioners of elections, and "TO FORWARD THEM BY MAIL" to the Returning Board. This done they were *functus officio* — they were dead in law — they could do nothing further in connection with the election.

In contemplation of the necessity for frauds, the supervisors of registration had been instructed* to disobey the law, and, instead of forwarding their returns *by mail*, to bring them in person to New Orleans. In the greater number of cases the supervisors had obeyed their party managers, instead of the law, and brought with them to New Orleans their returns. They were, as necessity dictated from time to time, instructed to make in New Orleans, and file with their returns, statements impeaching the legality, fairness, freedom, and peaceableness of registration *and election* in their parishes. For this purpose there was established in the custom house "an affidavit mill," where the supervisors swore to statements prepared for them by Republican managers, and negroes, by the scores, were brought from all quarters to make "their marks," and go through the form of qualifying to affidavits to sustain those sworn to by the supervisors. A committee of "visiting statesmen" had supervision of the lawyers who directed the manufacture of the so-called evidence.

* H. R. Mis. Doc., No. 31, 45th Cong., 3d Sess., p. 1460.

From beginning to end the whole business was illegal, even according to the election law of Louisiana. It was not what that law required. This fact every one of "the visiting statesmen" knew, and they deliberately became parties to the conspiracy which was formed to supply pre-texts for the Returning Board to assume jurisdiction, and to furnish it with a lot of *ex-parte* affidavits as substitutes for the evidence the law required.

With full knowledge of all these facts, "the visiting statesmen" proclaimed in New Orleans, and subsequently in their report to the President, that it was * " vital to the preservation of constitutional liberty that the habit of obedience to the forms of law should be sedulously incul-cated and cultivated, and that the resort to extra constitu-tional modes of redress, for even actual grievances, should be avoided and condemned as revolutionary, disorganizing, and tending to disorder and anarchy!"

Thus, while they preached the doctrine of rigid adher-ence "to the forms of law," they countenanced and en-couraged the widest departure therefrom. And one crime led to another. Having approved departures from the letter and spirit of the law, by the Returning Board, it be-came necessary to induce subordinates to make statements which the facts did not warrant. No matter how violent a partisan a man may be, he does not swear to lies for the mere fun of committing perjury for his party's sake. They had to be induced thereto.

John Sherman being shown a copy of a letter which James E. Anderson, supervisor of the parish of East Fe-liciana, had testified before the Potter committee, he had, in connection with D. A. Weber, supervisor of the parish of East Feliciana, received from John Sherman, that

* Senate Ex. Doc. No. 2, 44th Cong. 2d Sess. p. 32.

worthy declared, on his oath, that while he believed he did not write that particular letter, he would have written "some of the things" contained in the alleged copy if he had been asked so to do.

There were but three sentences in the letter. One acknowledged the receipt of a communication of even date from the two supervisors — the second, declared that Mr. Hayes and the country at large had been placed under great obligations by the actions of the supervisors, and the third, pledged, in the name of Mr. Hayes, rewards for the services performed. In effect, therefore, Mr. Sherman admitted to the Potter committee that he would have acknowledged in writing to such men, that they had placed Mr. Hayes under obligations and that they should be rewarded therefor. His language on the witness stand was — * "There are things in this letter that I would have written to them or any other men who were engaged in the performance of what I believed to be their duty, if I had been asked." The letter contained just two "things" — an admission of obligations and a promise to discharge them.

What had these men done, whereby they had placed Mr. Hayes under obligations which John Sherman would have been willing to — as Anderson claimed he did verbally and in writing — promise to see discharged? They had made,— not at the time and place and in the form required by law, — but in the custom house at New Orleans, statements, prepared by others, which were, in neither Anderson's nor Weber's case, filed with the commissioner's returns, and their consolidation thereof, with the Returning Board — but sometime after the filing of those records.

* Page 17, Vol. I, Rep. Potter Com. Mis. Doc. No. 31, H. R. 45th Cong. 3d Sess.

Mr. Sherman knew perfectly well that when the supervisors of registration filed their returns — either by mailing them, as the law required, from the parish town, within twenty-four hours after all the commissioners' returns had been received, or by handing them personally to the Returning Board — they ceased to have any official existence — that they were no longer supervisors of registration — or any other kind of officers of election. He knew that they had performed all their official duties and that any subsequent statements, made by them, impeaching the conduct of voters, and the character of the elections, were outside of the law — merely the acts of private citizens and ought not to have been received by the board.

But unless such statements were procured to be filed with the board it could have no sort of pretext for throwing out Democratic votes. The supervisors of registration knew this and hence they exacted consideration, or the promise thereof, for their work. Some of them added the crime of forgery to that of perjury — without apparently increasing their demands.

John Sherman was made Secretary of the Treasury in "recognition" of the important services he had rendered in Louisiana, and to satisfy the men who had assisted in the perpetration of the frauds that they would be rewarded. He was confirmed March 9, 1877. The place of Secretary of the Treasury is the post of most intrinsic importance in the Federal administration.

At that particular juncture its consequence was vastly increased by the funding operations which had been provided for by Congress in 1875. Hundreds of millions were involved and the opportunities for friends, and favored banks and bankers, to profit by the business were very great. These great opportunities were not neglected. One bank in the city of New York had the use of many millions of the government money for month after month, which was worth tens of thousands of dollars.*

Stanley Mathews was known to be, in a peculiar sense, the friend of R. B. Hayes. Very soon after his arrival in Florida W. E. Chandler telegraphed, in cipher, to the private secretary of Mr. Hayes to "send Stanley Mathews."† But Mr. Mathews was in New Orleans with John Sherman, Edward F. Noyes, James A. Garfield and others from Ohio and other Northern states. The request of Chandler was forwarded to New Orleans, but the presence of Mathews was deemed indispensable in Louisiana, and Edward F. Noyes, John A. Kasson, and Lew Wallace were sent to Florida.

* There were $740,000,000 of four per cent. bonds sold at par less a half of one per cent. commission, netting 99½ cents. Within a very short time the market value of these bonds advanced to 107—a profit to speculalors of $115,500,000! The principal purchaser at 99½ was the First National Bank of New York whose magnificent structure on the corner of Broadway and Wall streets is universally known as Fort Sherman. This bank with a capital of only half million dollars on June 14, 1879, owed the United States $128,109,071 for bonds. It was an institution of obscure and uncertain credit at the time its present owners came into control, which singularly enough, was of the same date as the incoming of the fraudulent administration. At a time when the four per cents were selling rapidly and the government could easily and safely have advanced the price Mr. Sherman announced that he had received subscriptions for all he could sell. The First National Bank was the subscriber for all that were for sale. There were $100,000,000 of 10.40 bonds held by the national banks and deposited as security with the government for circulation. They were called by Sherman and the banks had to replace them with four per cents. They could only get them of the First National Bank of New York. Within a week "fours" went up to 106.

Some of the national banks would not be fleeced and held off buying. This got the First National Bank of New York into temporary trouble and Mr. Sherman had to come to its rescue. The Treasurer of the United States Aug. 1, 1879, drew on the bank for $6,000,000. Mr. Sherman was in Maine making political speeches. The bank telegraphed him and he telegraphed the Treasurer to hold up. Mr. Sherman hurried from Maine to Washington and issued an order extending the time two months in which the pet bank could pay for its bonds. It got out of its temporary trouble, kept up the price of bonds, drew $800,000 interest on them while they held them, in addition to the premium at which they were sold.

† H. R. Mis. Doc. No. 31. 45th Cong. 2d Sess. p. 407.

Mr. Mathews took an active part in all that pertained to the fraudulent count by the Returning Board, and manifested the deepest interest in satisfying the claims of the carpet-baggers, after the fraud had been consummated, by the inauguration of Hayes. He was one of the Republican counsel before the Electoral Commission and was chiefly instrumental in inducing Southern democrats to defeat the movement in the House of Representatives, which had been organized to prevent the completion of the count of electoral votes. As the especial representative of Hayes he pledged the abandonment of Chamberlain in South Carolina, and Packard in Louisiana, in return for the seating of Hayes.

In pursuance of this understanding Mathews, on February 27, wrote Packard advising him that the Federal administration would have to withdraw the military support which sustained him, and assuring him that personally he and others should not go unrewarded. " It would be the duty," he said, " of the administration to take care that staunch republicans like yourself, against whom nothing disreputable can be alleged, should not suffer, and should receive *consideration and position* in some appropriate way."

This letter was written three days before the count of the electoral votes was completed, and was shown, before being dispatched to Packard, to prominent Southern democrats, as an earnest of good faith on the part of Mr. Hayes and his friends, that they would turn over the government of Louisiana and South Carolina to the democrats, if the Southern leaders would secure the defeat of the opposition in the House of Representatives to the completion of the count.

Mr. Mathews was also made the custodian of a shameful agreement * made in writing between Charles E. Nash, colored candidate for Congress in Louisiana, and James E. Anderson, supervisor of registration for the parish of East Feliciana, whereby Anderson undertook to suppress evidence establishing the fact that the democrats had fairly carried that parish and the state, and Nash in return was to use his influence to secure for Anderson the position of Naval Officer of the port of New Orleans.

Mr. Mathews obtained that agreement from Anderson and other documents he held, promising to secure him such "recognition" and "consideration" as would be satisfactory to him.

In return for these services Mr. Mathews was, by an arrangement made beforehand, elected to the United States Senate from Ohio, for the unexpired term of John Sherman, the succeeding term to be given to James A. Garfield, Mr. Mathews thereafter to be given the first vacancy on the bench of the Supreme Court of the United States.

In pursuance of this arrangement, Mr. Mathews was nominated for justice of the Supreme Court by Hayes in 1880, but the Senate declined to confirm the nomination. Hayes † requested his successor, Garfield, to nominate Mathews again which Garfield did in 1881, and by administration influence and the powerful coöperation of Jay Gould, and other railroad magnates, the confirmation of the nomination was secured. Mr. Mathews is now in the enjoyment of a seat on the bench of the Supreme Court and a salary of $10,000 a year.

James A. Garfield, accompanied John Sherman and Stanley Mathews to Louisiana in November, 1876. He was

---

* H. R. Mis. Doc. No. 31, 45th Cong. 3d Sess. p. 18.

† See N. Y. World for full particulars of this shameful transaction, March 10, 1884.

one of the most active, plausible, industrious, unscrupulous
of those invited by President Grant to go to that state. He
installed himself in the custom house where the affidavits
for use before the Returning Board were manufactured. As
he testified at Atlantic City in July, 1878,* he consulted
with witnesses and when he thought the subordinate affidavit draughtsmen had not done their work well he made
improvements therein.   Is it possible that Mr. Garfield
was misled by the unprincipled men with whom he was
thus associated ?   It is certain that some of the witnesses
he examined subsequently retracted their affidavits and
alleged that they were " pushed up to make them."†

D. J. M. A. Jewett, one of the shrewdest and most
capable of the Louisiana carpet-bag politicians, avers that
Garfield suggested to the Returning Board the plan to save
the five Hayes electors who ran behind by rejecting enough
polls from the returns of the parishes of Caldwell, Natchitoches, Richland, Catahoula, Iberia, Livingston, and Tangipahoa, to make up the votes lost in Bienville and Iberia
where only three electors had been voted for.

In accordance with the arrangement made with Mathews,
Garfield was elected for the long term in the United States
Senate.   He went to Chicago in 1880 as the friend of John
Sherman at the head of the delegation from Ohio, and
when the forces of Grant, led by Roscoe Conkling, had
successfully maintained for a week an unbroken front of
306, the managers of Blaine by a coup d'etat nominated
Garfield. His election was admittedly secured by the lavish
use of money in the October contest in Indiana, and the
November struggle in New York.

Chester A. Arthur, who managed the distribution of " the

* H. R. Mis. Doc. No. 31, 45th Cong. 3d Sess. p. 789.
† Ibid, p. 471.

soap," as he euphoniously termed it, subsequently, gave the credit of the success in Indiana to Stephen W. Dorsey of "Star Route" infamy.

William M. Evarts who in 1875, on the occasion of the interference of the military, under the orders of President Grant, with the organization of the Louisiana House of Representatives, unqualifiedly denounced that act as well as all the proceedings and acts of the Louisiana carpet baggers and Returning Board in the election of 1874, whereby the will of the people of that State was defied, went to New Orleans, at the invitation of the President, "to see that the board of canvassers make a fair count of the votes actually cast," and prostituted his reputation and fame, as a great lawyer, by countenancing the illegal acts of the same Returning Board whose conduct he had condemned in 1875.

No man knew better than Mr. Evarts that the Returning Board, under the Louisiana election law, was obliged "to canvass and compile" the returns of the commissioners of election from all polls whereat there had been "a fair, free, and peaceable registration and election," and that unless these commissioners had certified that the election *was not* fair, free, and peaceable, the Returning Board had no power whatever to go back of the same.   He knew, moreover, that the supervisors of registration were, in all things pertaining to the election, simply ministerial officers, and that it was their bounden duty to forward the returns of commissioners of election from every poll in their parishes to the Returning Board; and that they could not legally refuse to include any poll in their statement of the votes; and that the only irregularity they could report to the Returning Board was concerning the registration of the voters.

The fact was notorious that not one of the commission-ers of election in the entire state had reported that the election held on November 7th, was affected in any way by intimidation, acts of violence, or any of the other causes, which, the law said, *might* invalidate the same. He knew also that not one supervisor of registration had at the time and place, and in the manner required by the election law, certified that there had been any " intimi-dation, tumult, acts of violence, disturbances, bribery or corrupt influences " which had in any manner affected the " fair, free, and peaceable " character of the registration and election.

And, yet, Mr. Evarts united with John Sherman, James A. Garfield, and others, in a declaration made over their signatures, in New Orleans, and published to the world on November 16, 1876, that " it is, in our judgment, *so vital* to the preservation of constitutional liberty that the habit of obedience to *the forms* of law should be seduously incul-cated and cultivated, and that resort to extra constitutional modes of redress, for even actual grievances, should be avoided and condemned as revolutionary, disorganizing, and tending to disorder and anarchy."

This was mere hypocracy — nay, it was worse than the conduct of the Pharisees who took " tithe of the mint, the anise, and cummin, and neglected the weightier matters of the law."   It was deliberate, dishonest asseveration that they held in such sacred reverence *even " the forms " of the law*, that they would frown upon any departure therefrom, well knowing that the Returning Board would have to dis-regard " the forms," as well as the letter and spirit, of the law in order to count in the Hayes electors.   The asseveration was made to deceive the great public, and to cloak the contemplated frauds of the Returning Board in declaring chosen the Hayes electors who had been defeated at the polls by more than 7,000 votes!

Mr. Evarts united, also, with his co-defenders of frauds, forgeries, and·perjuries, in their report to the President which was as infamous for *suppressionis veri* as for *suggestionis falsi* contained therein. He was the leading counsel of Hayes before the Electoral Commission and strove with all his great ingenuity and eloquence to justify crimes which he had countenanced and encouraged in Louisiana, — if he had not been art and part therein. He was rewarded by being made the premier of the fraudulent administration.

E. W. Stoughton was no less conspicuous, though, less useful, because of his inferior capacity, in New Orleans, in the disreputable work of stimulating the Louisiana rogues to disregard law', justice, and right, and without adhering to even "the forms" prescribed by an unconstitutional law, to declare chosen the Hayes electors. He prepared the report to the President, commonly known as the Sherman report, because his name is the first signed thereto, justifying the monstrous conduct of the Returning Board. It was accompanied by the synopsis of the ex-parte affidavits prepared by Garfield and Courtlandt Parker. There were 375 printed pages of the affidavits, and in nearly every instance they were procured from ignorant negroes who did not know what they were swearing to, or did not care whether they were telling the truth or not. Those made by white men were in large part for "consideration" and "recognition" in the future.

The report itself was filled with misrepresentations, and falsehoods, and contained, among other shameless things, fulsome eulogies of, and certificates of good character for, the members of the Returning Board, two of whom were utterly characterless, while the other two were mulattoes, one of whom was a self-confessed petty thief, and the other an ignorant but willing knave.

For these services, as well as for the inconsequential part he bore in advocating the approval of the manifold frauds, forgeries, and perjuries by the Electoral Commission, he was made minister plenopotentiary and envoy extrordinary to Russia, which post he held from October 30, 1877, to April 12, 1872 — receiving in salary $77,626.25.

John M. Harlan, of Kentucky, was one of three persons, sent to Louisiana in the spring of 1877, by Hayes, to be present, in New Orleans, when, in pursuance of the agreement made by Stanley Mathews and others, on behalf of the fraudulent administration, the Federal troops were withdrawn from New Orleans, and the bogus Packard government abandoned to its fate. Mr. Harlan and his associates concluded, on their arrival in New Orleans, that it would be well to aid the democrats in procuring enough of the members of the Packard legislature who had been elected, without the aid of the Returning Board, to desert to, and join with, the Nichols legislature.

Packard had remained obdurate and would not respond to the appeal of Stanley Mathews, and insisted that his title to the governorship of Louisiana was neither better nor worse than that of Mr. Hayes to be President of the United States. It was, therefore, deemed advisable not to compel Hayes to openly admit the illegality of the Returning Board's acts, by abandoning Packard without some pretext.

The pretext was furnished by Harlan, and his co-commissioners, managing the breaking up of the quorum of Packard's legislature. This was accomplished by guaranteeing the seduced Packard adherents their pay in full, from January 1, 1877, by the Nichols government, and a bonus in cash. Mr. Harlan and his fellow-commissioners' appeals and arguments, unsupported by more weighty considerations, would doubtless have availed little with the corrupt cattle who adhered to Packard's fortunes.

Mr. Harlan * was rewarded for his services in successfully conducting this mission with a seat on the bench of the Supreme Court of the United States, his commission bearing date Nov. 24, 1877. The position is for life, with a salary of $10,000 a year.

Joseph R. Hawley, of Connecticut was a " visiting statesman " to Louisiana and played a subordinate, though doubtless, not an unimportant, part in giving moral (?) support to the " cogging, cozening, knaves " who counted in the Hayes electors. He was made commissioner to the Paris Exposition of 1878 with a salary of $10 per day and expenses.

John Coburn, a rural politician from Indiana, was serviceable in some capacity, in Louisiana, at the time of the Returning Board's operations and, as his reward, received the place of commissioner to lay off into lots government land at Hot Springs, Arkansas, salary $10 per diem and expenses.

Eugene Hale, and William D. Kelley, members of Congress from Maine, and Pennsylvania, were also " visiting statesmen " to Louisiana, to lend the weight of their names, position, and character, to bolster the acts of men like Wells, Anderson, Kellogg, and the other characterless conspirators engaged in stealing the vote of that state. Hale and Kelley received no promotion at the hands of the fraudulent administration they aided to make, but, doubtless they fared well in the general distribution of patronage.

* See testimony of H. V. Boynton, p. 396. H. R. Mis. Doc., No. 31, 45th Cong., 3d Sess. about Harlan's expectations before going to N. O. on this mission.

CHAPTER XII.

J. MADISON WELLS, president of the Returning Board,
was removed from the provisional governorship of Louisiana by General Phil. Sheridan in 1867, because he was " a
political trickster and a dishonest " man.   One of the
serious charges Gen. Sheridan preferred against him was an
attempt to dishonestly finger " some of the money " appropriated to repair the ruined levees.   The legislature had
passed two bills, one creating a board of commissioners to
supervise the repairing of levees, and another appropriating
$4,000,000 to defray the cost of the same.   Having passed
these bills the legislature adjourned before the governor
had approved or disapproved the bills.   Wells approved
the one appropriating the $4,000,000 but did not sign the

one creating the board to expend the money. He made a board of his own and issued some of the bonds provided for in the bill appropriating the money. This Gen. Sheridan properly characterized as dishonest. He also declared in a letter written to Secretary Stanton, June 3, 1867, as follows: " I say now, unequivocally, that Governor Wells is a political trickster and a dishonest man. I have watched him and his conduct has been as sinuous as the mark left in the dust by the movements of a snake. I say again he is dishonest."

With this record before them the Republican " visiting statesmen " pronounce the following general commendation on Wells' administration of Louisiana which General Sheridan so emphatically condemned: * " Under the Banks reconstruction scheme he was chosen lieutenant-governor on the ticket with the honorable Michael Hahn, who was elected governor, and upon the election to the Senate of the latter, a year after, Mr. Wells became governor of the State, to which office he was almost unanimously reelected under the reconstruction plan of President Johnson. His experience in public life has been great and varied, and his capacity to discharge the duties assumed cannot be questioned." Not a word about his removal by General Sheridan because of his general dishonesty and his unlawful attempt to finger " some of the money " appropriated for the repair of levees !

Notwithstanding the certificate of good character which " the visiting statesmen " gave Wells *after* he, in connection with Tom Anderson and the two mulattoes, had performed the rascally work of counting-in the Hayes electors neither the administration at Washington, the carpet-baggers in Louisiana, nor John Sherman and his associates felt sure of

* Senate Ex. Doc, No. 2, 44th Cong., 2d Sess., p. 6.

the Returning Board at the outset. The greed of Wells was notorious and his venality a matter of record. He was the holder of a large amount of state warrants * which were worth in the market about 30 per cent of their face value. Wells insisted that these must be cashed at their face and the money had to be raised for that purpose.

At the same time the Treasury Department at Washington sent a special agent post haste to New Orleans ostensibly to procure evidence against certain cotton claims but really to watch the Returning Board. † This agent of the

* H. R. Mis. Doc. No. 31,45th Cong. 3d Sess. p. 1426.

† The following official correspondence shows the purpose for which the government agent was sent to New Orleans, and also that he was implicitly trusted by high officials.

All Official Letters to this Office must be addressed to the "Commissioner of Internal Revenue," and in replying to Letters from this Office the marginal initials should be referred to.

TREASURY DEPARTMENT,
Office of Internal Revenue,
WASHINGTON, Nov. 11, 1876.

Sir:
    You are hereby assigned to the Revenue Agents' District comprising the states of Louisiana, Mississippi and Texas, with your station address at New Orleans.

You will at once proceed to New Orleans, and enter upon duty in the District to which you are assigned.

Respectfully,
H. C. ROGERS,
Acting Commissioner.

Jos. H. Maddox, Esq.,
    Revenue Agent,
        Washington, D. C.

H. E. W.   ———

OFFICE OF COMMISSIONER OF CUSTOMS,
WASHINGTON, D. C., Nov. 14, 1876.

J. H. MADDOX, ESQ.,
    Special Agent Int. Rev.,
        New Orleans, La.

    Dear Sir:
*   *   *   *   *   *

    I understand Gen. Logan did not go to N. O. as requested by the President. I saw Secretary Chandler yesterday with reference to what had been said to Collector Casey of N. O. about your going to La. to get the information about the purposes of the shot-gun democracy towards the returning board of that State and he said he had no special instructions.

It is apparent that the dem's. expect to prove (?) that the parishes show-

government was an old friend of Wells, a man of experience, courage, and ability. It did not take him long to ascertain what Wells was up to. The man "the visiting statesmen" eulogized in their report to President Grant was in the market. He wanted to serve his party friends if *they would pay therefor*, but if they did not *come down* according to his notion of the importance and value of his services he was willing to sell justice to his enemies and "make a fair count of the votes actually cast."

Inasmuch as Washington was the headquarters he thought it would be best for the government agent to proceed there forthwith and make known the situation. For that purpose Wells gave him first two letters, written Nov.

---

ing majorities for them have held fair elections and those opposed to them have been dishonestly conducted. I would suggest that their plan will be to hire "witnesses."

If you can get into their confidence and obtain proof of the perjury, and get witnesses from their own ranks you will do an invaluable service and entitle yourself to the gratitude of the country. It may be possible that the controversy will be brought up in the Senate, and in that case your proofs will tell. Another point was just suggested to me, as soon as they get their testimony manufactured, the mob of high-toned democrats who are there from the North, at the suggestion of Congressman Hewitt, will begin to flood the North with telegrams, giving the manufactured evidence the weight of their respectability, for the purpose of arousing the passions of the mob, against submission to the final result. You can easily ascertain this fact and suggest to Packard the advantages of anticipating their purpose by telegraphing North, an exposure of this purpose.

You need make no reports except to me, and when in your judgment you have finished the duties assigned you return here : this instruction is given, of course, on the assumption that you have no other, except what were based on my note of the 11th inst. to Gen. Sewall.

Write often.

Very respectfully, W. B. Moore.

Office Commissioner of Customs,
Washington, D. C., Nov. 27, 1876.

J. H. Maddox, Esq.,
No. 137 Bienville St., N, O.
My Dear Maddox:
I enclose copy of my communication to Hon. Secretary of the Treasury dated 24th inst. in which I ask to have you reimbursed for what you expect to pay for information. You can prepare your vouchers in accordance with the reasons set forth therein.

I called upon the President this A. M. but he said he was engaged on

29, and one written Nov. 21, * to exhibit to those most concerned. The two first differed slightly. One was a general letter of credit from Wells and was brief and to the
point. It ran as follows: " You fully understand the situation. Can you not advise with me relative thereto?"
The other, intended for exhibition to Republican leaders,
was more obscure, but there could be no mistake as to its

---

his message and would rather I would come next week. My object was to
talk of the S. S. Div.; of Judge Griswold's case, and other matters generally. And I did not want to talk under circumstances that would embarrass me, so, I suggested the delay myself.

You have heavy responsibilities on your shoulders and must encourage
the board to perform their duties manfully: the President's assurances to us
on Friday last, guaranteeing their safety, has received practical confirmation of his purpose to act in his order of this morning to stand by Chamberlain in South Carolina. Let me hear from you promptly.

Yours etc.,   W. B. MOORE.

OFFICE COMMISSIONER OF CUSTOMS,
WASHINGTON, D. C., Nov. 17, 1876.

JAS. H. MADDOX, ESQ.,
Custom House, N. O., La.
My Dear Maddox :

I have seen ex-Att'y-General Williams and he ap-
proves the suggestion that you be pressed for the office of Chief of the
Secret Service Division of the Treasury. I have not yet attempted to see
President Grant; the developments in the Dept. not yet having culminated
to a degree that would justify my approaching the President with reference
to the S. S. force.

There are grave reasons developing why a man unquestionably loyal
to the President should be at the head of that bureau ; one who has the pene-
tration to see the purpose of the traitors who are attempting to count Tilden in by intimidation and brow-beating the Returning Board at New
Orleans, and the courage to suppress them should they attempt to bring
their ku-klux tactics to Washington, should the controversy be transferred
to Congress.

*   *   *   *   *   *   *

If Louisiana is not counted for Hayes it is the purpose of every patriot
to urge on the Senate to throw out every state in the South where there is
proof of intimidation. This will effect Miss., Georgia, Alabama, and possibly Texas.

I have no fears of a conflict. My only fear is that there will be none.
The bold impudence of treason that now seeks to censure the Republican
party for wanting to keep them out of control needs another flogging and
they ought to be accommodated.

Direct to me care of the Commissioners of Customs.

Very truly,

W. B. MOORE.

* H. R. Mis. Doc. No. 42, 44th Cong. 2d Sess. p. 144. 131. 178, 180.

real meaning. Wells said : "Understanding the political condition of matters here from association with both political parties, and a friend of the President and a government officer, would it not be considered a part of your duty to go at once to Washington with as little delay as possible, and place before the President the condition and impending dangers of the situation ? Should you conclude by prompt action in the premises, allow me to commend you to Senator West, who is my friend, and with whom I trust you will freely communicate."

The letter of November 21 was addressed to Senator West, and was to be handed to him by the agent of the government. It was a most remarkable letter — clumsily cloaking the real designs of the writer in awkward and faulty language — protesting his own virtues, but to one like West, who understood the man, it in effect said — " there's millions in it; somebody may offer me my price; the faithful ought to be rewarded; how much can we make out of it ? A hint to the wise. You know how it is yourself."

Wells knew West — they knew each other. The career of both will long be remembered in Louisiana. West began his career as a supercargo on one of the vessels of Zacharie & Co., of New Orleans, and was dismissed for dishonesty. He left New Orleans between two days, and brought up in California where he barely escaped doing that state some service in the convict's garb. He entered the Union army and became a colonel of cavalry. At the close of the war he returned to New Orleans and was made supervisor of internal revenue, but his operations in California becoming known, Secretary McCulloch dismissed him. However, he became administrator of public improvements under Governor Warmoth, an office with almost unlimited opportunities for plunder. From this position West stepped into the

United States Senate. Senatorial honors in those days went cheap for cash in Louisiana.* Wells knew to whom he was writing when he penned the following letter: **

"NEW ORLEANS, La., Nov. 21, 1876.

My Dear Senator: I regret not seeing you when here: I wanted to say much to you which *would be at least imprudent to put on paper.* I trust, however, to meet you in Washington as soon as the canvass is over which is now on us. Our duties as returning officers have augmented to the magnitude of the destinies of the two great parties; may I not say the nation?

I fully comprehend the situation as well as my duty to the greatest living General — U. S. Grant: and not with my consent shall this oppressed people be governed by his paroled prisoners, aided by their white-livered cowards of the North. Let me, my esteemed sir, warn you of the danger.

Millions have been sent here and will be used in the interest of Tilden, and *unless some counter move*, it will be impossible for me or any other individual to wrest its productive results. The gentleman presenting this is fully aware of the moves, and if you will allow, will communicate freely. See our friends *and act promptly or results will be disastrous. A hint to the wise.* Strictly confidential.

Yours very truly,

J. MADISON WELLS."

Armed with these letters the agent of the government came to Washington and called upon the President and explained the situation in Louisiana.† The President was impressed with its gravity and sent the agent to see Zach. Chandler, giving him a card on which was written:

‡ " I wish the Sec. of the Int. would see Mr. Maddox Spl. agt, of the Treas. who has just returned from New Orleans, and has valuable information.

U. S GRANT.

Nov. 24th, 76."

* Tilden and Hendricks Campaign Text Book, 1876, p. 108.
** H. R. Mis. Doc. No. 42 Part 2, 44th Cong. 2nd Sess. p. 180.
† Ibid, p. 148, 155.
‡ See *fac-simile* of this card in Appendix.

What the interview with Chandler was we do not know, but the agent subsequently called upon Don. Cameron, Secretary of War, and explained to him that Wells was in the market and his price to the democrats was one million dollars.*

It may reasonably be presumed that Mr. Cameron, with his long experience at Harrisburg, concluded that the democrats would not pay that sum, and that Wells could be satisfied by the republicans for a much less amount. At any rate he gave the agent no encouragement.

Meeting an old friend, Col. John T. Picket, a distinguished ex-confederate, then living in Washington, the agent told him that he was authorized by Wells, in the event of the republicans failing to appreciate the value of his services, to dispose of the electoral votes of Louisiana to the democrats for $1,000,000.

Col. Picket, who knew the character of the Louisiana rogues, believed that justice *might be bought*, but could be had in no other way. He felt it to be his duty to lay the proposition before the National Democratic committee. He accordingly went to New York for that purpose, and the agent of the government communicated with Wells by telegraphic cipher that the negotiation was in progress and to "hold" things.

† Col. Picket submitted the proposition to Hon. Abram S. Hewitt, the Chairman of the National Democratic committee who unhesitatingly and indignantly rejected it.

Aside from this positive proof of the corruptibility of Wells, there is a great deal of indirect, as well as circumstantial evidence, to prove that Wells was anxious to be bought.

* H. R. Mis. Doc. No. 42, 44th Cong. 2d Sess. p. 148.
† Ibid, p, 133.

He was quite willing, as the testimony of Duncan F. Kenner,* of New Orleans, shows to sell the returns of the Democratic state ticket for $200,000 but would not agree to " count the votes actually cast " for the Tilden electors for that sum.   He had, at his own request two or three interviews with Mr. Kenner, on the subject of the return of the Democratic state ticket for that sum of money.   As will appear hereafter, in the account of the services of Jack Wharton ** and his reward therefor, the "dickerings " of Wells were fully known to Packard and other carpet-baggers and caused great uneasiness.

There is evidence tending to show that Kellogg † raised a considerable sum of money in New Orleans during the progress of the count by the Returning Board.   He related to a group of senators in one of the cloak rooms of the Senate chamber, in the presence of W. E. Curtis, ‡ correspondent of the Chicago *Inter-Ocean*, the circumstances connected with this transaction and claimed unequivocally that the money was used to secure favorable action by the Returning Board.   Subsequently Kellogg claimed that the money was for his brother-in-law, but this explanation was a very lame one and was entirely at variance with the story told to his senatorial friends.

The subsequent command which Wells and Anderson exercised over the Federal patronage of Louisiana, and the subserviency of the fraudulent administration to them, cannot be explained on any other theory than that the former dictated their terms and compelled adherence thereto.

The purchasing power of patronage is very great. There is a certain dignity connected with the dispensing of

---

* H. R. Mis. Doc. No. 42, 44th Cong. 2d Sess. pp. 376-387.
** Page, 275 post.
† H. R. Mis. Doc. No. 31, 45th Cong. 2d Sess. p. 666-7.
‡ Statement of Mr. Curtis to the author.

the favors of a great government which is very gratifying to men like Wells and Anderson. It gave them an importance and a political standing which money would not have given them. Their utter depravity and insensibility to shame made them, to a large extent, regardless of public sentiment and they would have sold their past grievances and along therewith the return of the Democratic electors and the state ticket for a much less sum than their asking price.

One hundred thousand dollars a piece, with " a sop " for " the two niggers " * as Wells termed his colored associates of the Returning Board, would have been thankfully accepted by Wells and Anderson. All they wanted was assurances from responsible parties that the money would be forthcoming and they would have come to an understanding without delay.

Failing to get assurances which Wells deemed satisfactory from Kenner, and the overtures to the National Democratic committee being spurned, there can be no sort of doubt that Wells and Anderson made the best terms they could with "the visiting statesmen" and the local carpetbag and scallawag capitalists.

There is no evidence that they had an understanding with "the visiting statesmen" other than that which subsequent developments furnished. Wells and Anderson and their relatives were rewarded with lucrative and commanding Federal offices. When the members of the Returning Board were indicted by the grand jury of New Orleans for the forging and falsification of the Vernon parish returns, John Sherman, James A. Garfield, Stanley Mathews, Eugene Hale, and Harry White, all " visiting statesmen," sent, Feb. 4th, 1878, to Tom Anderson, who was then

* H. R. Mis. Doc. No. 42, 44th Cong. 2d Sess. p. 145.

being tried for, and who was three days later convicted by an honest jury on which were two colored men, of the crime of forgery, the following dispatch: *

"The undersigned feel it due to you, under present circumstances, to assure you of our unhesitating belief that in the matter wherein you stand charged, you are altogether guiltless of any offense against law; that you are falsely accused and maliciously prosecuted; that the proceedings against you, though in the form of law, are without the substance of justice; that we, hereby, tender our earnest sympathies, and express our hope that the sense of justice and love of peace of the people of Louisiana, will protect you, and not permit the best interests of the whole country to be disturbed by a revival of sectional animosities. In any event we are confident that the American people will redress any injustice of which you may be the victim."

It may be confidently asserted that five distinguished men who had been honored by their fellow-citizens never before, in the history of the English speaking people, set their "signs manual" to so infamous a paper!

Let us briefly review a piece of antecedent history in connection with this message to Anderson. The democrats of the House of Representatives who felt deeply outraged by the partisan decisions of the Electoral Commission in the Florida and Louisiana cases organized a filibustering movement to defeat the count of the electoral votes. It was deemed a revolutionary movement by the more moderate Democratic representatives, who felt that their agreement to the Electoral Commission bill bound them to accept in good faith the result, notwithstanding the iniquitous rulings of the partisan commissioners. However, their sympathies were so strongly with their more impetuous brethren that it only required a manifest and il-

* N. Y. Sun, Feb. 12, 1878.

legal ruling of the President of the Senate during the opening of the returns from Vermont to carry the entire Democratic majority of the House of Representatives over to the side of the filibusters.

The House of Representatives received the official notice of the Electoral Commission's decision in the Louisiana case on Feb. 17, 1877. This was Saturday. The Republican plan was to proceed with the count that day and night till the next state, Oregon, from which there were duplicate returns, was reached. The filibustering movement began by the democrats voting that the House take a recess till Monday, Feb. 19th.

On Monday the joint meeting was resumed, when the protests to the decision of the Commission were presented and read and the Senate withdrew, and thereupon the House took a recess till Tuesday, Feb. 20. The debate on the Louisiana decision occurred that day. It was now apparent that the Democratic majority in the House could defeat the count by persisting in its filibustering. But eleven days remained in which it could be completed. There were objections to particular electoral votes from the states of Michigan, Nevada, Pennsylvania, Rhode Island, and Wisconsin, and duplicate returns from Oregon, South Carolina, and, it was claimed by the democrats, from Vermont also.

The programme of the filibusters was to secure one day by taking a recess and by debate on each of the states of Michigan, Nevada, Pennsylvania, Rhode Island, and Wisconsin. This would consume five of the eleven remaining days. It would be quite easy to dispose of the six days left with Oregon, South Carolina, and Vermont before the Commission. This programme was faithfully carried out until Vermont was reached, Wednesday evening, Feb. 28th.

The President of the Senate claimed that he had not received two returns from Vermont.

The democrats insisted that two had been sent. Mr. Hewitt, Chairman of the National Democratic committee, had received a duplicate of the Democratic return by mail, with a letter which stated that another had been sent to the President of the Senate. On Feb. 27, Mr. Hewitt called upon the President of the Senate and asked him if he had received two returns from Vermont. Mr. Ferry replied that he had not. Mr. Hewitt asked if there was not one addressed to him in the Post-office, and Mr. Ferry said that he did not know; all he knew was that he had not received one either by mail or messenger. Thereupon Mr. Hewitt drew from his pocket the return from Vermont and tendered it to President Ferry who refused to receive it, saying that Mr. Hewitt was not such a messenger as was contemplated by the law, and that the tender was made too late.

In the joint meeting on Feb. 28, when the State of Vermont was reached, Mr. Hewitt made a statement and presented the package purporting to be a return from that state. The presiding officer, the President of the Senate, refused to receive it, and then came the crucial test.

If the Democratic majority stood firm the two returns would have to go to the Commission, or the count would be at an end. If they went there, under the rules of that body, the democrats could easily consume the remaining three days. After a short struggle, formal objections were presented against receiving the one return which the President of the Senate had submitted, and the two Houses separated. The House by previous unanimous consent took a recess till 10 o'clock Thursday morning, March first. On that day the memorable contest over the vote of Vermont began. It was the crisis of the long struggle.

Immediately upon the reassembling of the House the point was made that there was not a quorum present, and two roll calls were gained by the filibusters, which, with points of order consumed two hours, and at 12 M. a new legislative day began. It was opened with prayer, and the Speaker directed the journal of the previous day to be read. A motion to suspend the rules and dispense with the reading was made which required a roll call. Then followed a wrangle over questions of privilege, all of which consumed time. Finally a resolution was offered requiring the President of the Senate to receive the package purporting to contain a return from the State of Vermont, and that it be, together with the one already opened, submitted to the Electoral Commission, and declaring that until this was done the House would not meet the Senate to proceed with the count.

Before this resolution was voted on, inquiry was made for the package which Mr. Hewitt had tendered to the President of the Senate in the joint meeting the previous day. This led to a startling statement, to the effect that the package had been carried off by the Secretary of the Senate, who refused to deliver it up on the ground that it was the private property of Mr. Ferry, President of the Senate. In the then temper of the House this was like touching a lighted match to a train of powder.

The scene that ensued was indescribable. The floor was crowded by senators and other privileged persons. It seemed impossible for the Speaker to make himself heard. The filibusters had up to this point been losing ground steadily during the preceding twenty-four hours, but now the tide turned in their favor, and it seemed impossible that any human power short of actual violence could check it.

Just then a Senate page appeared on the floor of the House and offered the package to Mr. Hewitt who refused to accept it. The page would not tell where he had received it, or who had sent him on his errand. The debate on the resolution above referred to proceeded and despite the efforts of the republicans to save themselves from the mistake made by the Secretary of the Senate in carrying off the package, the filibusters nearly carried the day. The resolution was lost by thirty-two votes. How this majority of thirty-two was obtained is not only interesting but bears directly upon the telegram above quoted from Sherman and others to Anderson.

The representatives of the Nichols government in Louisiana had, as far back as February the 16th, the date of the decision of the Electoral Commission in the Louisiana case, been endeavoring to secure some pledges from the friends of Hayes that if he was counted in the republicans of Louisiana and South Carolina would be abandoned. Stanley Mathews, ex-Governor Dennison, Charles Foster, and Lieutenant-Governor Young of Ohio were quite willing to give any pledges or promises to that effect, and Stanley Mathews a few days later wrote a letter to 'Packard foreshadowing the course of Hayes if he became President, a copy of which was shown to prominent Southern democrats.

But these assurances coming from the personal representatives of Hayes were not considered sufficient unless John Sherman and James A. Garfield joined in them. Inasmuch as they appeared reluctant to join in the arrangement, the Southern democrats, rallied by the representatives of Nichols and Hampton, entered heartily and solidly into the filibustering movement. Major E. A. Burke testified before the Potter committee in 1878 that notice was served on the friends of Hayes that unless the leading and prominent Republican leaders like Sherman and Garfield were brought to join in the pledges the electoral count would be defeated.*

.The action of the House on Saturday February 17, in taking a recess till Monday, the 19th, and in taking a further recess that day till Tuesday, the 20th, brought Sherman and Garfield to a condition of mind in which they were willing to discuss terms with Major Burke, and Representatives Ellis and Gibson of Louisiana, and Senator Gordon of Georgia who represented Wade Hampton of South Carolina.

On the 20th Senator Lamar of Mississippi was told that Mathews and Foster would both agree on behalf of Hayes that Packard should be abandoned if he was counted in. This Lamar communicated to Ellis in writing † and that same day Mathews and Dennison came to Burke, Ellis, and Gibson and proposed an interview with Sherman in the Senate finance committee room. Previous to this Mathews and Burke had agreed upon a memorandum of points which the Nichols government would guarantee if it was recognized by the Hayes administration provided it was allowed to come in.

Among other things was the following : ‡ " Desirous of healing the dissensions that have disturbed the State for years past, and anxious that the citizens of all political parties may be free from the feverish anxieties of political strife to join hands in honestly restoring the prosperity of

---

* H. R. Mis. Doc. No. 31, 45th Cong. 3d Sess. p. 971.

† Ibid. p. 973.

‡ Ibid, p. 1037.

Louisiana, the Nichols government will not engage in the persecution of individuals for past political conduct, but do not assume to grant immunity for crime." At the meeting with Sherman this memorandum was submitted to him and explained. He evidently did not like the last clause — " but do not assume to grant immunity for crime."

However, a conference was arranged to be held at Mr. Mathews' rooms at Wormley's Hotel * which took place on the night of the 26th of February. There were present Sherman, Garfield, Foster, Dennison, and Mathews on the part of the republicans, and Burke, Ellis, Levy, and Watterson on the part of Southern democrats. The latter guaranteed that the memorandum submitted to Mathews should guide the conduct of the Nichols government and the former pledged Hayes to recognize the Nichols government.

The agreement was reached on the night of the 26th,* but after that the filibustering in the House continued and the Southern democrats did not desert their Northern brethren till March the first when the test vote came on the resolution to compel the President of the Senate to receive and lay before the joint meeting of the two Houses the alleged return from Vermont.

What transpired between the night of the twenty-sixth of February and March 'first, we do not certainly know. But the impression very generally prevailed then, and has not been abandoned since by well-informed persons, that there was a formal ratification of the agreement reached at the Wormley Hotel Conference by Mr. Hayes in writing and that a more definite pledge was made on the part of the representatives of Nichols that the members of the Louisiana Returning Board should not be prosecuted.

* H. R. Mis. Doc. No. 31, 45th Cong. 3d Sess. p. 980.

Of course, if such an understanding was reached and put in writing all the parties to it would have the most powerful motives for concealing the fact. It would, if it could have been proved, have been sufficient to secure the impeachment of Hayes. It would on the other hand have damned politically the democrats who entered into it. No one of the parties thereto could have survived the disclosure of such a deliberate bargain and purchase and sale of the Presidency.

There was just about time — two days—for a messenger to have gone from Washington to Columbus and returned. At any rate during the roll call on the resolution aforesaid Burke, Ellis, and Levy were active on the floor of the House in securing votes against it. Burke came to Mr. Springer of Illinois who was active in the filibustering movement and urged him to desist, assuring him that they, the representatives of Nichols and Hampton, had " in black and white " assurances from Hayes that he would abandon Chamberlain and Packard.

Mr. Levy of Louisiana came to Mr. Hewitt and urged him to exert himself to stop the filibustering. Mr. Foster of Ohio was rushing about the floor of the House like a wild man importuning democrats to vote against the resolution. He urged Mr. Hewitt to see Speaker Randall and appeal to him to exert himself in the same direction. The combined efforts were sufficient to defeat the resolution, but the filibusters were still formidable, and it was not till 4 o'clock Friday morning, March 2, that the count was finally completed and Hayes and Wheeler declared to be President and Vice-President of the United States.

Returning to the telegram of February 4, 1878, to Anderson and comparing it with the memorandum agreed upon at the Wormley Hotel conference we will see that the senders of the former had the latter in their mind. The "hope" that they expressed therein, "that the sense of justice and love of peace of the people of Louisiana, will protect you, and not permit the best interest of the whole country to be disturbed by a revival of sectional animosities," was not only a reference to the agreement aforesaid but was intended to remind the Nichols government of its pledges.

The dispatch was sent just before the case against Anderson was submitted to the jury and was undoubtedly intended to have an effect on the jurors. There was a covert threat in it — to wit — that Anderson's conviction would cause "a revival of sectional animosities." But not content with sending this telegram they caused Hayes to instruct the Attorney-general to make application to Justice Bradley for the interference of the United States Court, Bradley being the justice assigned to that circuit. This was abandoned, however, for reasons which have never been made known.

The Supreme Court of the state, as will appear more fully hereafter, found a way to let Anderson out of jail. Wells, just as soon as he learned that criminal proceedings were to be commenced fled from New Orleans, and remained in hiding until the Supreme Court set Anderson at liberty.

As "recognition" of his services, Wells was allowed to hold the office of surveyor of the port of New Orleans from 1879 to 1882 and to receive in salary during that time $21,000, while his sons drew almost an equal amount from the Federal treasury.

Thomas C. Anderson, member of the Returning Board, was likewise a man of bad repute. He had engineered through the legislature, while he was a State Senator, during the reign of corruption under Warmoth, a bill to pay the claim of one Weil, for supplies, alleged to have been fur- • nished the State of Louisiana, in Confederate times. It was barred by the amendment of the Constitution of the United States as well as by the provisions of the constitution of Louisiana, but these provisions were of small moment to a carpet-bag and scallawag legislature when the job was sufficiently large to afford a liberal commission.

After the bill passed, and the claim was paid, Anderson was found to be the owner of it, and to have received the proceeds less the "divies" necessary to secure the votes to pass the bill. Anderson was made deputy-collector of the port of New Orleans in "recognition" of his services, August 27, 1877, and held the same until he was succeeded, July 2, 1885, by Hon. B. F. Jonas, who was appointed collector of the port of New Orleans, July 1, 1885. During the seven years, ten months, and six days Anderson held office for his services in 1876, in counting in the Hayes electors, he drew from the Federal treasury salary amounting to $22,500.

During the June term of the Superior Criminal Court for the parish of Orleans, State of Louisiana, in 1877, the grand jury, after a full and careful examination, directed the district attorney of the first judicial district to file an information against, J. Madison Wells, Thomas C. Anderson, Louis M. Kenner, and Gadane Cassannave for falsely and feloniously uttering and publishing as true a certain altered, false, forged, and counterfeited public record — to wit, the consolidated statement of votes, parish of Vernon, made by the supervisor of registration for said parish, whereby falsely and feloniously 178 votes were added to the number of votes actually cast for the Republican electors, and 395 votes were deducted from the number of votes actually cast for the Democratic electors by the voters of said parish.*

In pursuance of the order by the grand jury the district attorney, by direction of the court, filed the information. Thereupon J. Madison Wells fled from the city of New Orleans and hid in the swamps northeast of the city. And when the sheriff of New Orleans attempted to serve the writ of arrest on Thomas C. Anderson in the custom house on the 25th and 26th of January, 1878, he was first obstructed and then arrested by the United States marshal on a charge of attempting to injure property belonging to the United States.

A force of marines from a United States revenue cutter were stationed in the custom house, and all the doors leading to the rooms in which Anderson had taken refuge were barred, and United States deputy marshals were posted in front thereof. Upon the sheriff attempting to force his way into one of the ante-rooms a deputy marshal arrested him and carried him before Judge Billings of the United States District Court who declined to take cognizance of the case, whereupon the sheriff was taken before a United States commissioner who, upon an affidavit made by the chief clerk of the custom house, held him in recognizance for his appearance thereafter.

Two days later the United States District Attorney informed the sheriff that orders had been received from Washington to allow the warrant of arrest to be served on Anderson. The fraudulent administration upon reflection thought it would not be prudent to obstruct the course of justice in Louisiana. Public sentiment was not favorable to the exercise of such unconstitutional authority. Ander-

---

* "*Report of trial of Thos. C. Anderson,*" New Orleans, 1878, authority for all statements concerning that occurrence.

son, Kenner, and Cassannave were arrested in the office of the collector of customs on the 28th of January, 1878, and brought into court, and upon motion of the Attorney-general of the state a severance was had and the trial of Anderson proceeded. Kenner and Cassannave were held in bail in the sum of $5,000 each. Wells still remained in hiding.

The trial of Anderson lasted until February 7th when the jury brought in a verdict of guilty with a recommendation to mercy. A motion for a new trial was made and hearing had thereon, but it was overruled and Anderson was sentenced to two years at hard labor in the State penitentiary and to pay the costs of prosecution.

The trial was a perfectly fair one. The accused was defended by the first criminal lawyer of the state, Hon. H. C. Castellanos, a democrat, assisted by E. North Cullom and John Ray. The defense did not claim that there had not been an alteration, forgery, and falsification of the consolidated statement of votes for the parish of Vernon, but claimed that it was not a public record within the meaning of the law; that the only public and true record of the election held in Vernon parish on the 7th of November 1876 were the returns of the commissioners of the election at the divers polls in the said parish. It was also claimed that, while the consolidated statement of votes had been altered and forged and falsified, there was no proof of Anderson's connection therewith.

It was, however, clearly proved that Anderson was present at the session of the Returning Board, November 24, 1876, when the returns from Vernon parish were opened; that the consolidated statement showed that two of the Republican electors received no votes and the rest only two votes each, while the Democratic electors received 647 votes each; that there were no allegations before the board of fraud or intimidation affecting the vote of this parish. The original consolidated statement then before the board giving the vote, as above, was marked by one of the Democratic lawyers and it was produced by the proper custodian on the trial, identified by these marks, and it showed that the alterations had been made by adding 178 votes to the votes for Republican electors and by deducting 395 from the votes of the Democratic electors. The official vote as promulgated by the Returning Board on December 6, 1876, showed that these additions and subtractions had been made in the vote of Vernon parish. The burden of proof was, therefore, upon Anderson to show that he was not a party to this alteration, forgery, and falsification, of the record which had been made by the members of the Returning Board. This the defense utterly failed to do.

It was, moreover, proved, and not contradicted, that other records had been tampered with, altered, and falsified, by the Returning Board during the progress of the count, notably in the cases of the returns from De Soto and Ouachita parishes. The judge who presided at the trial was eminently fair and impartial in his rulings, and no exceptions were taken to his charge to the jury. There were two colored men on the jury.

The case being carried up to the Supreme Court it was held that the point made by the defense, viz.: that the consolidated statement made by the supervisor of registration was not the election return contemplated by the constitution and, therefore, the alteration of the same was not the forgery and falsification of a legal record.

This decision was applauded by the Republican press of the entire North. It was a consistent and just decision, and in harmony with the judgment of the United States

Senate which held in 1875 with Senator Edmunds that the election law of Louisiana was unconstitutional because it was not in accordance with section 48 of the constitution of the state. Article 48 makes the commissioners of elections *the* returning officers. Therefore the Returning Board was an unconstitutional body.

Anderson was made deputy collector of the port of New Orleans in "recognition" of his services, August 27, 1877, and held the same till July 1, 1885 — receiving during his seven years, ten months, and six days term $22,500!

Louis M. Kenner, mulatto member of the Returning Board, was made deputy naval officer of the port of New Orleans July 24, 1877, and held the place till January 9, 1882, when Kellogg secured it for one of his creatures who had rendered him more recent service in the Spofford-Kellogg contest. However, Kenner had been in the receipt of $2,500 per annum for four years and nearly six months — a total of $10,937!

Gadane Cassannave, the other mulatto member of the Returning Board, nearly three years after the great fraud had been consummated, thought he had cause of serious complaint against the administration he had helped to make. It happened in this way — the lawyers, who defended the members of the board in the criminal proceedings instituted by the state for the forgery of the Vernon parish return, obtained a judgment against them for their fees, and upon execution issuing, Cassannave was the only one found with property, neither Wells, nor Anderson, nor Kenner having anything in the parish of Orleans upon which the sheriff could levy.

Cassannave was an undertaker and his outfit was seized, and was about to be sold, whereupon he came to Washington and demanded relief. After some delay the money was

furnished through Shellabarger & Wilson, the private counsel of Hayes and Sherman.

At that time Cassannave stated that he had not desired
office for himself, and that his brother St. Felix Cassannave
who held a position in the custom house obtained the
same without his interference. On the other hand he asserted
that Wells, Anderson, and Kenner had a great many
of their relatives in the custom house. The following was
the list he gave *: C. B. Anderson, son of T. C. Anderson,
clerk, salary $1,400; Ben. Bloomfield, Anderson's son's
father-in-law, auditor, salary $2,500; Geo. L. Bloomfield,
brother-in-law of C. B. Anderson, clerk $1,200; Alex.
Wells, son of J. Madison Wells, deputy surveyor, salary
$2,500; S. S. Wells, another son, salary $1,800; R. B.
Rodenson, son-in-law, salary $1,600; Alex. Kenner,
brother of Louis M. Kenner, clerk, salary $1,600; Richard
Kenner, another brother, laborer, salary $600.

Cassannave came to Washington in no amiable mood and
served notice on Mr. Shellabarger, the legal representative of Hayes, that unless something was done forthwith he
"would expose the whole matter of the Returning Board
proceedings and go home and pocket the loss." He was
advised by that gentleman not to be too hasty, and to set
out his case in full in a letter to the President, which was
done for Cassannave by his attorney, J. Hale Sypher,
late carpet-bag statesman from Louisiana, now residing in
Washington, D. C.* On the 7th of August the letter
was delivered to Hayes and Sherman, and on the 15th the
money was telegraphed to New Orleans to stop the sale of
Casannave's effects by the sheriff.

The letter of Cassannave to Mr. Hayes, which brought
a prompt response in the shape of the required amount of

* N. Y. World. Aug. 19, 1879.

money, pointed out the propriety of making Wells, Anderson, and Kenner bear the costs of the prosecution. They had reaped the benefits of the work of the Returning Board — were in the enjoyment of lucrative offices bestowed upon them by the chief beneficiary of the Louisiana frauds. But the fraudulent administration did not dare to make Wells, Anderson, and Kenner meet their obligations. On the contrary it recognized the claim of Anderson that the fees of the lawyers who had defended the members of the Returning Board ought to be paid out of "funds to be sent from Washington." John Sherman it seems from Cassannave's letter was willing to recognize the justice of Anderson's claim to the extent of $100—which Cassannave thought, and very properly, was an exhibition of meanness unbecoming "the great Finance Minister of our government." Whether all the money required by Cassannave was made up by "assessments" on the members of the cabinet, or came out of Mr. Hayes' salary is not known.*

* "WASHINGTON, D. C. Aug. 7, 1879.

Mr. President:
     I have the honor to invite your attention to the following facts, upon which I respectfully solicit such relief as you may be able to offer me. In 1872 I was elected by the senate of Louisiana a member of the Returning Board of that state. I did not desire nor solicit the office, and I accepted it with great reluctance. In 1876 the grave and responsible duty of determining the result of the election for President of the United States devolved upon that board. Its deliberations were watched with profound solicitude by the whole country, while the leaders of the two great political parties hovered around it awaiting the result of its deliberations with that intense anxiety only known to expectants of the spoils of public office. The board found for the republicans, and the democrats, disappointed and chagrined, at once commenced criminal proceedings against its members. Counsel were employed to defend for a stipulated fee of $5,000, which Mr. T. C. Anderson assured me would be paid out of funds to be sent from Washington.
     At the conclusion of the prosecution counsel demanded their fee, which not being paid they instituted suit, and after a hearing in court, obtained judgment against all the members of the board. A writ fieri facias, copy herewith inclosed, issued, directing the sheriff to seize and sell sufficient property of defendants to satisfy the judgment of $5,000 less $1,875, The sheriff finding no property belonging to Anderson, Wells, and Kenner, seized my property and now holds the same subject to sale under his writ. If my property is sacrificed under that execution it will render me bank-

A. C. Wells, son of J. Madison Wells, was appointed
deputy surveyor of the port of New Orleans, Sept. 28,
1876, salary $2,500 a year. He held the office five years,
three months and six days, receiving during that time,
$13,125.

Samuel S. Wells, son of J. Madison Wells, held a place

---

rupt. I am a poor man and am unable to sustain such a loss. I have always assumed a full share of the responsibility attaching to the official acts
of the Returning Board, although I have never enjoyed any of the fruits
resulting from its findings, and in this connection I respectfully remind you
that I hold no office under your administration and have derived no pecuniary benefits whatsoever therefrom. But, on the contrary, I have sustained
considerable loss in my business on account of my identity with the board.
Messrs. Anderson, Wells, and Kenner, the other three members and their
numerous family connections are enjoying lucrative positions in the employ
of the government.

I protest against being mulcted for the cost of the criminal proceedings against the Returning Board while others enjoy the honor and emolu-
ments resulting from its decision. It is neither just nor honorable to impose this heavy burden upon me. It would be more becoming the beneficiaries of our acts to discharge this debt. Upon my arrival in Washington
two weeks ago, I was assured upon the promise of Assistant Secretary
Hawley that the amount required to satisfy the judgment would be raised
as soon as the Secretary returned. I called upon Mr. Sherman yesterday
and he proffered me $100 as the only relief he could offer me, which I was
compelled to decline out of respect for the great Finance Minister of our
government. I expect to take my departure for Louisiana in a few days,
and if any arrangement can be made of this matter to offer me relief, to
which, under these circumstances, I believe I am justly and honorably entitled, I will be under obligations to those through whose influence it may
be accomplished.

I am very respectfully,

G. CASSANNAVE.

Hon. John Sherman, Secretary of the Treasury:
DEAR SIR: I herewith inclose you a copy of an unofficial letter addressed to the President,

Very respectfully,

G. CASSANNAVE.

Washington, D. C., Aug. 7, 1879.

WASHINGTON, D. C., Aug. 13, 1879.
E. North Cullom, Exchange Alley, Custom House Street, New Orleans:
Should we send $1,000 more on Returning Board judgment will you
give reasonable time for balance.

SHELLABARGER & WILSON.

NEW ORLEANS, La., Aug. 13, 1879.
Messrs. Shellabarger & Wilson, Washington, D. C.:
If you will send me $250 more making a total of $1,750 and Cassannave
will give security not to dispose of his property I will wait till January 1.

E. NORTH CULLOM.

in the New Orleans custom house, from May, 1877 till 1882 at a salary of $1,400 a year, and received during that time $7,000.

Charles B. Anderson, son of Thos. C. Anderson, has held a place in the New Orleans custom house since 1877, recieving a salary of $1,400 a year, making a total of $11,200.

York A. Woodward, a clerk of the Returning Board who, with G. B. Davis, assisted James F. Littlefield, to execute the orders of J. Madison Wells in altering, forging, and falsifying the returns from Vernon parish, was appointed a clerk in the New Orleans custom house, Oct. 8, 1877, salary $1,400 a year. Feb. 11, 1878, he was promoted to be assistant deputy surveyor under J. Madison Wells, salary $1,600 a year. In 1882 he was transferred to the U. S. Mint, New Orleans, salary $1,250 a year.

Charles S. Abell, secretary of the Returning Board, has an interesting history. He is a native of Ohio and came to Louisiana in 1869 from North Carolina as an agent of the Freedman's Bureau. He resigned and was made an assistant assessor of internal revenue at Shreveport, La., and while in this office was elected to the legislature from Bossier parish in which he had not been, even as a visitor, ten consecutive days. After serving one term in the legislature he was appointed division superintendent of public education for the fourth district which included the Red River parishes.

The school law enacted by the carpet-bag legislature, placed the entire control of the school fund and the management of the educational system in the hands of the governor. He appointed a general superintendent and division superintendents, and they constituted the local school boards for every parish in the state. The people had no more voice in the school management than they had in the affairs of Turkey. The school fund was systematically plundered and there was scarcely a pretense in many parishes of keeping the schools open.

From the school board, Abell went into the Returning Board at a salary of $7 a day, and also held at the same time a position as flour inspector. When the Packard government broke up Abell was appointed a clerk in the New Orleans custom house at a salary of $1,200, and July 9, 1878, was promoted to $1,600 a year. On July 1, 1885, he was a $1,200 clerk in the custom house, having been there continuously from 1877. His total pay in that time was $8,266.59.

As secretary of the Returning Board Abell had charge of the reception of returns filed by the supervisors of registration, or as they came by mail. He was, in connection with other clerks, caught falsifying the records in the cases of returns from the parishes of De Soto and Ouachita. He knew of the forgery and falsification of the returns from Vernon parish. His previous history proves that he was an unscrupulous and unprincipled man who could be safely trusted by the members of the Returning Board to do any disreputable and unlawful work assigned him.

Judge G. B. Davis, a clerk of the Returning Board has also an interesting history. He, too, came to Louisiana as an officer of the Freedmens Bureau. A native of Massachusetts, he was from 1865 in the service of the Freedmens Bureau till it was wound up, and then became a deputy collector of internal revenue, and served in this capacity till 1876, when he was employed as a clerk by the Returning Board. During part of the time he was in the internal revenue service from 1870 to the summer of 1876, he was also parish judge of East Baton Rouge.

This was an important judicial office and yet Davis had never been admitted to the bar and knew nothing whatever of the civil law which prevails in Louisiana. During the time he was parish judge he lived in open, flagrant adultery with a colored woman whom he had arbitrarily divorced from her husband. Davis and Abell, fair specimens of the carpet-bag office-holders, were made judges and legislators by appointment or through the manipulation of the Returning Board.

After his service as a clerk of the Returning Board terminated, Davis was employed as a clerk in the office of F. A. Woolfley, the United States commissioner, who had been the chief administrator of oaths for the "outrage mill" in the custom house during Nov. 1876. Subsequently he was employed in the custom house.

He assisted York A. Woodward and Jas F. Littlefield to execute the orders of J. Madison Wells in falsifying and altering the Vernon parish returns. Having charge of the clerks compiling the returns he directed them to bring up the vote for any Republican electors running behind to that of those having the greatest number. In compiling, the consolidated statements of the supervisors of registration were used, and when, as was frequently the case, several of the Republican electors in different parishes did not receive as many votes as some of their colleagues did, Davis ordered the clerks to make the vote for electors even by erasing and putting in the highest figures. These alterations on the consolidated statements were fortified by making corresponding changes on the tally sheets and on the commissioners' returns.

W. H. Green, colored, was the minute clerk of the Returning Board. His duty was to keep a journal of the proceedings of the board during the open sessions when the

visitors were present — the object being to make a show
of regularity and deliberateness in the conduct of the canvass. But this was all sham.

The real work of the Returning Board was done in
secret sessions and there no minutes were kept. The compiling clerks under Davis made the votes of all Republican
electors equal and Abell looked after the details of the
throwing out of polls. Green, however, on account of his
former connection with the board was implicitly trusted,
and assisted in the clerical work of compiling. He was
appointed a clerk in the custom house, Sept. 20, 1877, and
two years later was made an inspector at $3 per day.

Charles Hill, a clerk in the state auditor's office was
detailed for clerical work to the Returning Board. He
was also the bearer, in place of Thomas C. Anderson, of
the forged certificates of electoral votes to the President of
the Senate, leaving New Orleans Dec. 29th, 1876, and arriving in Washington January 3d, 1877. Anderson had
carried the first and defective certificate to Washington and
on discovering its defects, after advising with "leading
friends" there, brought it back to have it "fixed." Not
being able to return with the forged certificate Hill acted
in his place.

Hill testified to the Potter committee that Kellogg
gave him a letter to Zach. Chandler and that Anderson
gave him one to Mr. Ferry, President of the Senate. The
record kept by the President of the Senate of the receipt of
electoral certificates credits Anderson with being the
bearer of the one received January 3d, 1877. The object
of this was to make his record tally with the well-known
fact that Anderson had been appointed by the electors,
Dec. 6, 1876, messenger to carry their certificate of electoral votes to the President of the Senate. Hill was ap-

pointed store-keeper in the New Orleans custom house, Dec. 15, 1877, at a salary of $1,460 a year, and held the place one year and nine months.

John Ray was the counsel of the Returning Board. The law made no provision for a legal adviser to the returning officers. The legal presumption, of course, was that where such extraordinary powers were bestowed upon a body of men the Senate would select them with a view thereto. But in addition to their notorious bad character and violent partisanship, the men chosen were utterly ignorant of the law and without the remotest conception of judicial functions. The selection by them of John Ray as their legal adviser was not for the purpose of having a man learned in the law to guide them in the exercise of their great powers for justice's sake, but to aid them in their contemplated defeat of justice.

John Ray was one of the natives who early joined the alien-spoilers of the state to profit by the plunder of the people. He was a lawyer of some ability but without character in his profession, or in the ordinary affairs of life. His connection with various gigantic schemes of plunder was open and notorious. His part in the attempted stealing of the Vicksburg, Shreveport, and Texas Railroad, and the participation therein of John Luedling, the chief justice of the state, illustrates the general demoralization of public and private morals which carpet-bag and scallawag rule had brought about.

That corporation had been subsidized by the state and had been plundered by the men to whom its management was confided. Not content with this they determined to cheat the bondholders and steal outright the whole concern. For this purpose, Ray and Luedling formed a combination with other scoundrels and, availing themselves of legal forms, carried through their nefarious enterprise. They thought they were secure and laughed at the remonstrances of those they had despoiled. The riot of official and private debauchery had continued so long unchecked that they imagined the day of judgment would never come.

But their victims in this case appealed to the United States courts and after many delays finally got the decision of the Supreme Court of the United States thereon. The opinion of the court was unanimous, and, to all who desire to read a record of villainy unparalleled in the judicial history of any country, reference is made to Jackson v. Luedling, 21st Wallace, United States Supreme Court reports. After giving the history of the transaction the court says:

"Were there nothing more in this case than is narrated by the brief history thus given, which is uncontradicted, it would be difficult to characterize the transaction as anything less than a great wrong perpetrated by the agency of legal forms. The great body of the bondholders could have known nothing of the proceedings to sell the mortgaged property and discharge their lien. Their residence was remote and the sale was hurried as fast as the forms of law permitted. Not a day was lost. They were not afforded an opportunity to bid at the sale, or to pay off Gordon's small claim of $720. Neither they nor their trustee were consulted. The sale was made in a village far in the interior. It was advertised in only one local newspaper, and not a day longer than the law required. The appraisement was made at the last moment, and it was obviously intended to facilitate a hasty sale for a nominal price.

"Onerous and illegal conditions of sale were exacted from other bidders, but not from these purchasers, who paid nothing except to themselves. A property upon

which had been expended nearly $2,000,000, together with
a large stock subscription, a large grant of lands, and considerable movable property was bought for $50,000 by the
very persons who defeated a sale for a much larger price
($500,000) and the purchase money was retained by them-
selves. *   *   It is impossible to sustain such a
transaction. Throughout it was grossly inequitable. That
the property was sacrificed by means of an unlawful and
widespread combination is abundantly proved, and that
the directors who were parties to it, and who became the
purchasers, were guilty of an inexcusable violation of confidence reposed in them admits of no doubt.* "

* U. S. Rep. 21 Wallace pp. 621-2, 631.

CHAPTER XIII.

William Pitt Kellogg's interest in the result of the Returning Board's
   work: His character delineated: He assisted in the alteration of
   the affidavit of Supervisor Kelley: His part in the forgery of an
   ante-dated set of electoral certificates: His knowledge of the forging of the names of Levissee and Joffroin, two absent electors, to
   the electoral certificates: Kellogg took into his confidence William
   M. Evarts, E. W. Stoughton, Zach. Chandler, and Senator Morton: The knowledge of the forgery must have been known to the
   other so-called Republican electors: Kellogg's negro messenger
   threatened to "peach" and was taken care of by Kellogg: Kellogg
   had to buy his seat of the Returning Board Legislature: He filled
   the New Orleans custom house with the rascals in order to get
   them to retract affidavits: How Kellogg was saved from indictment
   and conviction for bribery while a senator by George Bliss: How
   the Hayes electors were rewarded: Packard got "consideration
   and position."

WILLIAM PITT KELLOGG, Governor of Louisiana, by virtue
of the illegal order of United States District Judge Durell,
and the unlawful enforcement thereof by Federal troops,
acting under orders from President Grant, was the head
and front of the local conspiracy to deprive the people of
that state of their choice of Presidential electors and immediate rulers.

Kellogg's direct personal interest to be subserved was to
secure a legislature that would elect him to the United
States Senate. The entire machinery of election was subject to his control. He made the supervisors and assistant
supervisors of registration for every parish and ward. He

dictated the appointment, by the supervisors and assistant supervisors, of all the commissioners of election. The state registrar of voters and his clerks were named by him.

Few shrewder and more adroit men have ever wielded such vast political power. He was utterly unscrupulous, thoroughly corrupt, and full of wiles. He was plausible, affable, and resourceful. Personally mean and grasping, he was liberal with the people's money and content with a fair share of the common plunder. In dealing with a man like Wells who was passionate, revengeful, and violently partisan, but greedy for money and power, Kellogg was without an equal. He knew the right chord to touch and the right suggestion to make. He could flatter, fawn upon, appeal to, and cajole a subordinate who owed everything to him. He rarely resorted to dictation. He preferred to wheedle, to promise, and to tempt. He had one failing which would have brought to grief in a short time, a less plausible fellow. He was a notorious liar, and always cheated when he had the opportunity. Those who knew him best would not trust him without guarantees of some kind. Wells and Anderson knew him through and through and admired his skill and cunning, but while they would be captivated by his address, his cleverness in suggestions, they never failed to demand sponsors or an equivalent in hand.

There were few if any disinterested followers in Louisiana politics. Even the negroes, who by nature were grateful, soon ceased to display gratitude after they had trained a little while under scallawag and carpet-bag politicians. With rare exceptions they were cheap in price. Pinchback, in whom white blood predominated, a natural-born gambler, was high-priced. Dunn, a full-blooded African, alone had worthy ambition, but he was not incorruptible.

A few of the supervisors of registration, like Grady of Ouachita, Grant of Morehouse, Anderson of East Feliciana, and Scott of Claiborne, could not be controlled by Kellogg's assurances and promises unguaranteed.   Hence, it is doubtless true that these men had to be impressed and awed by interviews with visiting statesmen.   There is no positive evidence of this except the unsupported statements of James E. Anderson, and the hearsay declarations of D. J. M. A. Jewett.

Kelley, supervisor of Richland parish, could not be induced by Judge Campbell, Jewett, or Blanchard, Kellogg's executive clerk, to swear to a false statement about the registration and election in his parish.   Kellogg labored long and faithfully with him, but exerted all his arts in vain. They were compelled to accept the inadequate statements he was willing to make and bring them up to the required standard by forgery — interlining, after the innocent things had been sworn to, the falsehoods he would not swear to.*

Forgery and falsification of records were slight obstacles to the Louisiana politicians of the Kellogg kidney.   When Wells wanted to return as elected candidates for local offices in Vernon parish and had neglected to have so-called evidence of intimidation provided, he promptly altered, falsified, the returns by changing the Democratic votes to the Republican candidates.   When Tom Anderson brought the certificates of electoral votes to Washington and was told by the President of the Senate† that the sealed envelope in which they were contained did not have endorsed thereon what the law required, he went to his hotel, broke the seal, which he had no right whatever to do,

* H. R. Mis. Doc. No. 31, Part 2, 45th Cong. 3d Sess. pp. 171 to 1778.
† H. R. Mis. Doc. No. 31, 45th Cong. 3d Sess. p. 539.

and finding, upon consultation with "leading friends,"* that the certificates were not made out in accordance with the Constitution of the United States, he took the first train for New Orleans.

Immediately upon his arrival Anderson hastened to Kellogg and explained the dilemma they were in. What was it? The Constitution requires that the electors shall make "*distinct,*" that is separate "*lists,*" or certificates of votes cast for President and for Vice-President. They had embodied the votes for President and for Vice-President in one "list" or certificate. The laws of the United States requires that there shall be three of those "lists" or certificates made out and signed by each of the electors, and that each of these certificates shall have appended the certificate of the governor of the state, signed by him, countersigned by the secretary of state, and attested by the great seal of the state, certifying that the electors had been "duly chosen."

The law also prescribes that the electors "duly chosen" shall meet on the first Wednesday in December and proceed to vote by "distinct" ballots for candidates for President and for candidates for Vice-President, and thereupon make, then and there, the "distinct" — separate — "lists" or certificates of all the persons voted for for President, and of all the persons voted for for Vice-President. This done the electors are *functus officio.* They are dead in law, just as effectually and conclusively as if they were dead physically. If they have failed to comply with the provisions of the law, or of the Constitution, and the same is not discovered that day and corrected before they have finished, there is no legal way of correcting the error, mistake, informality, or non-compliance with the Constitution or the laws.

* H. R. Mis. Doc. No. 31, 45th Cong. 3d Sess. p. 258.

Anderson knew this. He was undoubtedly advised thereof by "leading friends" in Washington. Kellogg knew it. But they were not going to lose the Presidency after all they had done, all the chances they had taken, when they could quietly manufacture certificates in due form. It was true they had less than two days in which to do this, because, they must be in Washington on or before January 3, 1877. To reach there the messenger must leave New Orleans at 5:20 P. M. December 29th.

Two of the late electors, A. B. Levissee, and Oscar Joffroin, were not in New Orleans, and could not be got there before 5:20 P. M. December 29th. But that was not an insuperable obstacle. Kellogg had clever penmen at his command — the genuine signatures of Levissee and Joffroin could be imitated. This would be forgery, but the making out of new certificates of the electoral vote would be forgery! If they had to steal a sheep why hesitate at stealing a lamb?

They might be discovered? They could trust one another, and "leading friends" in Washington. The President of the Senate, Mr. Ferry, would know that something had been done, but he was too discreet to ask questions. Who would suspect such a crime? The very magnitude of it — its seeming impossibility would prevent even suspicion.

The business of preparing new certificates for the signatures of the electors, and of the governor's certificate of their election, all in triplicate, was intrusted to H. Conquest Clark, Kellogg's private secretary. He performed the work with dispatch, secrecy, and exactness — even to *facsimile* reproductions * printed from the same type and including counter signature of secretary of state and impres-

* H. R. Mis. Doc. No. 31, 45th Cong. 3d Sess. p. 258.

sions of great seal. He arranged an " upper room " in the State House, and the late electors who were accessible were notified to be on hand and sign their names the requisite number of times.

They came Dec. 29th, one by one, slipping in quietly, and secretly going to the upper room.* They signed in order as they originally appended their signatures, Dec. 6th. There was the necessary interval of coming, between the one who had signed before Levissee, and Joffroin, and the one signing after, so that those signatures could be forged. The crime was systematically, deliberately, orderly, committed. Levissee's and Joffroin's signatures were each forged six times.

The work was done and the messenger took his departure for Washington on the 5:20 P. M. train, Dec. 29, 1876, and reached there in due season and turned over to the President of the Senate, Mr. Ferry, the package containing the forged electoral votes. † One of the forged certificates of electoral votes was also sent by mail to the President of the Senate, and an attempt was made to substitute one of the forged sets for that one deposited Dec. 6 with the judge of the United States District Court, New Orleans.

" The friends in Washington " who knew of this crime observed discreet silence. The fact that a set of certificates of electoral votes had been prepared and dated back twenty-three days was known to the President of the Senate, Mr. Ferry, to John Sherman, to Hale and Frye of Maine, on January 3, 1877, and also to Zachariah Chandler. Kellogg gave Morton to understand that it would

---

* H. R. Mis. Doc. No. 31, 45th Cong. 3d Sess. p. 263-264.

† Ibid, part 2, pp. 50, 53, 54.

not do to depend upon the set of certificates of electoral votes last received by the President of the Senate.*

Anderson admitted that, before he opened the envelope, on Christmas day in Washington, containing the certificate made Dec. 6, he had talked with some friends.** † Clark testified that Anderson told him "leading friends in Washington" thought the lists ought to be on two sheets instead of one. Of course, "leading friends" knew that a new set was to be manufactured and dated back. Again, it is perfectly certain that several persons knew there was "something" wrong, about the certificates which were in form correct.

The original intention of the conspirators was undoubtedly to suppress the one of Dec. 6th, which came to the President of the Senate by mail. But this had to be abandoned because the United States district judge‡ at New Orleans would not allow the package purporting to contain electoral votes first deposited with him to be withdrawn and another substituted in its place.

When the two Houses of Congress met in joint convention Feb. 12, 1877, and the State of Louisiana was reached

* H. R. Mis. Doc. No. 31, Part 2. 45th Cong. 3d Sess., p. 711.

Q. "You say that when you came to Wahington, after the election of 1876, you had a conversation with certain friends in regard to the election certificates. With whom was the conversation to which you have referred to held?" A. "After I came to Washington and after the Electoral Commission had reached in its deliberations the State of Louisiana, I stated to two or three (I do not recollect the number) of our friends that the certificates, three or more in number, were not executed at the times they were apparently executed. I had not thought to interfere in any manner with the matter before, but when I arrived here the law had passed both Houses creating the Electoral Commission; and when the matter came before that Commission (or about that time) I thought it proper to state that fact, and I did so, to Mr. Evarts, to Mr. Stoughton, perhaps to Mr. Chandler, and certainly to Senator Morton."

** Ibid. p. 540.

† Ibid. p. 258.

‡ Ibid. p. 1106.

the President of the Senate * produced first the genuine Kellogg certificate of electoral votes, second, the McEnery certificates, third, two Kellogg — (forged) — certificates, and fourth, a burlesque certificate signed by John Smith, stating the vote of Louisiana belonged to Peter Cooper.

This last was ordered to be suppressed and no reference thereto to be made in the record of the proceedings. It was the first time in the history of the counting of electoral votes that a burlesque of this kind had been attempted, and coming as it did from New Orleans, it would seem that it was sent for a purpose. An incident of this kind would naturally tend to divert attention from the appearance of three, instead of two, Kellogg certificates of the Hayes electoral votes.

The democrats suspecting nothing wrong in the form of the certificates themselves appear not to have examined them at all. They had prepared beforehand their objections to counting the vote of Louisiana, as the act creating the Electoral Commission required, and all the electoral certificates, together with the objections, went to the Commission. There none of the originals were read but all ordered to be printed. The President of the Commission, N. Clifford, numbered the certificates as follows — The genuine Kellogg certificate, " No. 1, N. C;" the McEnery certificates, No. 2, N. C;" the two Kellogg — (forged) certificates, " No. 3, N. C."

Senator Morton, member of the Commission, who knew from Kellogg that No. 3, " would not do to depend on," moved that certificate No. 1 — the genuine — one which was not in form as required by the Constitution of the United States — should be counted. His motion, thus technically made, was put and carried 8 to 7.

* Electoral count, pp. 205 to 211.

Nobody — none of the Democratic lawyers, members of the Commission, managers on the part of the House, observed that one of the Kellogg certificates was fatally defective because it did not comply with the specific requirements of the Constitution.   Mr. Morton and his Republican colleagues knew of this defect, but they thought it better to count their man in on a constitutionally defective certificate than on a forged one.

And singularly enough it so happened, or was so designed,* that in printing the record of the proceedings of Congress and of the Electoral Commission the forged certificates did not appear at all.† Two copies of the one constitutionally defective certificate appear in the record.   So far as the published proceedings of Congress and of the Electoral Commission show we would not know that two other sets of certificates from the Kellogg electors were before Congress and the Commission.   It is scarcely possible that this could have been accidental.   Is not the conclusion irresistible that the omission was by design ?

That the forging of the names of A. B. Levissee and Oscar Joffroin was possible without the knowledge, the approval, the instigation of Kellogg, an honest and intelligent person cannot admit.   Neither can it be conceived possible that all the other Hayes electors who signed on Dec. 29 were without knowledge of the absence of Levissee and the whereabouts of Joffroin.‡   They would naturally be put on inquiry as to Levissee and Joffroin when they came to sign.

* H. R. Mis. Doc., No. 31, 45th Cong., 3d Sess., p. 116.

† Ibid, p. 420.

‡ Sheldon admitted that he knew they were not in the city on Dec. 28 and asked Kellogg who said he had sent for them : that Kellogg told him the 29th they had arrived — which Sheldon must have known was not true, because he knew that it was physically impossible to get them there in that time.

They knew why these second certificates had to be gotten up. *

If their inquiries were evaded the evasive answers would only tend to excite suspicions. It must be concluded, therefore, that Burch, Joseph, Sheldon, Marks, and Brewster, knew of the absence of two of their colleagues. Knowing their absence, of course, they knew that somebody would have to forge their signatures. But who was to do the forging, or who did do it, they may not have sought to know.

It is absolutely certain that it could not have been done without Kellogg's knowledge, and it is almost equally certain that it was not done without his approval or instigation. Would any one of his subordinates have voluntarily forged the signatures? Men do not commit a crime of this kind without an object. What object would one of Kellogg's clerks have to do this forging? To render his party a great service? Men do not render their party such criminal service without the hope or expectation of reward. In this case the reward could only come through Kellogg. Before one of his clerks, except Clark, could know that the forgery was necessary he would have to be informed thereof. This information could alone come through Kellogg or Clark. Is it probable that a clerk would volunteer the commisssion of the crime to the governor's private secretary? Scarcely. He would want Kellogg to know that he had rendered the all-important service.

The negro messenger, † Thomas S. Kelley testified that B. P. Blanchard, Kellogg's executive clerk, forged Joffroin's name, but this testimony was given under circumstances, and the story was so improbable, that the con-

* H. R. Mis. Doc., No. 31, Part 1, 45th Cong., 3d Sess., p. 1274.
† Ibid. pp. 1148-9.

viction is irresistible that Kellogg prompted it. Kelley
undoubtedly knew a great deal about the forgery. He wrote
to Hon. Clarkson N. Potter, June 9, 1878 * that he knew,
and, if protected, would tell all about the crime and point
out the men who did it. Kellogg learned of this letter, and
sent a colored man, named James D. Kennedy,** an employé of the sergeant-at-arms of the Senate, after Kelley.
Kelley arrived in Washington July 1, 1878. The fact of his
being there was concealed until the committee of which
Potter was chairman had left Washington for the summer.

Kellogg maintained Kelley in Washington until December 16, 1879 † when he had his name placed on the pay-
roll of the New Orleans custom house. This continued
until March 4, 1880, when Kellogg had Kelley appointed a clerk in the second auditor's office, where he
secured him two promotions. These things Kellogg did
for some purpose. He suffered Kelley to be more than a
year without government employment and manifested no
interest whatever in his welfare until he learned that Kelley
was about to "peach." Blanchard ‡ was dead at the time
Kelley testified that he forged Joffroin's name. The crime—
or one of the crimes—Kelley only swearing to the forging of
Joffroin's signature—being laid at a dead man's door, what
further object had Kellogg in taking care of Kelley? The
character of Kellogg is too well-known for any one to
credit him with gratitude!

To obtain his reward—the seat in the United States
Senate—cost Kellogg a deal of trouble. After the Returning Board had counted in a majority of Republican

* H. R. Mis. Doc. No. 31, Part 1, 45th Cong. 3d Sess. p. 1132.
** Ibid. pp. 1115-16.
† Records Appt. Divis. Treas. Dept. Washington, D. C.
‡ H. R. Mis. Doc. No. 31, 45th Cong. 3d Sess. p. 1440.

candidates for the legislature, and Packard, was installed as governor, the great body of the people of Louisiana declined to recognize the bogus concern. They quietly inaugurated Governor Nichols and the legislature elected by them, and the authority of this government was recognized throughout the state, while the other exerted no power whatever outside the State House.

There was absolutely no money in the treasury of the bogus government. Its script was worth nothing. To keep the legislature together Kellogg had to cash the members' certificates for pay.* He had also to buy outright the votes of the ungrateful ones, who seem to have been a large majority. He was given promptly, on the fourth of March, on the motion of James G. Blaine, Senator from Maine, the prima facie right to the seat in the Senate.

But Hayes' commission to New Orleans broke up Packard's and Kellogg's legislature and certified to the legal organization of the Nichols legislature. That legislature elected Henry M. Spofford, senator from Louisiana for the term beginning March 4, 1877. He contested Kellogg's right to the seat, and among other things which he proved invalidating the so-called election of the sitting senator, was the bribery of a number of the members of the bogus legislature electing him. This proof of bribery was in form of affidavits made by many of those who had been bribed. To get these witnesses to retract Kellogg had to have them appointed to places in the New Orleans custom house, and to prevent others 'from "peaching" he had to secure them positions in this common refuge for scoundrels, forgers, and perjurers.

The Republican majority in the Senate of the United States, to preserve the symmetry of its record — to avoid

* Senate Mis. Doc. No. 79, 46th Cong., 2d Sess., pp. 21 to 35.

stultifying its action in voting to ratify the decision of the Electoral Commission in the Louisiana case — refused to oust Kellogg and seat Spofford. And still Kellogg's troubles were not at an end.

Before his term in the Senate had expired—to be exact, four years after he was seated on motion of Senator Blaine—the evidence was discovered proving beyond the possibility of doubt that Colonel J. B. Price, a mail contractor in the Star Route service, had paid Senator Kellogg $20,000 in drafts on the future pay of two star routes, San Antonio to Corpus Christi, and Indianola to Corpus Christi, Texas, in consideration for Kellogg procuring from Thomas J. Brady, Second assistant Postmaster-general and one of "the visit- . ing statesmen" to Florida, an increase of pay for carrying the mail over said star routes.*

The records of the Post-office department showed that the order making the increase of pay was made the day after the drafts aforesaid were given to Kellogg by Price. The records of the sixth auditor's office showed that the drafts had been paid as they fell due. Price confessed that he had given the drafts to Kellogg for his influence with Brady, and the banker, with whom the drafts were deposited by Kellogg for collection, testified that he had collected the money on the drafts and had paid one-half to Kellogg and one-half to Brady.

The discovery of this evidence was made not only before Kellogg's term in the Senate had expired, but within the three years succeeding the payment to Kellogg by Price of the drafts.† Not only his expulsion from the

* Record U. S. vs. William Pitt Kellogg, charged with receiving a bribe while a U. S. Senator. Washington, Govt. Printing Office, 1884, pp. 67 to 74, 75 to 101, 102 to 113.

† H. R. Mis. Doc., No. 38, Part 2, 48th Cong., 1st Sess., pp. 75, 76, 77, 353, 354, 355, 431 to 468.

Senate, but his conviction for misdemeanor under the statutes of the United States, and punishment by fine and imprisonment, would have been an absolute certainty, if the government had proceeded forthwith to have him indicted therefor.

George Bliss* who was the special counsel for the government in the Star Route cases, in full and complete charge of the same, having the entire confidence of the President, Chester A. Arthur, and the Attorney-general, Benjamin Harris Brewster, deliberately suppressed the evidence against Kellogg. And, to make good his work of suppression, he intrigued, lied, and maligned, until he drove out of the Star Route cases the counsel for the United States, who had originally discovered and worked up all the evidence in those cases including that against Kellogg.

However, at a later period the late Hon. R. T. Merick,† of Washington, was employed to conduct in court some of the Star Route cases, and his attention being called to the fact that Bliss had deliberately suppressed the evidence against Kellogg, he insisted that the case against him should be investigated by the grand jury of the District of Columbia. But he foolishly consented that Bliss should represent the government before this grand jury.

The result was, of course, that no indictment was found. Bliss introduced the case to the grand jury, as was afterwards proved, before a congressional committee, by a member of the grand jury, and a witness present at the time, that "it was a grave and serious thing to indict a Senator of the United States."‡

* H. R. Mis. Doc. No. 38, Part 2, 48th Cong. 1st Sess. pp. 431 to 468.
† Ibid. pp. 431 to 468, also pp. 75, 76, 77.
‡ Elias S. Hutchinson, Foreman of the Grand Jury — as to Bliss dec-

Finally, after the lapse of nearly a year, and the expiration of his term in the Senate, all the ingenuity of Bliss, and the indirect, but potent, influence of the administration, failed to save Kellogg from indictment. * However, a stupid draughtsman of the indictment, a very poor specimen of the Philadelphia bar, imported to Washington by Attorney-general Brewster, was the means of saving Kellogg from the penetentiary.†

In drafting the indictment, instead of pleading that Kellogg had received upon such and such dates the proceeds of such and such drafts payable in future at such and such dates in lawful money of the United States, he set forth that he received lawful money on such and such dates and his proof showed that at a period anterior to the three years' limitation in criminal cases Kellogg had received certain drafts payable at certain specified dates in the future.   The court, thereupon, sustained Kellogg's plea of the statute of limitation as a bar to the prosecution, and he escaped merited punishment in the convict's garb, but his self-confession of infamy was coincident with his permanent retirement from public life.

J. Henri Burch was one of the Republican electors-at-

---

laration that it was a serious matter to indict a U. S. Senator—p. 429 of Mis. Doc. No. 38, part 2, 48th Cong., 1st Sess.

Q. " Did you in that Grand Jury Room hear Mr. Bliss say that it was a very serious matter to indict a Senator of the U. S. ?"   A. " Well, I don't think he said it was a *very* serious matter.   He certainly said it was a serious matter."

Q. " Did he say that before the Grand Jury ?"   A. " Yes."

Q. " Can you give all that he said in that connection?"   A. " I could not, but I remember that language.   I would not attempt to repeat the conversation going with it."

Q. " It was made before your deliberations as to whether you would, or would not find an indictment?"   A. " Yes, sir ; before our deliberations."

See Testimony of John H. Mitchell, pp. 416-417, same Doc.

* Ibid. pp. 353 to 355, 431 to 468.

† Record U. S. vs. Wm. Pitt Kellogg, Washington, Govt. Printing Office, 1884.

large. The character of the men whose names ornamented the Hayes electoral ticket in Louisiana, their standing in the community, is illustrated by the sort of a "recognition" this elector-at-large obtained for his services in the great fraud. — He was made a clerk in the New Orleans custom house with a salary of $1,400 a year. He held the same from March 24, 1879, till his death, April 17, 1883.

Peter Joseph, one of the Hayes electors in Louisiana, was also provided for in the custom house, at a still lower rank than Burch was rewarded with. Joseph was made first an inspector at $3 per diem, and a year later was made captain of the night watch at the same rate of pay. He continued to hold the place July 1st, 1885.

Morris Marks, an Israelite, associated with Burch and Joseph on the Hayes electoral ticket in Louisiana, fared better than they did. He, probably, owed his good fortune to the fact that with his native, characteristic shrewdness he not only knew more than they did, but knew what his knowledge was worth.

It would have been difficult to conceal from a fellow like Marks the facts concerning the forging of Levissee's and Joffroin's names to the certificates of electoral votes December 29, 1876. He came to Washington at an opportune time — just when McLin and Dennis of Florida were unbosoming themselves and the Potter committee was being created by the House of Representatives. He went back to New Orleans commissioned collector of internal revenue for the State of Louisiana. He held that lucrative office until the 13th of September, 1883 receiving in all as salary $19,557. But that was not all the "recognition" he received — he was made register of the United States land office and has continued to draw $500 a year and a commission of 1% on all moneys received.

A. B. Levissee, of Shreveport, La., was a Hayes elector, and originally a decent man. He, as well as Oscar Joffroin, were not in New Orleans on Dec. 28, and 29, 1876, when the bogus electoral certificates were made out and signed in an "upper room" of the State House.

Levissee was in Shreveport and it would have been a physical impossibility for him to have reached New Orleans at that season of the year even if he had been requested to come. As elsewhere related, his name was forged six times by some one of eight or nine men who were aware of his and Joffroin's absence.

Levissee was not immediately provided for by the fraudulent administration, probably, on the theory that he ought not to have put his friends to the trouble of forging his name. However, Levissee came to Washington in the summer of 1878 and soon made it so very interesting that an agent of the department of justice hunted him up one day and wanted to know what would stop his mouth. Levissee replied "an office with good pay and not much work." He got it. He was made a special agent of the Treasury, salary $7 per day and head-quarters at San Francisco, California. He held this till July 15, 1881.

Lionel A. Sheldon, formerly of Ohio and who carpet-bagged thence to Louisiana, was one of the Hayes electors. He rendered service during the count by the Returning Board as a confidential intermediary between the visiting statesmen and his "carpet-bag and scallawag" associates. He received no regular "recognition" till his friend Garfield became President, when he was made Governor of the Territory of New Mexico. He held the office four years and five months and drew from the Federal Treasury, $11,487.-50.

O. H. Brewster was one of the Hayes electors in

Louisiana. He lived in Monroe, La. He learned there that a depraved, disreputable negro woman, named Eliza Pinkston, had made an affidavit before John A. Dinkgrave in which she charged certain persons with having murdered her husband and her child and alleged that they shot, cut, and beat herself. Brewster hunted up Pinkston and took her to New Orleans, where she was exhibited and examined before the Returning Board in the presence of "the visiting statesmen."

But between the time Pinkston made her affidavit before Dinkgrave in Monroe, and her appearance before the Returning Board in New Orleans her story was entirely changed. It was greatly enlarged and amplified with harrowing and horrifying details, and the various crimes of murder, outrage, and attempts at murder, were charged upon an entirely different set of people. Those last accused of the crimes were the leading young men and active democrats of Ouachita parish. The original affidavit was filed with the Returning Board on Nov. 23d, but when Pinkston came in person with a new and more startling story, the original affidavit was destroyed and another of the date of Dec. 2d substituted therefor.

It would have been embarrassing even to Louisiana politicians to have had found on the files of the Returning Board two affidavits by the same person, each contradicting the other. It is unnecessary, perhaps, to say that the Pinkston incident has been proved by overwhelming and unimpeachable evidence to have been not only false, but to have been gotten up deliberately for effect on the public mind.

Brewster was rewarded for his services by being immediately reappointed to the Federal office which he had to resign in order to apparently qualify as a Presidential Elector — the position of Surveyor-general of Louisiana.

S. B. Packard was the Republican candidate for Governor of Louisiana. He was a native of Maine and was made United States Marshal of Louisiana by President Grant. He had executed the orders of the President, through Attorney-general Williams, to enforce the " decrees and mandates of the United States courts," so opportunely given just before issuance of Judge Durell's infamous midnight order in Dec. 1872, whereby Kellogg was made governor without regard to the fact that he had been defeated by the people, and John McEnery, who was elected, had been granted the certificate of election by the legally constituted authority. As United States marshal, Packard had been the efficient ally of Kellogg and his creatures in oppressing and robbing the unfortunate people of Louisiana.

It required the disfranchisement of a less number * of the citizens of Louisiana by the Returning Board to count in Packard as governor than it did to make a majority for several of the Hayes electors. When Hayes reaped the fruit of the frauds, forgeries, and perjuries committed in Louisiana by assuming the Presidency, and Kellogg obtained his seat in the United States Senate on the certificate by Packard that he had been duly chosen by the legislature — the same legislature that was made by the Returning Board at the very time the Presidential electors were ground out, — it is not surprising that Packard should have felt confident that the fraudulent President and the Senate of the United States would be compelled to sustain his pretentions to be governor.

Packard declined to step down and out at the request of Stanley Mathews, who had, on behalf of Hayes, agreed that Packard should be abandoned in order to secure the

* H. R. Mis. Doc. No. 31, 45th Cong. 3d Sess. p. 1441, 1454, 1455.

assistance of certain Southern democrats in the House of Representatives to complete the count of the electoral votes, in spite of a minority of determined democrats who were exerting every parliamentary expedient to prevent the ratification of the wicked decision of the Electoral Commission.

It, therefore, was necessary, since Packard would not abandon his share of the fruits of the Louisiana conspiracy, to get rid of him in another way. This was accomplished by Hayes* sending a commission to New Orleans, of course, without any authority of law, to manage the fraudulent administration's abandonment of its twin relic of fraud — the so-called Packard government of Louisiana. This commission consisted of John M. Harlan, of Kentucky, Wayne MacVeagh, of Pennsylvania, and John C. Brown, of Tennessee.

On its arrival in New Orleans this commission found that the friends of the Nichols government could seduce a number of the negro members of the Packard legislature and that in this way the quorum of the former could be broken. The Packard legislature never had a legal quorum. Some of the members thereof were honestly elected but not enough to make a quorum. To supply the requisite number to make a quorum the Returning Board counted in candidates who had been defeated at the polls. The quorum of Packard's legislature having been broken by inducing legally elected members to desert to Nichols, the Federal troops were ordered to their barracks outside the city and Packard and his few remaining followers deserted the State House as rats leave a sinking ship.

Notwithstanding all his vaporings Packard gracefully

* H. R. Mis. Doc. No. 31, 45th Cong. 3d Sess. p. 832.

kissed the hand that smote him and accepted, what Mathews had termed, "consideration and position" in the shape of the Liverpool consulate which was worth quite $15,000 a year. He held the place seven years and pocketed not less than $105,000.

CHAPTER XIV.

The rewarding of the registration officers: Hahn and McArdle were taken care of: George L. Smith's services and pay therefor: Lewis, Badger, and McMillan get their "sops": The character of Jack Wharton: His evidence as to the corruptibility of J. Madison Wells: His mouth sealed by the U. S. marshalship: Hugh J. Campbell's services and reward: H. Conquest Clark, Kellogg's private secretary: His share in the forging of electoral certificates: Still a pensioner of the government: Thomas S. Kelley, Kellogg's negro messenger, still a clerk in the second auditor's office of the Treasury department: Hardy and Smith paid for their rascality: C. L. Ferguson, his services and reward.

MICHAEL HAHN was state registrar of voters, the chief executive officer under the registration act. But in reality this officer was little more than a figure-head. The governor had the appointment of all the subordinate registration officers. The state registrar's power was merely supervisory, and practically the duties of the office were discharged by his chief clerk, James P. McArdle, assisted by D. J. M. A. Jewett, who was an expert in the manipulation of election and registration statistics as well as of election returns.! The census of 1875 was taken under the direction of McArdle and Jewett, and the results manipulated by them to show the largest possible number of negro voters in the state.

Hahn had been the first provisional governor of the state under the Constitution of 1864 and was not an inherently bad man. He was weak, irresolute, and without moral courage. So far as he dared in the campaign of 1876 he yielded to the requests of the Democratic leaders for fair rulings, but the registration officers, being independent of him, obeyed Jewett who was secretary and manager of the Republican committee on canvassing and registration.

Sometime in May, 1878, Hahn came to Washington and demanded recognition. The Potter committee was soon after appointed in pursuance of a resolution passed by the House of Representatives and the fraudulent administration was terror-stricken thereby. Hahn, Levissee, and some others of the Louisiana crowd were immediately assured that they would receive their long deferred recognition. Hahn was appointed superintendent of the United States mint at New Orleans June 25, 1878. He was not confirmed by the Senate and December 18, 1878, yielded his place to his successor—having received only $1,750.

James P. McArdle was chief clerk and real head of the state registrar's office. In connection with D. J. M. A. Jewett he manipulated the census returns of 1875 and managed the registration of voters in 1876. He was invaluable after the election, when the supervisors of registration came to New Orleans, in stimulating and encouraging them to obey the behests of the party leaders who insisted that false affidavits should be made to order for the Returning Board. McArdle, Jewett, and Blanchard were the first to see the supervisors on their arrival in New Orleans, because they naturally came direct to the office of the state registrar to render their accounts and draw their pay.

McArdle was appointed October 6, 1877, a laborer in the custom house at a salary of $600 a year, and August 12, 1880, was appointed to a clerkship at $1,200 per annum. On the record in the appointment division of the Treasury department at Washington, under McArdle's name, is the following memorandum in lead pencil — "not to be removed — D. J. M. A. Jewett interested; letter on file April 10, 1880." Diligent search of the correspondence files of the Treasury department failed to reveal Mr. Jewett's letter. It had been removed, doubtless by some one interested in its suppression.

George L. Smith was a carpet-bagger who established himself in Shreveport, Louisiana, as the editor and proprietor of a newspaper which he started in order to be made state printer for that locality. The printing law authorized the governor to appoint a state printer for each parish in the state and all the general laws enacted by the legislature, as well as all local transactions by the parish authorities, and the proceedings of all corporations and municipal bodies, had to be published at rates fixed by the printing board in these local journals.

Smith made money at the expense of the general public and was elected to the Forty-third Congress from the fourth congressional district of Louisiana. He was a candidate for reëlection in 1876. Kellogg gave him commissions signed in blank for such supervisors of registration as he might select for the different parishes in his district.

After the election Smith gathered his supervisors at Shreveport and accompanied them to New Orleans. One of the supervisors, C. L. Ferguson, of De Soto parish, had forwarded his returns, as the election law directed, by mail to the Returning Board. The others carried their returns with them to New Orleans. Arriving there Smith had them deposit the same with the cashier of the Post-office, D. D. Smith, who locked them up in the Post-office vault.*

The returns from De Soto parish which had come for-

* H. R. Mis. Doc., No. 31, 45th Cong., 3d Sess., p. 1442.

ward by mail were stopped in the New Orleans Post-office. On the night of November 24th, 1876, according to the testimony of D. J. M. A. Jewett, Smith, Ferguson, of De Soto, T. H. Hutton, supervisor of Bossier, and John T. Morrow, supervisor of Webster, D. D. Smith, cashier of the Post-office, Saml. Gardner, citizen of Webster parish and Fred E. Heath, and himself, met in the postmaster's private office. D. D. Smith unlocked the vault and produced the returns from De Soto, Bossier, Caddo, and Webster parishes.

It was found on examination that the votes cast at certain polls in these parishes would have to be thrown out to create Republican majorities. George L. Smith then and there had the supervisors make affidavits, which were draughted by Jewett, against the returns from the selected polls. These affidavits were done up with the parish returns and sent forward to the Returning Board the next day. In the case of Bossier parish, T. H. Hutton, the supervisor, falsified the record by interpolating on his consolidated statement, which had been sworn to before the clerk of the district court of the parish, a statement impeaching the freedom, fairness, and peaceable character of the election at polls 1, 3, 5, 7, and 8. The interpolation was made above the jurat so as to appear to have been made at the parish town before the oath was taken.

For this and like services George L. Smith was, May 4, 1878, appointed collector of the port of New Orleans, and held the office till February 20, 1879, when he was succeeded by A. S. Badger. The amount of Smith's " recognition " in cash was $5,541.73.

James Lewis was one of Kellogg's police commissioners. The metropolitan police of New Orleans was, by an act of the legislature, passed during Kellogg's term, as governor, made a part of the state militia. It was the only body of efficiently organized and drilled men in the state which could be relied on by the carpet-bag authorities. It was composed mostly of foreigners, discharged soldiers of the Union army. They were paid by taxes imposed upon the citizens of New Orleans, and so long as their pay was liberal, and promptly received, they would, like any other mercenaries, obey orders. They served as guards about the State House during the count by the Returning Board, but their most valuable service was rendered during the registration of voters in New Orleans, and on election day, by assisting the supervisors of registration in preventing white voters from registering and aiding in the false registration and voting of negroes.

Lewis was appointed naval officer of the port of New Orleans, January 9, 1877, and held the office till Dec. 27, 1880. On January 4, 1882, he was appointed superintendent of custom-house warehouses which he held till May 4, 1883. He received "recognition" to the amount of $9,999.93.

A. S. Badger was an officer in the Confederate army and achieved some distinction in the service of the rebel government. He was appointed by Kellogg commander-in-chief of the Louisiana militia and organized and rendered efficient the metropolitan police already described. He was a brave man and one of the most respectable of the Louisianians who joined, for selfish considerations, the carpet-bag oppressors and plunderers. He was in command of the state militia at the time of the count by the Returning Board. He was made Postmaster of New Orleans, by Hayes, July 19, 1878, and was appointed collector of customs, Feb. 20, 1879, and continued in that office till July 1, 1885. His total salary was $43,800.

18

W. L. McMillan was a native of Ohio. He migrated to Louisiana and joined his political fortunes to those of Henry C. Warmoth, the first carpet-bag governor of the state. He was a liberal republican in 1872 and was elected to the United States Senate in 1873 by the McEnery legislature, but the Senate did not recognize his election, nor that of Pinchback, by the Kellogg legislature, as legal. In 1875 McMillan joined the Kellogg party because Hayes was an Ohio man. He was active and unscrupulous and assisted, to the extent of his ability, during the fraudulent count by the Returning Board, and was appointed by Hayes pension agent at New Orleans with a salary of $3,400 per annum.

Jack Wharton, a native of Maryland who settled in Louisiana before the civil war, and served with Gen. Pillow in the Confederate army, was another of Warmoth's adherents who joined Kellogg's party in 1874. He was made Adjutant-general of the state militia by Kellogg.

In 1868 and '69 Wharton lived in Northern Louisiana and was accused of participation in a massacre of negroes in Bossier parish in 1868.* He was a prime favorite of the debauchees who formed the official social life of New Orleans during the flush times of carpet-bag rule. He was of the Joe Miller order of story-tellers and his vulgar jests and broad stories gave him the reputation of a wit among the depraved men and women who constituted the court circle of New Orleans in that era of official and private immorality.

To provide a place for Wharton, J. R. G. Pitkin, an unscrupulous partisan, but a gentleman in breeding, was removed from the United States marshal's office. Wharton came to Washington soon after the inauguration of Hayes

* H. R. Mis. Doc. No. 31, 45th Cong. 3d Sess. p. 1436.

and remained during the summer and fall of that year. He was a constant visitor at the White House in company with George A. Sheridan, another Louisiana buffoon and vulgar story-teller. Mr. Hayes found Wharton's society congenial, either on account of his wit, or his narratives of the heroic service he had rendered as Adjutant-general of the Louisiana militia during the critical period of the Returning Board's count.

Doubtless Wharton also narrated the part he played, with a government agent, in having the demands of J. Madison Wells for money satisfied. When Wharton was examined by the Potter committee he reluctantly related how he went with this agent to Packard and told him that unless Wells * was satisfied he was afraid he would not go straight. He admitted that it was the general understanding that Wells compelled the state authorities to cash at par a lot of state warrants, which he held, when they were worth, in the market, only 25 or 30% of their face value.* He also admitted that he had written a letter in which he said — " I have seen Packard and talked to him fully. He thinks that old Wells is trying to get all he can, be it little or much ; that Wells would sell out to either side." * He testified that that statement, as made in his letter, was true ; that he correctly reported Packard's language.

Wharton, after a great deal of evasion and prevarication, admitted that it was proposed to give Wells a local office, which would be in Packard's * gift, if he became governor, worth from $30,000 to $40,000 a year. He " saw Packard every day " and " in the general talk Packard expressed a good deal of mistrust as to Wells. Packard fluctuated. Sometimes he believed more and sometimes less." * From all which it is quite evident that

* H. R. Mis. Doc. No. 31, 45ht Cong. 3d Sess. p. 1426-1431.

Wharton could have told a great deal more than he did to the committee. He had been made marshal and his mouth was sealed. It was only by the most rigid cross-examination, conducted by Gen. Butler, that a small part of the truth was extracted from this reluctant witness.

Wharton was appointed marshal Dec. 3, 1877 and held the office till his death in 1881, recieving in fees about $30,000.

Hugh J. Campbell was a native of Iowa, from Scotch Presbyterian stock settled in Pennsylvania. He went to Louisiana after the war and became one of the most unscrupulous and vindictive of the carpet-bag politicians. He was elected to the state senate in 1868, and was the author of the original election law of 1870, which was changed in none of its essential features, save as to the composition of the Returning Board, by the act of 1872. His advocacy in the state senate of the legislation in favor of the New Orleans, Jackson, and Great Northern Railway Company, was purchased by the agent of Henry S. McComb.* He was appointed a judge of one of the civil courts of New Orleans by Kellogg. His services after the election of 1876, as one of the counsel employed in the custom house to manufacture so-called evidence for the Returning Board, were highly appreciated by John Sherman and other "visiting statesmen." He addressed an elaborately prepared letter to Sherman which accompanied the report made to the President by the "visiting statesmen." It narrates the history of the Louisiana election law and boldly justifies its monstrous provisions and defends the conduct of the Returning Board.

Campbell, according to the testimony of Kelley, supervisor of Richland parish, as well as by the evidence of

* H. R. Mis. Doc. No. 211, 42d Cong. 2d Sess. pp. 475 to 482.

Jewett, was largely concerned in the crime by which a harmless statement made by that officer was converted into an intimidation affidavit.* Among the chief concocters of outrage and intimidation stories Campbell was *primus inter pares.* He was able, unprincipled, and terribly vindictive. He was canny where self-interest was concerned. In the spring of 1877 he came to Washington as the representative of Packard, and, seeing that the abandonment of his client, by the fraudulent administration, was inevitable, he did not forget himself. He secured the office of United States District-attorney for Dakota Territory, in May 1877, which he held for two full terms. The fees of the office are large and amounted to not less than $48,000 during his two terms.

H. Conquest Clark went to New Orleans originally as the correspondent of the New York *Herald* and became the stenographer and private secretary of Kellogg. By Kellogg's direction, on the return of Tom. Anderson from Washington on the 28th of December, 1876, bringing back the void electoral certificate of December 6th, 1876, Clark undertook the preparation of a certificate of electoral votes for President, and a certificate of electoral votes for Vice-President.

Although the time for this work was short Clark had these two certificates, in triplicate, printed from the same type and on the same kind of paper † the originals were. He got up the governor's certificate, which the law requires shall be attached to the certificate of electoral votes, certifying that the electors had been duly chosen, and made them appear as if made and executed on December 6th, instead of December 29, although they had to have, in

---

* H. R. Mis. Doc. No. 31, Part 2, 45th Cong. 3d Sess. pp. 1462-'64-'65.
† Ibid, p. 258.

addition to the governor's signature, the counter-signature of the secretary of state and the impression of the state's great seal.

Having gotten the electoral certificates ready for the signatures of the late electors then in New Orieans Clark arranged an "upper room"* in the State House, to which the individuals could go, one by one, to affix their names. Two of the late electors, A. B. Levissee and Oscar Joffroin, were not in the city † and provision had to be made for the forging of their signatures to the certificates. Clark arranged the order of the "stealing up" to the upper room by the men who were obtainable, so that their signatures would appear on the forged certificates in the same sequence as on the original of December 6th.

At the proper time, when the signatures of Levissee and Joffroin were to be forged, the stealing up stairs was interrupted for a season. The work of forging having been finished the fellows who were to sign last stole up to the upper room and wrote their names. The object of this was, in the event of discovery at any time in the future, the last signers could swear that when they signed the names of Levissee and Joffroin were written above theirs.

Clark remained with Packard until his bogus government tottered over and disappeared, and then came to Washington where he was provided with a clerkship in the internal revenue bureau through Kellogg at a salary of $1,800 a year. He held this place till November 14, 1882, when he was made secretary of the Alabama claims commission. He still holds this position.

B. P. Blanchard was executive clerk to Kellogg while he was governor. He was originally state registrar of

* H. R. Mis. Doc. No. 31, Part 2, 45th Cong. 3d Sess. p. 260.
† Ibid. pp. 92, 1135.

voters before Hahn was appointed. As an expert statisti-
cian he was reputed to have few equals. He trained
McArdle, who was Hahn's chief clerk in 1875 and 1876.
During the campaign of 1876 he was the chief adviser of
McArdle and Jewett in the manipulation of the registration
of voters.

After the election Blanchard devoted his entire time to
the management of supervisors as they came to New
Orleans with their returns. Jewett testified * that when
they had failed to induce Kelley of Richland parish to
make an affidavit, Blanchard and himself took him to Kellogg's house for an interview with the governor. The
policeman, who was on night duty all through this period
at Kellogg's house, testified that Blanchard and Jewett
were almost nightly at Kellogg's in consultation with him
and frequently Blanchard was there till a late hour working
on papers which looked like election returns.

Thomas S. Kelley the mulatto messenger to the executive office, while Kellogg was governor, swore † before the
Potter committee that, to his personal knowledge, Blanchard forged Joffroin's name to the certificates of electoral
votes made December 28th in the upper room of the State
House December 29, 1876. Jewett ‡ swore before the
same committee that this was impossible because Blanchard
and himself were devoted friends and kept no secrets from
each other; that Blanchard being dead Kelley laid the
crime on him.

It does not matter who did the deed, inasmuch as it
could not have been done without the fore-knowledge, instigation, and approval of Kellogg. It is a matter of small

* H. R. Mis. Doc. No. 31, Part 2, 45th Cong. 3d Sess. p. 1447.
† Ibid, p 1147.
‡ Ibid, p. 1440.

concern whether Blanchard or Kelley or Clark did the forging — they were all Kellogg's creatures and tools.

Blanchard was appointed a clerk in the New Orleans custom house October 29, 1877, at a salary of $1,400. He died of yellow fever October 11, 1878.

W. R. Hardy was one of the lawyers who directed the manufacture of affidavits in the custom house for use before the Returning Board. He was appointed an inspector of customs in the New Orleans custom house August 28, 1877, at a salary of $3 per day and held the office for five years — realizing $5,835.

D. D. Smith was the cashier of the New Orleans Post-office, and was present[*] on the night of November 24, 1876, in the postmaster's private office, when George L. Smith, C. L. Ferguson, T. H. Hutton, John W. Morrow, Saml. Gardner, D. J. M. A. Jewett, and Fred. E. Heath made changes and alterations in election returns, got up affidavits, and did divers other villainy.

The returns were in D. D. Smith's custody locked up in the Post-office vault which he unlocked and produced therefrom the package of papers. He had no right whatever to have the custody of election returns — they should have been in the charge of the Returning Board. He was retained as cashier of the Post-office until George L. Smith was made collector of the port of New Orleans when he was appointed a clerk in the custom house and held the same till December 27, 1882 — salary $2,500 a year.

C. L. Ferguson was made supervisor of registration of De Soto parish by George L. Smith, who had blank commissions for that purpose from Governor Kellogg. He mailed his returns from Mansfield, La., but instead of the Returning Board receiving them, they found their way into

* H. R. Mis. Doc., No. 31, Part 2, 45th Cong., 3d Sess. p. 1442.

the custody of D. D. Smith, cashier of the New Orleans Post-office, who kept them in the vault thereof until the night of Nov. 24, 1876, when they were produced for inspection by George L. Smith, and D. J. M. A. Jewett, Ferguson being present. *

At the same time and place T. H. Hutton and John W. Morrow, supervisors of Bossier and Webster parishes, were present to "doctor" the returns from those parishes. Jewett says that on inspection it was found that a Republican majority could not be created without getting rid of the votes cast at polls 1, 3, 5, 7, 8, De Soto parish; that he draughted an affidavit for Ferguson embodying the necessary facts — such as Ferguson and Smith furnished: that Ferguson swore to the affidavit he had drawn, and this was rolled up with the returns, the envelope restored to its original appearance, and the package went to the Returning Board the next day by letter carrier.*

Jewett swore he was positive that the envelope bore "registration marks" showing that it had come by registered mail from Mansfield, and that it was addressed to the Returning Board. The proceedings of the Returning Board for Nov. 25, as published in the Sherman report show that on that day the returns from De Soto parish were opened and that Messrs. Burke and McGloin, Democratic counsel, detected the affidavit bearing date Nov. 24, along with the supervisors return, which purported to have been mailed at Mansfield on Nov. 14th.† Thereupon, there was confusion, and Chas. S. Abell, secretary of the board, prompted by E. W. Stoughton, "visiting statesman," began lying in the most vigorous manner. The fact, however, is disclosed by the record that the affidavit made in

* H. R. Mis. Doc. No. 31, Part 2, 45th Cong. 3d Sess. p. 1442-3.
† Senate Ex. Doc. No. 2, 44th Cong. 2d Sess. pp. 88-9.

the post-office on the previous night, as detailed by Jewett, was in the package containing the De Soto returns.

These facts prove that the " registered package " coming forward from Mansfield to the Returning Board was either stopped in the New Orleans post-office, or if received and receipted for by the secretary of the Returning Board, was delivered to George L. Smith, the supervisor, or to D. D. Smith, who put it in the vault of the post-office and retained it until it was "fixed " on the night of Nov. 24th.

Ferguson was appointed by George L. Smith to a place in the New Orleans custom house at a salary of $800 a· year which he held as long as Smith remained collector.

CHAPTER XV.

The services and reward of "a roper-in" for a snake show : The difficulty Kellogg had in getting an affidavit from M. J. Grady : Grady's
services and reward: James E. Scott, supervisor of Claiborne, had
to be "induced" to make an affidavit: James E. Anderson and the
trouble he gave carpet-baggers and visiting statesmen : How he
was feared by Sherman, Evarts, Stanley Mathews, and Hayes: A
long list of minor rogues —Moore, Kempton, Maloney, Leon,
Rowan, Underwood, Creagh, Brim Loan, Howard, and Swazey,
their services and the rewards they received : Thomas S. Kelley,
the hold he had upon Kellogg : How he has been cared for : The
two Dinkgraves, Norton, Dumont, Chapman, Sheradin, Twitchell,
Delacey, Souer, Dickerson, Brown, Milon, de Joie, Jones, and
Johnson — what they did and what they got.

F. A. CLOVER came to New Orleans from Mississippi,
where he had been a carpet-bag member of the legislature,
as the manager of a snake show. His education in Mississippi, and training as a "roper-in" for a snake show,
seems to have suggested to Kellogg his eminent fitness for
the supervisorship of the parish of East Baton Rouge. Accordingly Kellogg made him supervisor of registration for
that parish.

When the election was held on the 7th of November
Clover thought it would be a good thing to throw out the
returns from polls numbered 1, 3, 4, 5, 6, 7 and 11 and get
rid of 1,136 Democratic votes. The election law makes
it obligatory upon the supervisor of registration to forward

to the Returning Board the returns from every poll made
by the commissioners of election and to embrace them all
in his consolidated statement of the votes of the parish.
He had no discretion whatever, but must perform the ministerial duty confided to him.   But Clover, without any
evidence whatever from the commissioners of the respective
polls aforesaid — without any allegations from anyone that
the elections held thereat had not been fair, free and peaceable, refused to consolidate the votes and to forward the
commissioners' returns to the Returning Board.

It was necessary that the Board should have some evidence — or what purported to be evidence — before them.
Clover had made out his consolidated statement at Baton
Rouge and swore to the same and deposited a duplicate
with the clerk of the district court.   He did not make, on
the consolidated statement, any remarks concerning his refusal to compile the votes from polls 1, 3, 4, 5, 6, 7 and 11.
When he reached New Orleans he discovered that he
should have done something of this kind.   He had his returns with him and interpolated above the jurat made in
Baton Rouge the statements concerning the rejected polls
which he thought would be plausible reasons for their rejec-
tion.   This was forgery — falsification of a public record.

The Returning Board accepted the work of Clover as a
final adjudication of the case, refused to send for the returns and ballot-boxes for the polls rejected, and not only
refused to count the votes there cast, but threw out those
from polls 13 and 14.

Clover like Ferguson not only escaped punishment for
his crime, but he was rewarded by being made assistant
weigher in the New Orleans custom house at a salary of
$1,200 per annum and held the office for five years, ten
months and twenty-two days — receiving in all $7,373.

M. J. Grady was made supervisor of registration for Ouachita parish by Kellogg. He brought his returns to New Orleans and Jewett testifies was only induced after repeated interviews with Kellogg, and, as Blanchard informed him, with " visiting statesmen," to make an affidavit impeaching the fair, free, and peaceable character of the election in Ouachita parish.

Jewett says that Grady was actuated by fear, but that was not true. He was not a resident of Ouachita parish and had formerly been employed in the New Orleans custom house. It is evident that he wanted guarantees that he would be rewarded for forswearing himself. He was induced to make the required affidavit. He knew nothing of the Eliza Pinkston affidavit made in Monroe, La., before Dinkgrave, or of the occurrences Pinkston narrated therein, at the time he filed his returns with the Returning Board, for on Nov. 23d he wrote to Chas. S. Abell, secretary, as follows — " Please find enclosed the affidavit of Eliza Pinkston which I received too late to file with my returns. Please see that it is filed with my returns."

The record of the proceedings of the Returning Board, as published in the Sherman report, shows that Grady did not file his returns till two days after this letter was written. It is evident, therefore, that after Pinkston was brought to New Orleans, and it was determined to have her tell a story entirely different from the one she swore to before Dinkgrave in Monroe, that Grady withdrew his returns from the custody of the Returning Board, in order to suppress the original affidavit of Pinkston, and overlooked his letter of November 23d to Mr. Abell.

For his services Grady was first made register of the United States land office at Monroe, La., March 1, 1877, and July 10, 1878, was appointed deputy collector of internal revenue for part of Northern Louisiana.

James E. Scott was a clerk in the New Orleans Post-office when he was appointed supervisor of registration for Claiborne parish.

Jewett testified that Scott was reluctant to make an affidavit alleging " intimidation " in that parish and only consented, after much solicitation, to forswear himself. He finally made an affidavit — or swore to one which had been prepared for him, impeaching, in a vague way, the character of the election at polls 1, 2, 3, 5, 11.

Jewett says " no fact was stated which under a fair construction of the law would have given the board jurisdiction." The board threw out the votes of poll 3.

Scott after he made his affidavit resumed his duties as a $900 clerk in the New Orleans Post-office and was stlll there July 1, 1885.

James E. Anderson, who was appointed supervisor of registration for the parish of East Feliciana, was a native of Pennsylvania and was taken to Louisiana by J. Hale Sypher, also a Pennsylvanian who had carpet-bagged to New Orleans.

Anderson held a position in the New Orleans custom house at the time he was made supervisor of East Feliciana. He was an unprincipled young fellow, but bright, smart, and boasted " the cheek of an army mule." He was inquisitive, prying, suspicious, and always on the alert to discover what was going on among the politicians. His presumption was great, and from the day he landed in New Orleans he expected in due time to come to Congress.

Anderson was anxious to be made supervisor of East Feliciana, because he thought he could make himself serviceable to the member of Congress from that locality,

Chas. E. Nash, a colored man. But when he reached the parish he discovered that while Nash's negro friends wanted an election held, the white republicans did not want one.

Both sides wanted Anderson to act with them, and when he took sides with the colored leaders the white men tried to run him out of the parish. Anderson alleged that they waylaid him one night and attempted to kill him. He left and came to New Orleans where, as he averred, he soon discovered that Kellogg, Jewett, and the rest of the Republican managers, did not want an election held in certain parishes, including East Feliciana.

The democrats insisted upon Anderson's return and finally Kellogg gave him a written order to go back, but Jewett, so Anderson swears, and Jewett more than half admits, told him to stay in New Orleans. He finally went back and completed the registration and appointed the commissioners of election. He avers that Kellogg urged him to manage to have all the negroes vote at a few polls which could be so located as to enable the bulk of them to attend on election day, and to have disturbances created at the Democratic polls whereby the votes cast there could be thrown out. This he did not attempt.

It would have been quite easy to have executed such a plan if there had been perfect accord between the colored and white leaders and all the negroes were determined to vote the Republican ticket. Neither of these conditions existed.

The election was fair, free and peaceable, and the democrats carried the parish by a large majority. Anderson made his returns in due form and mailed them to the Returning Board as the law directs. He came to New Orleans, and all the testimony agrees that he proclaimed that there was no just ground for contesting the election in his parish.

There is disagreement as to whether he made the protest, or affidavit, which appears in the Sherman report. Anderson swears that he did not, and Pitkin and Campbell that he did.   But Pitkin says that after he had made it Anderson wanted to withdraw it, and raised a great row, because he was not allowed to have it.   Burke testified that Anderson came to him and offered for a sum of money to furnish the evidence which would establish beyond controversy that the election was fair, free, and peaceable, and was honestly won by the democrats.   There can be no question that Anderson's conduct caused the republicans serious uneasiness.

It would have been embarrassing to have a supervisor go back on them after he had made an affidavit.   There can be no doubt that every effort was made to control him. He was restored to his old place in the custom house at a salary of $1,400 a year November 17, 1876.

C. E. Nash, the colored candidate for Congress, entered into a written agreement with him on November 21 wherein he stipulated to secure for Anderson the appointment of naval officer of the port of New Orleans in consideration "that the said Anderson shall suppress evidence showing that the said parish of East Feliciana was fairly carried by the Democratic party at the election held November 7, 1876, thereby electing the entire Democratic state ticket and Congressmen."

Anderson asserted that the Nash agreement was of little moment so far as he was concerned; that he was only induced to forego his purpose of exposing the conspiracy to count in the Hayes electors and the Republican state ticket, congressmen, and members of the legislature by the written assurances he and a friend, Don. A. Weber, supervisor of the parish of West Feliciana, received from John Sherman.

It is not worth while to consider the probabilities of Anderson's story about the Sherman letter as he detailed it with great elaborateness and many evident contradictions to the Potter committee. The only important question we are concerned with is, would John Sherman have written such a letter as Anderson claimed he did? Upon this point Sherman himself has foreclosed inquiry. When called as a witness by the Potter committee, while giving it as his best recollection that he had not written the original of the copy which was shown him, he volunteered the declaration that he would have written "some of the things" in the letter it if he had been asked to do it. No doubt he would. Anderson was dangerous. He had to be quieted!

All the subsequent dealings with Anderson by Stanley Mathews, John M. Harlan, Sherman, Evarts, and Hayes himself, prove that they considered him dangerous and wanted to quiet him. They appointed him consul to Funchal but he would not accept. He placed a high value on himself and the more efforts they made to satisfy him the higher he advanced his pretensions. They finally decided that he would not keep faith; that he was merely leading them on step by step and meant to betray them in the end and, therefore, dropped him. Then he unbosomed himself, and, to break the force of his disclosures, it was necessary to prove him a great scoundrel and an awful liar. But in doing this his late friends only did what those who handle pitch do — defiled themselves!

W. J. Moore, was assistant supervisor of registration of the seventh ward, New Orleans. The record of his connection with the custom house, as it exists in the appointment division of the Treasury department, is interesting on two accounts, first, because, it shows the kind of men Kellogg appointed as registration officers, and second, because it proves that Moore drew two salaries at the same time. From June 20, 1875, to April 12, 1876, he drew a salary of $600 per year, and from June 17, 1875 he drew $2 per day as a night inspector. After the election he was made a guager in the internal revenue office and held the place till July 13, 1880.

A. W. Kempton was commissioner of election at poll No. 2, eleventh ward, New Oleans. He arbitrarily refused to sign the returns, and thereby gave the assistant supervisor an opportunity to refuse to include the return from this poll, in his consolidated statement. He had no right to so do, but any pretext was sufficient to excuse a violation of law, provided, thereby Democratic electors were disfranchised.

Kempton's reason for refusing to sign the return was that he had been intimidated after the votes had been cast and counted. It was a mere subterfuge — the object was to get rid of 413 Democratic votes. He was rewarded by an appointment in the custom house at a salary of $720 a year, which he held till September 6, 1878. For twenty-five days he drew double salary, having been made August 12, 1878, an assistant weigher at $1,200 a year. On the record of the appointment division of the Treasury, under Kempton's name, appears this memorandum in lead pencil — "not to be removed — D. J. M. A. Jewett interested — letter on file April 10, 1880." This letter, which was on file April 10, 1880, cannot now be found in the correspondence files of the Treasury department.

P. J. Maloney, assistant supervisor of registration of the fourteenth ward, New Orleans, was at the same time an employé in the custom house. He was transferred to the internal revenue service October 6, 1878, where he remained till January 1, 1881.

Thos. Leon, assistant supervisor of registration of the eighth ward, New Orleans, was an employé of the custom house — a night inspector — salary $3 per day.

T. H. Rowan, assistant supervisor of registration, tenth ward, New Orleans, was at the same time a custom house employé and held on till 1883, salary $3 per day.

Napoleon Underwood, assistant supervisor of registration, twelfth ward, New Orleans, was appointed night inspector, custom house, April 23, 1878, $3 per day salary.

Patrick Creagh, assistant supervisor of registration, third ward, New Orleans, was at the same time clerk of a police court. He was appointed June, 1879, storekeeper, custom house, salary $1,460 a year and was still drawing the salary July 1, 1885.

A. J. Brim, assistant supervisor of registration, second ward, New Orleans, was at the same time an employé of the custom house. He arbitrarily and illegally refused to consolidate with the returns from other polls the vote cast at poll No. 6 whereby 248 Democratic electors were disfranchised. He continued to hold his place in the custom house till August 12, 1877.

W. F. Loan, assistant supervisor of registration, fifteenth ward, New Orleans, was chief of Kellogg's metropolitan police, a state as well as municipal, a state constabulary as well as city, organization. It was especially intended to serve partisan purposes, and was unscrupulously used to assist the registration officers in 1876 in affecting a fraudulent negro registry in New Orleans. As a reward for his services, Loan was appointed January 19, 1877, inspector in the custom house at a salary of $3 per day, and May 7, 1878, was promoted to be assistant weigher with a salary of $1,200 per annum. July 1, 1885, he was still in the New Orleans custom house.

R. C. Howard, assistant supervisor of registration, fourth ward, New Orleans, was at the same time a clerk in the post-office of that city with a salary of $720 per year, and, unless recently discharged, still holds the place.

George A. J. Swazey, was a negro member of the legislature from West Feliciana parish for a number of years. He was a notable example of the influence of evil surroundings and corrupting examples on the negroes. He is about one-fourth white and was one of the most useful tools Kellogg had in the legislature. He and Louis J. Souer were the "bosses" of the negro members of the legislature, and regulated the price of their votes. They made contracts and delivered "the goods." Swazey was efficient in 1876 in marshalling negroes to the custom house for "the affidavit mill." He brought his men trained to answer affirmatively all questions propounded to them. Souer and Swazey "corralled" and held the negro legislators for Kellogg when that worthy was elected to the senate in January 1877. When Spofford contested Kellogg's seat Swazey was the latter's chief lieutenant in managing his negro witnesses.

Swazey was, July 1, 1885, a night inspector in the custom house at $2 per day having held office continuously, with the exception of nine months, for five years.

Thomas S. Kelley was the negro messenger of the executive office under Kellogg. He is a spruce and intelligent mulatto.

When the Packard government went to pieces in the spring of 1877, Kelley was neglected. His extravagant habits soon consumed all his substance and when the Potter committee began its work of investigating the frauds of 1876, Kelley indicated his purpose of telling what he knew about the forgery of electoral votes in December, 1876.

He wrote to Hon. Clarkson N. Potter from Lake Providence, Louisiana, where he was staying, on June 9, 1878, stating that, if protected, he would tell who forged the names of A. B. Levissee and Oscar Joffroin to the certificates of electoral votes manufactured in the State House December 28 and 29, 1876.

On June 22, Kelley was subpœnaed to appear in New Orleans to testify before a sub-committee of the Potter committee, but the very day the subpoena was served on him James D. Kennedy, a negro employé of the sergeant-at-arms of the Senate, arrived at Lake Providence, having been sent by Kellogg, and induced Kelley to go to Washington with him. Kennedy furnished the money for expenses. Arriving in Washington Kelley was maintained at Kellogg's expense, the money being paid through John A. Walsh, a banker at 916 F street who had recently come from New Orleans where he had been the chief financial supporter of the Packard government.

From July to Dec. 16, 1879, Kelley was supported by Kellogg through the medium of Walsh. On Dec. 16, 1879, Kelley was placed on the pay-roll of the New Orleans custom house, although he was then in Washington and remained there for more than three months rendering no service in New Orleans.

The record of the appointment division of the Treasury department shows that Kelley was appointed a clerk in the New Orleans custom house on Dec. 16, 1879 and that he continued on the pay-roll there until March 4, 1880, when he was appoinied on the recommendation of Kellogg by direction of John Sherman a clerk in the second auditor's office, Washington, D. C., at a salary of $1,000 a year. On Oct. 30, 1883, at the instance of Kellogg, he was promoted to $1,200 a year, and he is now a second-class clerk in the same office receiving a salary of $1,400 per annum.

When Kelley was examined by the Potter committee January 11, 1879, he said he knew positively that A. B. Levissee and Oscar Joffroin were not in New Orleans Dec. 28 and 29, 1876; that being the messenger of Kellogg he, with H. Conquest Clark, had charge of the forged certificates of electoral votes on those days and that no signatures were attached to the same till Dec. 29; that they were on that day kept in a room on the third floor of the State House and that the late electors except Levissee and Joffroin went up, one by one, either in his company, or with H. Conquest Clark, and signed their names; that he did not see all who signed, but saw them in the State House and two of them, Brewster and Joseph, he sent after; he declined to say, whether or not, he forged the names of Levissee and Joffroin, his reason therefor being that if he admitted he did people would say he was a fool for admitting it, and if he said he did not, nobody would believe him. He would not say that his answers would criminate him. He requested a few days delay in which to consult counsel, which was granted him. He professed to be familiar with the signatures of Levissee and Joffroin and said he was positive those purporting to be theirs on the second set of certificates of electoral votes were not genuine.

Levissee had testified June 6, 1878, that he signed but one set of certificates, and on being shown what purported to be his signatures on a second set, he said they were forgeries, and very poor and awkward imitations; that he left New Orleans on the 22nd or 23d of December, 1876, and on the 28th and 29th he was in Shreveport, Louisiana.

On January 14, 1879, Kelley again appeared and was examined by the Potter committee. He then said that he did not forge the signatures of A. B. Levissee and Oscar Joffroin to the forged certificates of electoral votes on December 29, 1876; after much fencing and prevaricating, he said that B. P. Blanchard, Kellogg's executive clerk, forged Joffroin's signature.

Kelley's story of how he knew this was altogether improbable. He said he came into the "upper room" in the State House where the certificates were and found Blanchard sitting at the table; that he, Kelley, went to the fireplace and took a seat. Presently Blanchard remarked: "How is that for high?" whereupon, he, Kelley, got up, went to the table and saw the papers before Blanchard, Joffroin's name was written, and the ink not dry; that not another word was spoken; that when he came into the room he did not observe that Blanchard was doing anything save sitting at the table — did not notice any papers; that he did not see Blanchard writing after he sat down at the fire, and did not look up or look round, till he heard "how is that for high," coming from Blanchard.

Being subjected to a most rigid, skilful cross-examination by Gen. B. F. Butler, Kelley was made to appear in a very bad light as a witness. Any one who reads this examination will be convinced that the witness was lying from beginning to end.

John H. Dinkgrave, a resident of Monroe, Louisiana, was the commissioner before whom was executed the original affidavit of Eliza Pinkston — the one which M. J. Grady, supervisor of Ouachita parish, forwarded to the Returning Board, November 23, 1876, and which was suppressed, and another, prepared in New Orleans, December 2, 1876, telling a different story, was substituted. Dinkgrave was appointed deputy collector of internal revenue at Monroe, La. Salary $1,500 a year.

W. H. Dinkgrave, who was also a party to the Pinkston fraud, was appointed a clerk in the New Orleans custom house April 2, 1879, salary $1,600 a year, and held the place till he resigned October 11, 1882.

Geo. L. Norton, assistant adjutant-general of Kellogg's militia, at the time of the count by the Returning Board, was appointed supervising inspector of steamboats at a salary of $3,000 a year.

A. J. Dumont, chairman of the Republican campaign committee of Louisiana in 1876, was appointed an inspector of the New Orleans custom house, May 7, 1878, and March 24, 1879, was made a deputy collector of customs, salary $3,000, which place he held till he committed suicide in June, 1885.

Sam'l. Chapman, sheriff of East Feliciana parish, and in charge of negro affidavit-makers from that parish, in 1876, held a position in the New Orleans custom house from Oct. 6, 1877, to April 22, 1878, salary $600 a year.

George A. Sheradin, a native of Ohio, a Louisiana carpet-bagger, a personal friend of R. B. Hayes, who helped to consummate the frauds in Louisiana by which the electoral vote of that state was secured, was appointed by Hayes recorder of deeds for the District of Columbia, an office worth $10,000 a year, May 25, 1878, and held the same for four years, and also enjoyed large emoluments from fraudulent contracts under Thos. J. Brady, Second assistant Postmaster-general.

W. H. Twitchell, a state senator from parish of Natchitoches, Louisiana, for several years, was appointed consul to Kingston, Canada, in 1877, salary $1,500 a year and extra fees.

It was shown during the investigation by the Potter committee that Twitchell was one of the most corrupt of the carpet-bag members of the legislature; and it was proved in the Spofford-Kellogg contest that he admitted the purchase of his vote for Kellogg.

W. J. Delacey, a member of the legislature who voted for Kellogg in 1877, admitted in an affidavit that he was paid therefor. Upon retracting this affidavit — that is after swearing that he swore falsely in the affidavit — he was appointed an inspector in the New Orleans custom house, salary $90 a month.

Lewis J. Souer, a member of the legislature counted in by the Returning Board, admitted in the Spofford-Kellogg contest that in order to keep a quorum present till Kellogg could be elected United States Senator, he cashed at par members' pay-certificates which could not be sold for anything on the market. He was appointed an appraiser in the custom house, salary $3,000.

Vincent Dickerson, Chas. F. Brown, A. E. Milon, Aristidie de Joie, Milton Jones, J. J. Johnson, who made affidavits in which they confessed to having been bought to vote as members of the legislature for Kellogg to be United States Senator, were all appointed to places in the New Orleans custom house upon retracting their affidavits. There were in all 34 * members of the Packard legislature who voted for Kellogg appointed in the New Orleans custom house — the refuge for almost every scoundrel in Louisiana, who had anything to do with the great fraud of 1876.

* See Senate Mis. Doc. No. 79, 46th Cong. 2d Sess. pp. 21 to 35, for all that relates to the period previous to Kellogg's putting witnesses in custom house.

CHAPTER XVI.

The Roll of American dishonor : The centennial era of the Republic
  disgraced : The apology of the instigators and promoters of the
  Great Fraud analyzed : The facts which have been proved against
  " the visiting statesmen :" The Florida case : The Louisiana case:
  A shameful story : The dishonesty of the defense put forward by
  " the visiting statesmen :" Their names linked for all time to those
  of the Louisiana and Florida rogues: Retributive justice: How all
  the chief beneficiaries of the Great Fraud feared exposure : Mathews
  and Jim. Anderson : General Grant knew the Louisiana rogues
  and was prepared to believe them capable of any villainy,

THE roster of visiting statesmen, of the Returning Board
rascals and their relatives, of the state officers, and of
subordinate rogues; the recounting of their many crimes,
their frauds, perjuries, and forgeries by which the electoral
votes of Florida and Louisiana were counted for Hayes
and Wheeler; the enumeration of the rewards bestowed
upon the instigators and promoters, the aiders and abettors,
and the perpetrators of those crimes, might appropriately
be termed the Roll of American dishonor.   What a shameful record it is!

There have been periods in the political history of
England when parliamentary elections were a mockery,
and the prostitution of patronage, and the bestowal of the
monarch's favors were a scandal and disgrace.   But the
history of English politics will be searched in vain for examples of political infamy, of official degradation compara-

ble to those which disgraced the centennial era of our Republic.

The most disgusting feature of the story of the great fraud of 1876 is the justification the instigators and promoters thereof have attempted.

Their apology has been and is that southern rebels deprived the negroes of their suffrages; that to protect the freedmen in their political rights election laws were enacted by the carpet-bag legislatures of certain southern states which enabled constitutional power to be exerted in purging the ballot-boxes; that they simply advised and encouraged the execution of these laws.

But it has been conclusively shown that, in the case of Florida, the board of state canvassers had not the power to do aught but accept the returns of the county canvassers and canvass and compile the vote from the same; that the county returns gave the Tilden electors a majority of all the votes cast; that the grossest frauds were committed by the republicans in many counties, and that in every instance these frauds were accepted as true returns by the state canvassers; that the perpetrators of these crimes were rewarded for their services; and that the proof of these frauds were furnished by the guilty parties who confessed their guilt. It has been further proved, beyond controversy, that the state canvassers were procured to violate their oaths of office and to peril their souls by the promise and pledge of rewards to be given them by Hayes.

In the case of Louisiana it has been demonstrated, first that the election law was not in accordance with the constitution of the state; that the Congress of the United States so decided, the Senate and the House of Representatives, each voting separately on different cases, so held; that it was so held by the highest court of Louisiana.

Second, it has been established that the election law, waiving its constitutionality, prescribed certain forms and methods whereby the Returning Board might be vested with jurisdiction in specified cases, and that, in not one single instance in which the Returning Board in 1876 assumed jurisdiction and exercised the power of rejecting votes, did it acquire that jurisdiction and exercise that power, in accordance with the forms or the letter and spirit of the election law.

It has been shown that the election was fair, free and peaceable; that the so-called evidence to prove the contrary was manufactured by wholesale.

It has been proved that the instigators and promoters of the frauds in Louisiana knew that these "forms" had not been observed and that the Returning Board had no jurisdiction; that it did not pretend to follow the mode of procedure prescribed by the law; that to give the Returning Board *colorable* jurisdiction the crimes of forgery and perjury were committed; that these crimes must have been with the knowledge, if not by the connivance of the men who were invited to go to Louisiana by President Grant, " to see that the Returning Board make a fair count of the votes actually cast."

And what an array the enumeration of these crimes and the perpetrators thereof makes! What a shameful story the history of the rogues is! Beginning with Kellogg, the governor of Louisiana, and coming down to the insignificant officials, there is an unbroken procession of graceless scamps. Take for instance the men who were counted in by the Returning Board as members of the legislature in order to give Kellogg a colorable title to a seat in the United States Senate. Was there ever such an exhibition of turpitude and political immorality witnessed by English-

speaking people ?   A score of the wretches make affidavits
to the effect that they were bought like sheep in the sham-
bles by Kellogg.   Then Kellogg buys them to swear they
had forsworn themselves, and pays them with places in the
New Orleans custom house!   And the Federal patronage
thus disbursed was that of the department of the government over which John Sherman presided.   Thirty-four of
the characterless rogues, who had for a brief period made a
quorum of a sham legislature, and by their votes had given
Kellogg a claim to a seat in the Senate of the United
States, were at one time on the pay-roll of the New Orleans custom house!

And, notwithstanding the proof of these things was incontestible, a partisan majority of the Senate would not
kick Kellogg out of the Senate.   Not only this, but the
whole power and influence of a Republican administration
was wielded to prevent the indictment of this carpet-bag
rogue for accepting a bribe while a Senator!

The hollow-heartedness, the dishonesty, of the defense
of the conduct of the Republican " visiting statesmen "
to Louisiana, was made manifest to the whole world by
their agreement to abandon Packard in order to secure
votes in the House of Representatives to defeat Democratic filibusters and complete the counting-in of Hayes
and Wheeler.   All of the prominent visiting statesmen from
John Sherman down were parties to this bargain.

Hayes, himself, in lamenting his defeat on the night of
November 8th, 1876, hypocritically proclaimed that his
only regret was for the poor negroes, and the following
February consented to and ratified the arrangement made
by Stanley Mathews, John Sherman, Charles Foster, and
James A. Garfield with the representatives of Nichols and
Hampton whereby in return for the completion of the elec-

toral count and the seating of Hayes, Packard and Chamberlain were to be abandoned.

Honorable men will justify the conduct of the representatives of Louisiana and South Carolina in ridding their people of the awful calamity of carpet-bag and scallawag rule, but upon what ground can the justification of Hayes and his party friends be placed ?

If intimidation prevented the Hayes electors from securing a majority of the ballots in the boxes how was it with Packard ? He received over a thousand more votes than five of the Hayes electors !

The truth was confessed perforce by the men who were responsible for the Returning Board frauds. They did not dare to assume the further responsibility of continuing by military power the indefensible rule of carpet-baggers and scallawags in Louisiana and South Carolina!

They knew, better than the rest of the world, the enormity of that rule. They were far better acquainted with the real characters of the carpet-baggers and scallawags than the rank and file of their party was, and they felt that it would be no longer possible to defend the wholesale plundering, the general corruption, the petty thieving and rascality of their southern allies. The public was beginning to know the truth.

But one thing these Republican politicians did not reckon upon, the linking throughout all time of their names with those of the Kelloggs, the Andersons, the Wellses, the Jewetts, the Dennises, the McLins, *et id omne genus*. They were compelled not only to eulogize and defend these rogues *ex nescessitate rei*, but they had to reward them for the base services they rendered.

Retributive justice, in the guise of the members of the Louisiana Returning Board, and of the legion of other rogues, was daily and hourly reminding Hayes and his cabinet of the crimes they had been art and part of.

How all these honorable (?) gentlemen dreaded the exposure, which was constantly impending, is strikingly illustrated by the experience of Stanley Mathews with Jim. Anderson. Without breeding, utterly devoid of the instincts of a gentleman, a typical political bummer and striker, indicating by his habitual speech his low origin and lower manner of life, Anderson quickly impressed the lawyer, statesman, and jurist with the firm conviction that the reputation of the late " visiting statesmen," and the stability of the whole fabric of the fraudulent administration were at the mercy of the late supervisor of registration for the parish of East Feliciana ! This is no exaggeration. The facts warrant even a stronger statement.

Jim. Anderson did not make the acquaintance of Mr. Mathews in New Orleans while the latter was there in the capacity of a " visiting statesman." He first met Mathews in Cincinnati in the latter part of March, 1877. It is doubtless true that Anderson was a quite frequent visitor at the headquarters of the " visiting statesmen " in New Orleans. He was " cheeky " and realized that a fellow of his calibre would, in all human probability, never have another such opportunity to make a political " stake." He knew that the Presidential election turned upon the electoral votes of Louisiana. He knew, moreover, that those votes could not be given to Hayes unless the members of the Returning Board monstrously perverted the election law. He was smart and unscrupulous, and quickly discovered that the supervisors of registration were the sole dependence of the local and national Republican leaders.

The commissioners of election had honestly performed their duties and had not reported intimidation, acts of violence, and corrupt influences, simply because there were none to report. For the same reason the supervisors of registration had not reported cases of intimidation prior to the election. How then was the Returning Board to obtain jurisdiction and secure pretended evidence upon which to base their contemplated action? The supervisors of registration could by forswearing themselves lay a false foundation. The whole structure of the intended fraud must be bottomed on perjury and forgery!

"Red-headed Jim," as Anderson was popularly known, knew his fellow-supervisors, and while he was quite certain that they would not hesitate at the commission of any crime, he firmly believed that they would insist upon guarantees of protection and pledges of adequate rewards. He knew that the local leaders of his party would be liberal with guarantees and profligate with promises, but niggardly in performances. His first scheme was to get promises and then to make assurance doubly sure by having them guaranteed by the " visiting statesmen."

Anderson formed an alliance offensive and defensive with Don. A. Weber, a scallawag supervisor of registration for the parish of West Feliciana. The evidence of concert between these two worthies is conclusive. Weber was quite as mercenary and unscrupulous as Anderson. Their coöperaion was absolutely necessary to the success of the dangerous undertaking which had been determined on by the desperate party leaders. Anderson began by securing from Charles E. Nash, candidate for Congress, an agreement in writing which was as follows:

"NEW ORLEANS, Nov. 21, 1876.

By an arrangement entered into this day between James E. Anderson, supervisor of registration for the parish of East Feliciana, Louisiana, and Charles E. Nash, member of Congress from the sixth

Congressional district of Louisiana, it is agreed that the said Anderson shall suppress evidence showing that the said parish of East Feliciana was fairly carried by the Democratic party at the election held November 7, 1876, thereby electing the entire Democratic state ticket and Congressmen. In consideration of which the said Nash agrees to secure for said Anderson the position of naval officer at the port of New Orleans, Louisiana.

(Signed) JAMES E. ANDERSON.
C. E. NASH.

The above agreement was signed in our presence this 21st day of November, 1876.

(Signed) J. M. TOMLINSON.
O. B. MORGAN."

The next move of Anderson was to obtain from one or more of the "visiting statesmen" a guarantee that pledges and promises would be kept if Hayes became President. That he was verbally assured that they would be kept cannot be doubted. It is unnecessary to discuss the probability of Anderson's story about Weber and himself receiving such assurances in writing from John Sherman. This question has been considered elsewhere.

Anderson was in Washington to witness the inauguration of Hayes and get his reward. He had abandoned the idea of becoming naval officer at New Orleans and wanted a consulship. Nash and Dr. Darrall, another Congressman from Louisiana, urged Anderson's claims, and Hayes directed that his case be made "special" for "a consulship in a warm climate."

But Anderson was too impatient to tolerate the tardy routine of the State department and posted off to New Orleans. He stopped in Cincinnati and called on Mr. Mathews. Anderson's account of the interview which followed is interesting :

"I called on Mr. Mathews. I went into a general history of the

20

election in Louisiana. I told him what part I had taken, of the manner in which the election in East Feliciana had been conducted and in the state : told him they had thrown out my parish on a forged protest : that they made me promises which they had not fulfilled and had no intention of fulfilling : in fact, told him the whole story of the whole thing right through : went into all the details, with the exception that I omitted any mention of Mr. Sherman's name. I did not mention his name at all."*

Mr. Mathews was impressed by Anderson's " whole story " of the Louisiana election. He asked Anderson to leave with him the Nash agreement. He gave Anderson a note of introduction to John M. Harlan who was one of the commissioners sent by Hayes to supervise the abandonment of Packard's sham government. A few weeks later Mr. Mathews wrote to Anderson, who was still in New Orleans, assuring him that he had " the best reasons for saying that sooner or later, and as soon as practicable," he would " be able to obtain " for him " a satisfactory appointment, either at home or abroad."

Harlan was also impressed by Anderson's story, and when he came North he coöperated with Mathews in his efforts to prevent the exposure they both believed the fellow could make. Mathews wrote Anderson on the 27th of April, 1877, from Cincinnati, saying that he had " conferred with General Harlan, having travelled with him from Philadelphia here." He continued — " we both concluded it would be better to wait now until the extra session of Congress, which will be called to meet June 4th, when I will be in Washington regularly, and situated so as to give the attention to your application which I have promised, and when I do, no doubt I will be able to secure your appointment to some foreign position which will be agreeable to you."

* H. R. Mis. Doc. No. 31, 45th Cong. 3d Sess. p. 23.

On the 14th of May Mr. Mathews gave Anderson a letter to the Secretary of State in which he said, among other significant things, "that the circumstances in which Mr. Anderson has been placed, and in which he has been compelled to act a very difficult part, are such as to give him very strong claims upon the administration in the public interests, and I do most earnestly urge that some satisfactory public employment may be found for him at once."

This letter brought an appointment to the consulship at Funchal, salary $1,500 a year and fees. This was indignantly spurned by Anderson who sent an insulting telegram to Mr. Mathews and followed it with an impudent letter. Notwithstanding this unmannerly and ungrateful conduct on Anderson's part Mr. Mathews continued to manifest a deep interest in the fellow's behalf, and continued his efforts to secure him "a satisfactory appointment." But in the meantime Anderson had been talking and threatening, and Sherman and Hayes were afraid to do anything for him, believing that he was being used by democrats to entrap them.

The only reasonable explanation and defense of Mr. Mathews' part in this scandalous business was made by his nephew, Hon. Henry Watterson, who claimed that his uncle was striving "to save his party friends from a scandalous exposure, knowledge of which had reached him. No one pretends that he participated in the Louisiana frauds. He was in New Orleans but a few days."

But short as Mr. Mathews' visit was to New Orleans in November, 1876, he must have been cognizant of, and privy to, transactions between his fellow "visiting statesmen" and the Kellogg crowd, which prepared him to believe Anderson's story. He had repeated interviews with Hayes and Evarts and Sherman in Anderson's interest. If they were not afraid of Anderson's threatened revelations why did they not quiet the apprehensions of Mr. Mathews. His only object was to serve them and his party. It is not possible that there could have been any bond of sympathy between the cool, calculating lawyer and the political bummer and striker!

It is not strange that from Hayes down the fraudulent administration and its friends should have been in constant dread of an exposure by some one of the many Louisiana villains. They knew the character of the men they had to deal with. They knew of the crimes these men had committed to make Hayes President. If their knowledge was not criminal it was so nearly so that the public would not discriminate in their favor.

General Grant, who had learned by costly experience the character of the Louisiana carpet-baggers and scallawags, was not deceived by the defense which the "visiting statesmen" made for themselves and their allies. He thought that in the case of Florida his party was entitled to the benefit of the doubt, but the Louisiana frauds were so gross and indefensible that he was determined not to assume any responsibility therefor.

He had great confidence in General Sheridan and remembered his unsparing condemnation of J. Madison Wells when constrained in 1865 to remove him from the provisional governorship of Louisiana. When Mr. Maddox, the government agent who had been sent to New Orleans to observe the conduct of the members of the Returning Board, reported, November 24th, 1876, that Wells was for sale and was "dickering" with both sides, President Grant promptly sent the agent to Mr. Chandler. General Grant had no doubt of the truth of Mr. Maddox's report. He knew that Wells was capable of any villainy.

There can be no question that when General Grant came to review in the calm repose of private life the political events of the eight years of his administration he was ready to condemn unequivocally the many and desperately wicked excesses of the rule of the carpet-baggers and scallawags in the southern states. And who is not? Who does not fervently thank God that the Pattersons, the Kelloggs, the Dorseys, the Wests, the Warmoths, the Moseses, and all that they represented have disappeared from national as well as southern politics? Where is the conscientious, self-respecting citizen of the Republic who can recall without feeling the blush of shame tingle on his cheeks the riot of corruption, the debauching of public and private morals, which were the result of the reign of the carpet-bagger and scallawag in the South?

If any there be who are not satisfied that the elimination of the carpet-bagger and scallawag was a God-sent deliverance let them read the history of Louisiana politics from 1865 to 1876 in the succeeding chapters.

CHAPTER XVII.

Review of Louisiana carpet-bag politics : Lincoln's plan of reconstruction : The first provisional government : The illegal attempt to
amend the constitution of 1864 : The New Orleans riot and massacre the result of incendiary appeals to the negroes : Gen. Hancock's
benificent rule : The election of Warmoth and the enactment of registration and election laws : The character and purpose of these
laws : Analysis of the laws : Senator Edmunds pronounces the election law in conflict with the State constitution : The character of
Warmoth : He delineates the characters of his opponents : Universal corruption : The Custom House party : The attempt to impeach Warmoth : The use of the troops : The Carter-Warmoth
war :

THE history of the election in Louisiana in 1876, and
the enormity of the illegal methods, the monstrous perversion of the principles, and the flagrant disregard of "the
forms" of law, the perjuries, forgeries, and divers other
crimes by which the will of the people of that State, peaceably and honestly expressed at the polls, was nullified
and the perpetrators thereof were rewarded cannot be fully
understood and adequately appreciated without reviewing
the preceding political occurrences.

The plan of reconstructing the government of the
Southern States devised by President Lincoln and suggested
by him in a message to Congress in 1863, differed widely
from that subsequently adopted by the leaders of the Republican party. Mr. Lincoln affirmed in the last public
utterance he made that his plan was " distinctly approved

by every member of his cabinet." Speaking of his policy Mr. Lincoln described it as follows :

" Some twelve thousand voters in the heretofore slave State of Louisiana have sworn allegiance to the Union ; assumed to be the rightful political power of the state; held elections; organized a free government; adopted a free state constitution, giving the benefit of public schools to black and white, and empowering the legislature to confer the elective franchise upon the colored man. This legislature has already voted to ratify the constitutional amendment recently passed by Congress, abolishing slavery throughout the nation. These twelve thousand persons are thus fully committed to the Union, as to perpetual freedom in the States — committed to the very things the nation wants — and they ask the nation's recognition and its assistance to make good that committal. Now if we reject and spurn them, we do our utmost to disorganize and disperse them. We in effect say to the white man : ' you are worthless, or worse; we will neither help you, nor be helped by you.' To the blacks we say : 'this cup of liberty which these your old masters hold to your lips we will dash from you, and leave you to the chances of gathering the spilled and scattered contents in some vague and undefined when, where, and how.' If this course discouraging and paralyzing both to the white and black, has any tendency to bring Louisiana into proper relations with the Union, I have, so far, been unable to perceive it. If on the contrary, we recognize and sustain the new government of Louisiana, the converse of all this is made true. We encourage the hearts and nerve the arms of the twelve thousand to adhere to their work, and to argue for it, and feed it, and grow it, and ripen it to a complete success."

The idea thus indicated by Mr. Lincoln was that when-

ever any considerable body of the people of any Southern
State took the oath of allegiance to the United States and
gave evidence of their acceptance of "the very things the
nation wants" by organizing a free government, adopting a
free state constitution, giving the benefit of free schools
equally to black and white, and empowering the legislature
to confer the elective franchise upon the colored man, they
were entitled to the nation's recognition and assistance. It
is fair to presume that if Mr. Lincoln had been permitted
to live and supervise the rehabilitation of the Southern State
governments he would have adhered to his deliberately
formed policy. It will be noticed that the tone as well as
the tenor of his remarks, quoted above, indicate that the
subject had been carefully considered, had been much discussed, and his views were the result of mature reflection.
It is no secret that his policy was not approved by many
prominent leaders of his party in Congress, and his language is indicative of some feeling on his part. His plan
of reconstruction had been criticised because it did not require the enfranchisement of the negro as a condition
precedent.

Mr. Lincoln thought that suffrage should be gradually bestowed instead of by a sweeping enactment. In
the same speech, from which the above extract is taken,
he clearly indicated that the colored man must show some
progress before he would be entitled to that boon. His
language also conveys the idea that the right of suffrage
must come from the States. He said, "the colored man,
too, seeing all united for him is inspired with vigilance and
energy, and daring to the same end. Grant that he desires
the elective franchise, will he not attain it sooner by saving
the already advanced steps toward it (the right of the legislature of Louisiana to confer it) than by running backward

over them ?"   In reply to those who had said that twelve
thousand voters were but a mere handful, and a poor beginning at reconstructing the state, he replied by a characteristic and pointed illustration.

" Concede," he said, " that the new government of
Louisiana is only what it should be as the egg to the fowl,
we shall *sooner* have the fowl by hatching the egg than by
smashing it."

It is not to be presumed that the radical leaders in Congress would have yielded their views without a struggle, but
there can be no doubt as to what the issue would have been
if the contest had been between them and Mr. Lincoln.
He was the one great figure of the time and would have
continued to be, as he was the people's idol. He was essen-
tially a man of the people.   He had in a greater degree,
than any one of his time, the power of putting things
within the comprehension of the masses.   His direct and
simple form of speech, his homely and forcible illustrations,
and his facility of condensation and classification, enabled
him to carry conviction to the people in a wonderful way.
But unfortunately for the whole country, and especially for
the South the assassin's bullet did its fatal work just as the
angel of peace was spreading her white wings over the
land.   The Louisiana experiment, in which Mr. Lincoln
felt such a deep interest, proved a disastrous failure through
the machinations of unworthy men who obtained power and
were encouraged to resort to illegal and desperate methods
by radical congressmen.   There was but a feeble minority
in both Houses of Congress.   The radical element of the
Republican party dominated the Senate and House of
Representatives.   Andrew Johnson was obstinate, imprac-
ticable, without tact, and his judgment of men was often
utterly at fault.

The provisional government of Louisiana which Mr. Lincoln wanted Congress to recognize as the constitutional government of that State was created by a convention called in 1864 under a proclamation of Gen. N. P. Banks in command at New Orleans. This was a novel way of setting up a state government, it is true, but *inter arma selent leges*. The convention met and formulated a constitution which was submitted to the people and ratified by them — by a respectable body of those within the Federal jurisdiction. After hostilities ceased and the authority of the national government was everywhere recognized, this provisional government exercised jurisdiction over the whole state. Its authority was recognized — obeyed — by all the people. But in 1866 a class of men obtained control who have since proved to be characterless. In November, 1866, J. Madison Wells was elected governor. He was a man of violent temper. Before the war he was one of the terrors of the Red River country. He was a Union man and suffered persecution, but as his hand was against every one who was unfriendly to him, his troubles were not altogether due to his political sentiments. He was dishonest, unprincipled, and vindictive. Michael Hahn was the first governor of the provisional government although he had been an original secessionist. His ability was limited. His conversion to Union sentiments was due to motives, neither high nor honorable. From 1864 to 1884 he was in one capacity or another a pensioner either upon the State or the Federal government. Rufus K. Howell, who was made associate justice of the Supreme Court by Wells, J. King Cutter, Dr. Dostie and several others had been secessionists but, on the capture of New Orleans by General Butler, joined Hahn and became violent agitators and advocates of the punishment of rebels. Henry C. Warmoth was a needy adventurer in New Orleans and loud in advocacy of a military government. William Pitt Kellogg, made Collector of the port of New Orleans by President Johnson, was discreetly an advocate of the President's policy of admitting the state to full participation of the benefits of the Union. E. H. Durell, district judge of the United States, was likewise temporarily an advocate of Johnson's policy and opposed to reconstruction.

There was naturally a large turbulent element in New Orleans. The population was a mixed one. Before, during, and since the war the good name of the city has suffered on account of the many bad characters who have occasionally obtained a temporary ascendency there. Immediately after the war the number of these desperadoes was largely increased. They have been, as their interests inclined them, the partisans of first one and then another political party. The disbanded Confederate armies threw upon society many restless and reckless young men. Discharged Union soldiers, of bad character, swelled the ranks of the dangerous classes. A race of mixed blood, the product of various Latin progenitors, live on the islands and along the coast of the gulf who are termed Dagos. They are fruiters and fishermen. For a few dollars many of them can be hired to wield the assassin's knife.

* In 1866 the violent leaders determined to make a new constitution and provide therein for the disfranchisement of all late rebels and the enfranchisement of all the negroes. They could not accomplish this by legal methods, because, they could not control the legislature, which alone, under the provisions of the constitution of 1864, might provide for its amendment. Therefore, they determined to reconvene the constitutional convention of 1864, despite the fact, that

* H. R. Report, No. 16, 38th Cong. 2d Sess. pp. 37 to 61.

it had been defunct two years.   After consultation with
radical members of Congress, a call was issued by Judge
Howell, on the refusal of the former chairman, Judge
Durell, to act, convening the convention in New Orleans
on the 30th day of July, 1866.   There was no concealment
of the purposes of these violent men.   They openly proclaimed their intention to punish rebels and to do this the
negroes should be given the right of suffrage.   The night
before this so-called convention was to assemble, Dostie,
Cutler, Howell, and others, addressed mass meetings of
negroes and gave expression to their sentiments in unrestrained language.   Their speeches were inflammatory to
the last degree, and the most foolish and wicked advice was
given to the poor negroes.   If these men were sane they
must have desired to provoke an outbreak and secure the
slaughter of the people they professed to love.   They took
no steps whatever to secure the protection of the military.
They must have known what the consequences were likely
to be if they scattered firebrands broadcast among the in-
flammable material, composing in large part, the population
of New Orleans.

The next day the convention met in Mechanics Institute. The negroes rallied by their pretended friends gathered
in large numbers and paraded the streets.   A riot started—
no one could tell how or why — the result —: a large number of negroes killed and many wounded. The police force
did most of the killing.   It was a dastardly and bloody massacre. An attempt, of course, was made to prove that it was
a premeditated conspiracy on the part of prominent late
rebels to kill all the Union men and teach the negroes a
terrible lesson.   But this failed signally.   There was no
evidence produced to justify even a suspicion of this.   On
the other hand there were circumstances and facts proved

which gave the color of truth, at least, to the charge that a disturbance was not unexpected and was rather courted by the promoters of the convention scheme. J. Madison Wells prudently kept out of harm's way. Dostie was the only one of the incendiaries who lost his life.

The New Orleans riot of July 30, 1866, was a fortunate occurrence for the Republican leaders who were bent upon reconstructing the Southern States. It was the most unfortunate event for Louisiana and the whole South that could possibly have happened. That it would have been prevented if the respectable citizens had suspected its possible occurrence, cannot be doubted by reasonable men. The consequences thereof would be apparent to all reflecting minds. The reconstruction measures placed Louisiana along with the rest of the South under absolute military rule. Fortunately, however, for the people of that State, General Hancock was assigned to the command of the fifth military district which included Louisiana. For a few brief months they enjoyed a government, military though it was, regulated by law. Upon assuming his duties the general announced * "that the great principles of American liberty are still the lawful inheritance of this people, and ever should be." And he illustrated his words by his deeds, so long as he was suffered to remain in that command. He maintained the right of trial by jury, the privilege of the habeas corpus, the liberty of the press, the freedom of speech, the natural rights of persons and the rights of property. He proved that to be true which he declared in his famous order, namely: "that free institutions, while they are essential to the prosperity and happiness of the people, always furnish the strongest inducements to peace and order." He sustained the regular civil tribunals and all crimes and of-

* General orders No. 40, Nov. 29, 1867.

fences committed were referred to them for consideration and judgment. The result was perfect order and universal contentment. A constitutional convention was held which framed a new constitution. It was adopted and state officers were elected. Before this occurred, however, General Hancock was compelled, on account of the measures taken by radical congressmen who were deeply incensed at his conduct, to ask to be relieved of his command.

Henry C. Warmoth, a brilliant, but unprincipled adventurer, was the first governor elected in Louisiana under the reconstructed government. Handsome in person, engaging in manners, eloquent and persuasive in speech, possessing a quick, fertile brain, insensible to fear, and resourceful in expedients, he was the beau ideal of a political freebooter. The opportunities for self-aggrandizement and almost unrestrained looting were unrivalled. The Federal patronage was vast, and the chance to profit by frauds upon the national revenue to be collected was practically unlimited. Illicit distilling was so open and notorious, that revenue agents intrigued for details to New Orleans in order, in a few months, to enrich themselves. The Custom House was the gateway to affluence and political power. William Pitt Kellogg, who was Collector of Customs from 1865 to 1868, accumulated a fortune and secured from the legislature elected along with Warmoth a seat in the United States Senate. The military power was now in hands less scrupulous than Gen. Hancock was. But there was no occasion for its exercise. The claim has been made that there was a great deal of violence and much bloodshed in Louisiana during 1868 and 1869. There was doubtless some lawlessness and bloodshed. There is always more or less in every community. In portions of Louisiana there had always been turbulent classes. The worst of them were, however, from the beginning acting with the carpet-baggers. This was true of Rapides parish, the home of the Wells' family. But it is a noteworthy fact that during the months of Gen. Hancock's command there were no massacres, no lawlessness that attracted public attention. The necessity for political capital did not exist then. The government was one of law and order and not one for plunder.

The organized system of spoliation which was inaugurated with the establishment of carpet-bag rule worked so satisfactory that the only concern of the spoilers was to make its continuance certain. That was impossible unless they could grasp all power, local as well as general, and provide the way to retain it in spite of the will of the people. Preparatory to this scheme "the outrage mill" was set to work. It was charged that fair electious could not be held because of intimidation and violence. This was a pretext. The object was an excuse to invent and put in operation election machinery, which would enable them to maintain control of the parish, municipal and state offices. Their purpose was to fasten upon the intelligent, respectable and property-owning class a government which was to regulate the local concerns of the parishes, towns and cities as well as the affairs of the state, the burdens of which were to be borne by citizens who were to be practically disfranchised. It was necessary to secure the co-operation of a few unprincipled white men, natives of different parishes, or carpet-baggers recently settled in the interior towns, and, therefore, they were assigned the local pickings and stealings. But this made it necessary to provide, that whatever local officers were elective should be really named by the central power. All political authority, the distribution of vast and widely ramifying patronage, the valuation of property, the assessment and collection of all local and general taxes, the management of public schools, the building of school-houses, the employment of teachers, the construction and repair of highways and bridges, the administration of justice—everything pertaining to the local government was to be centered in the governor, whose will could only be regulated by a Senate which was always subservient.

The men who originated this scheme knew that its maintenance would be a difficult and dangerous undertaking. They based their hope of success upon three things—first, the control of the large negro population, second, the countenance and protection of the Federal government, and third, the fact that the white population was not altogether of Anglo-Saxon lineage and had, moreover, long been accustomed to the civil law and many of the institutions peculiar thereto. A pure Anglo-Saxon community, with its traditional folkmote, its cherished right of local self-government, could not have been kept in subjection to an alien rule of this kind.

Registration and election laws* were enacted in 1870 which supplemented each other. The first, delegated to the governor the appointment of the persons who determined who should vote, and the second, invested a Returning Board composed of the governor, lieutenant-governor, secretary of state, and two senators named in the act, with the power to count the votes and declare who had been elected. The act was unconstitutional because it made persons not contemplated by the constitution Returning officers. But this was of no consequence to the conspirators against the liberties of the people, because the entire judiciary was appointed by the governor, and the judges were his creatures. Moreover, a political court had been created which was invested with exclusive original jurisdiction in all cases of summary

* Senate Report, No. 457, 42d Cong. 3d Sess. pp. 35 to 75.

process, and in all proceedings instituted to try contests for office.

The governor, by the registration law, appointed by the advice and consent of the Senate a State Registrar of Voters, who was to be paid $3,000 a year out of the state treasury upon his own warrant, one chief clerk at a salary of $1,500, and one assistant clerk at a salary of $1,200 per annum. The chief clerk could perform the functions and discharge all the duties of the registrar in his absence or disability. Quarters, and all blank books, stationery, and all expenses were to be paid for on the warrants of the registrar. The sextons of all cemeteries in the parish of Orleans were to report the interments of all males of twenty-one years and over, and whatever other statistics the registrar might require he was authorized to obtain and report to the legislature annually. This general authority was held to cover a quadrennial census of the state which was made the basis for election frauds. The governor also could appoint, within two months of any general election, for each parish in the state, except Orleans and Jefferson, one supervisor of registration, and one assistant supervisor for each ward of New Orleans and for each part of Jefferson, as divided by the Mississippi river. These officers were to receive $5 per day for each day they were employed, which might be till ten days after the election. They could have two clerks, each at a salary of $3.50 per diem. They were to open one office in each parish, but they could go to different points to give facility for registration if they deemed it necessary. In New Orleans they were to keep open their offices for fifty days prior to the election, but must close ten days before, and in the parishes twenty days prior to, and close nine days before the day of election. They were to give notice of the appointed time and place of registration. They were the sole judges of the right of electors to register and their certificates alone gave citizens the right to vote. Parish judges not only could afford no relief to the citizen unlawfully deprived of his rights, but if they attempted to do so they were liable to a fine of not less than $500, six months' imprisonment and impeachment and removal. The governor could at his pleasure remove supervisors and assistant supervisors. The supervisors appointed three polling officers, known as commissioners of elections and any number of assistants who had the power of constables. It was required that a general registration should be held in 1874 and no one could vote on a certificate issued prior to that date.

The election law provided that each parish and each ward of the city of New Orleans should constitute an election precinct and that the supervisors and assistant supervisors should determine the number of polling places but were only required to establish one for each justice of the peace's ward outside New Orleans. The commissioners of election were to receive the ballots of registered voters, and to preserve the peace with the assistance of their assistants, and could order the arrest and confinement, until after the close of the polls, of any persons they adjudged guilty of disorder. They were to keep a list of the names of the persons voting, numbering the voters from one to the end, which they were to sign and swear to as correct, immediately on the close of the polls. The ballots were to be counted at the close of the election, then and there, in the presence of bystanders, without moving the boxes, and the tally lists, lists of voters, and ballots were to be placed in the boxes and committed to the custody of the clerks of the district courts.

A duplicate of the count of votes was to be forwarded to the Supervisor of Registration together with a full statement, under oath, verified by three citizens, respectable and qualified voters, of any riot, tumult, acts of violence, intimidation, disturbance, bribery or corrupt influence preventing or tending to prevent a fair, free, peaceable election, and of the exact number of qualified electors thereby deterred from voting. The Supervisor of Registration was to make a consolidated statement of the vote of his parish, in duplicate, and attach to each "by paste, wax, or some adhesive substance, that the same can be kept together," first a statement, made and sworn to, by himself, and corroborated under oath by three respectable witnesses, qualified voters, of "any riot, tumult, acts of violence, intimidation, and disturbance, bribery or corrupt influence at any place within said parish, or at or near *any place of registration, or revision of registration,*" which " prevented or tended to prevent a fair, free, peaceable and full registration ;" and, second, the statements of the commissioners of election as to any like occurrences at *the time of the election.* One copy of these duplicate consolidated statements with the attachments, he was to deposit with the clerk of the court after swearing to both before him, and the other he was to forward *by mail* to the Returning Officers together with the returns from the commissioners of elections, their tally sheets and lists of persons voting.

Within ten days after the closing of the elections the Returning Board was to meet in New Orleans to canvass and compile the statements of votes made by the commissioners of elections. They were to continue in session till such returns were compiled, and at such meeting the presiding officer in the presence of the other members should open the said statements and compile *first* the statements from all polls and voting places at which there had been a fair, free, and peaceable registration and election. In the event of any statement, as required by law, from the Supervisor of Registration *affecting the registration*, or from the Commissioners of Elections *affecting the election*, or both, they were not to canvass, count, or compile such statements of votes, thus affected, until all statements from other polls or voting places were canvassed and compiled. This being done they were to proceed to investigate the statements of the supervisor *as to interference with registration*, and the statements of commissioners *as to occurrence at time and place* of election, and if they were fully convinced by evidence that for any of the causes specified the purity and freedom of election at such poll or voting place was interfered with they should "not canvass or compile the statement of the votes of such poll or voting place, but shall reject it from their returns."

It will be observed that the power and influence of the governor over elections was almost unlimited. He appointed, practically, all the election officers. The Supervisors of Registration were his creatures. Their dictum as to the right of voters to register was absolute. And after the election they and their appointees, provided they could secure three respectable citizens, qualified electors, to join with them, might invalidate the election at any poll or polls. The Returning Board officers were the final arbiters, it is true, but they were also his creatures. But the proceedings of these officers must be regular and in strict conformity to the law. The Supervisor of Registration *could protest* ONLY *to acts affecting the registry* of voters, and the Commissioners of Election *only to acts affecting the voting*. It was true, nevertheless, that the courts, presided over by creatures of the governor, were of no avail to the citizens, if the forms of law were not observed in exercising the tremendous power thus vested in a few men.

That the election law was clearly in conflict with the constitution of the State admits of no doubt. A majority of the committee on privileges and elections of the Senate of the United States, among whom were some of the ablest Republican lawyers of that body, say of it: * "This act is in conflict with the constitution in several particulars: first, the constitution provides that the returns of the election of all members of the legislature shall be made to the Secretary of State. And article 48 provides that the returns of every election for Governor shall be sealed up and transmitted to the Secretary of State, who shall deliver them to the Speaker of the House of Representatives then next to be holden, and that the members of the general assembly — that is, both houses of the legislature — shall meet in the House of Representatives to examine and count the votes for governor and lieutenant governor."

Senator Edmunds in a speech made in the Senate, March 16, 1875; in combating the theory advanced by some of his Republican colleagues that the "returns" spoken of in the constitution of Louisiana, might be held to mean the "returns" made by the Returning Board said, after quoting article 48, of the constitution:

†" In the light of that language, can any senator stand up here and say that he believes that the word "returns" as used in that constitution, means, or can mean, any other thing than the local official papers taken at the time in every voting district and precinct in the state, and that in Louisiana, as I believe in Indiana, and certainly in Vermont and Massachusetts and many other states, the votes of the people, taken on the same day, and before a thousand different officers in different places, are by a statement to be sealed

* Senate Report No. 457, 43d Cong. 3d Sess. p. V.
† Cong. Record, Part I, Vol. IV, p. 65.

up and transmitted to the sovereign power of the state, that by them, and not by any judgment of any intervening authority, the original evidence of what the will of the people has been, shall receive examination, and that by them the result shall be declared?"

The political adventurers thus entrenched in office behind this unconstitutional law, exercising, nevertheless, supreme, though illegal, control over the ballot-box, flourished exceedingly until those who were the beneficiaries of the Federal patronage became jealous and envious of Warmoth and his followers. The quarrel began in the fall of 1870, and continued with varying fortunes to the respective sides till it culminated in December, 1872, by the complete overthrow of Warmoth. But from 1868 to 1871 the carnival of plunder was enough to satisfy both the State House and Custom House ringleaders. The inception of the quarrel was probably the desire of James F. Casey, the brother-in-law of President Grant, who was collector of customs at New Orleans to be made United States senator. There had been, and there promised to be, ample spoil to satisfy the small number of chief adventurers no matter how voracious they might be. They have testified before Congressional committees concerning each other's villainy, and from this data their characters will be delineated.

Warmoth had an appreciation of printer's ink and besides subsidizing the press of the entire state by the judicious distribution of the publications paid for out of the state treasury, founded an official organ of which he owned one-third, and in one year bestowed upon it $700,000 for public printing. He, in 1867, secured the funding of a debt against the state which had been incurred under Confederate authority and was outlawed by the constitution of 1868 to the amount of $290,000. He was accused of having an interest in every job and scheme of plunder that was put through the legislature. As will be seen hereafter he displayed wonderful familiarity with legislative corruptions. He was unquestionably the source of all power — an autocrat uncontrolled save by his own will. The legislature was under his undisputed and absolute sway for two years. Whatever bill he favored became a law, and with his opposition no legislation could be obtained. The judiciary were likewise his creatures and tools. Warmoth made no pretense of immaculateness. He was always frank and bold. He once said to a delegation of bankers: "I don't pretend to be honest. I only pretend to be as honest as anybody in politics." He, however, on that occasion proved himself to be quite as honest as the New Orleans bankers. They had endeavored to buy legislation, and Warmoth mercilessly exposed them. He told them the truth when he declared that "corruption is the fashion" in Louisiana. A corrupt government inevitably demoralizes the entire community. One of his most eloquent opponents, the speaker at one time of the House of Representatives, thus describes Warmoth :*

"Who is Henry Clay Warmoth? I knew him before he was governor. He came in your midst poor and an adventurer, and he has been elected to office, and gradually, by corruption and all the questionable means resorted to by the political demagogue, abusing the confidence of a simple-minded and confiding people, he has acquired and holds power more despotic than any king in Europe, and patronage more abundant and potent than any five governors in the Union. Through the registration and election laws he makes voters and controls elections. Through his patronage he poisons public virtue and cor-

* New Orleans *Picayune.*

rupts public officers; and through the metropolitan police, militia, and constabulary laws, he intimidates and coerces those whom he cannot corrupt. With executive powers the greatest possible, he has nefariously absorbed, in many instances, judicial power, and manipulated and controlled the legislative department of the State; and all this for the perpetuation of his power, and the aggrandizement of his partisans, rather than for the public weal."

Mr. Warmoth delineated the characters of his principal opponents in his turn.* He testified that James F. Casey, collector of the port of New Orleans, was interested in the act to incorporate the Shed Company, which monopolized the front levee from Common to Poydras streets, New Orleans, and taxed all merchandise landed at the steamboat wharves; that Casey was in charge of the corruption fund to secure the passage of the bill. This act Warmoth vetoed. But Casey and others associated with him passed a warehouse bill, over Warmoth's veto, which gave the concern $1,400,000 of State bonds.

S. B. Packard, then United States marshal, subsequently candidate for governor in 1876, secured the passage by bribery of a paving bill which would have taken from owners of property in New Orleans and the State treasury for one street $1,250,000, and Warmoth vetoed it notwithstanding he was, as he claims, offered $50,000 to approve it.

John Ray, of whom we will hear more hereafter, and Luedling, chief justice subsequently of the state, secured the passage of a bill which gave their railroad from Vicksburg to Monroe, Louisiana, $546,000 in state bonds; and also the incorporation of the Louisiana Levee Company with authority to build fifteen million cubic yards of levees at 60 cents a cubic yard, and to assess a tax of 10% on the cost of the

* H. R. Mis. Doc. No. 211, 42d Cong. 2d Sess. pp. 395 to 401.

property of the state for twenty-one years and to issue its bonds endorsed by the state in anticipation of the taxes.

It was proved by other witnesses that a Mr. H. S. Kimball,* procured legislation in behalf of the New Orleans, Jackson, and Great Northern Railroad Company, by the bribery of P. B. S. Pinchback, Hugh J. Campbell, Mortimer Carr, and other legislators. One witness testified as follows: "I have seen money paid to members of the legislature by one or two different parties. I was asked, in one instance, to go with a party who told me he had a large amount of money to pay out; as he supposed some members would object to giving him a receipt, he asked me to go along as a witness." This same witness testified that he knew members of the legislature to accept notes in part payment for their services and votes. Bartley Campbell, author and dramatist, who was at one time official reporter of the Louisiana assembly, while Warmoth was governor, states that on frequent occasions he had seen money paid to legislators on the floor of the House to secure the withdrawal of their opposition to certain measures. It was proved that H. S. Kimball disbursed, to secure railroad legislation at one session of the legislature, $80,000. The expenses of the general assembly which in 1861 had only been $175,000 were in 1871 increased to nearly $1,000,000. That year the State tax was $2 on every $100, and in the city of New Orleans $5 on every $100 of assessed valuation of property. George A. Sheridan, a favorite of Warmoth, received in one year as collector of taxes fees amounting to over $60,000.

This saturnalia of jobbery and corruption, with the attending public and private immorality, lasted for two years

* H. R. Mis. Doc. No. 211, 42d Cong. 2d Sess. pp. 474 to 481.

without any disturbance to the harmony of the rogues.   In 1870 Warmoth having obtained the registration and election laws which vested in him absolute power, determined to perpetuate his sway.   The constitution provided that the governor should be ineligible for the four years succeeding his term of office, but this was a trifling obstacle to a man who had been made master of the ballot-box and the counting of the votes.   He simply had his legislature provide a constitutional amendment making him eligible and went through the form of submitting it to the people. The Custom House branch of the carpet-bag party were alarmed by this bold move of Warmoth.   They had grown rich and the patronage they controlled gave them potent political influence provided by any means they could clip the wings of the governor.   They endeavored to defeat his constitutional amendment in the legislature but failed. They sought to have it voted down by the people, but the election machinery was too perfect and worked too smoothly. The ratification was secured without difficulty.

The secretary of state, who was by law a member of the Returning Board, was indiscreet in announcing his opposition to Warmoth, and he was promptly removed and his successor appointed.   This was an act of usurpation.   The secretary of state had been elected on the same ticket with Warmoth and could only be removed by impeachment. Constitutional provisions never stood in the way of these political freebooters.   The courts being the only restraint upon the governor during the recess of the legislature, Warmoth always saw to it that the judges were his pliant tools. The appeal of the secretary of state to the courts resulted in his prompt non-suiting.

The Federal patronage party realized that their only way of defeating Warmoth was to wrest from him the control of the party organization. But to do this it was absolutely necessary to have the sympathy and coöperation of the President. The first step was to detach Casey, collector of customs, who being the President's brother-in-law had his confidence. Warmoth had flattered Casey with intimations, perhaps with promises, that he should be elected to the United States Senate in 1871, but so confident was he of his own strength that he suffered one of his creatures who was administrator of public improvements in New Orleans, John R. West, to walk off with that prize. Casey was bitterly disappointed, and was ready to join Packard, Kellogg, and the rest of the anti-Warmoth gang. They knew how to flatter and wheedle him. He was a jovial, agreeable fellow without any moral stamina and possessing very limited abilities. Intent upon his personal enrichment and political elevation he readily became the facile instrument of the adroit, unscrupulous men who surrounded him. One of the radical defects of President Grant was his total inability to judge men. His devotion to those he liked blinded him to any of their shortcomings. He had suffered the inconveniences of extreme poverty and he was always ready to assist one of his relatives to better his fortunes. He had made Casey collector of the port of New Orleans because he was poor, and he would have been exceedingly gratified if Warmoth had made him United States Senator. He was piqued when the promised work was not performed. Casey was supplied with the requisite stories of Warmoth's insincerity, faithlessness, and general treacherousness, and plied the President therewith. The President was in the mood to accept them as gospel truths, and gave his sympathy and coöperation unreservedly to the anti-Warmoth faction.

A state convention was to be held in New Orleans, August 19, 1871, to appoint a Republican state central committee.   Packard was chairman of the then existing central committee, and issued the call for, and called to order, the state convention.   He did not indicate where it was to be held in his call, but the day before the meeting he announced that it would be held in the custom house.   The same day he made a requisition on the commanding general of the military district for troops and the commander at the barracks was ordered to supply him.*   One company of infantry were marched to the custom house on the morning of August 19th and, with a hundred more deputy marshals, Packard guarded every approach to the United States court room and admitted no one till he had packed the convention with the delegates selected by himself and friends.   Warmoth and his friends, who were admitted to the custom house, but held in the corridors, between files of soldiers and deputy marshals, until Packard was ready to admit them to the court room, refused to take part in the packed convention and withdrew and held a convention of their own elsewhere.   Complaint was made to the President by Warmoth and his faction of the conduct of Packard and of the use of troops and deputy marshals for political purposes.

The President, according to Judge Dibble's evidence, said he would investigate the matter, but he never did.   It was Dibble's opinion that the President " had come to the conclusion that anything was justifiable to overthrow Governor Warmoth."   The Packard, Kellogg, Casey, combination, named their central committee and claimed to be the regular Republican party.   They were in control of the organization and began preparations to impeach Warmoth.   The control of the House was in their hands and by presenting articles of impeachment against the governor his functions

* H. R. Mis. Doc. No. 211, 42d Cong. 2d Sess. pp. 136–7.

were suspended until he was acquitted. This would have made the lieutenant-governor, a colored man, and an adherent of the Custom House party, acting-governor. But Dunn died and Warmoth called, instead of an extra session of the legislature, the senate only to meet in extraordinary session. Warmoth succeeded by the bribery of a senator, who voted the first time for the Custom House candidate, in having Pinchback elected lieutenant-governor.

The regular session of the legislature met on January 1st, 1872, and Packard and Casey by putting seven senators on the revenue cutter, Wilderness, and keeping them out of the way of the sergeant-at-arms, prevented a quorum in the senate. The House met and by a vote of 49 to 45 confirmed Carter, the speaker of the previous session, for the ensuing one. This was simply a test vote, for the legislature being biennial with two sessions, of course, the speaker elected at the beginning of the term held over unless the House proceeded to a new election. The next day, however, on the motion to approve the journal of the preceeding day, the vote was 46 for and 49 against. The Custom House faction knew that Warmoth had "got in his work" during the night and a row ensued. A motion to elect a new speaker was made and declared carried by Mortimer Carr, but force being opposed to the installation of the new speaker, the House adjourned in a tumult.

Thereupon Packard procured warrants, from a friendly United States commissioner, for the arrest of Warmoth, Pinchback, several senators, and eighteen members of the House on a charge of conspiring to resist the execution of the laws of the United States. It was an infamous proceeding but it accomplished its purpose. The next day Packard's deputies entered the State House and began making the arrests. The Warmoth members, thrown into confusion nearly all left the hall whereupon, without a quorum, the Custom House faction unseated seven War- moth members and admitted six of their fellows, but they stopped short of impeaching Warmoth and adjourned. He was equal to the emergency with a like unconstitutional proceeding. He issued a proclamation convening the legislature in extraordinary session that same day. Notice was given only to his friends. The senate met, but being without a quorum, the Warmoth members of the House assembled and, procuring the attendance of a quorum, pro- ceeded to wipe out the proceedings of the morning, to de- clare the office of speaker vacant and to elect a new, and to expel from the House the old one. Thereupon ensued the famous Carter-Warmoth war. For three weeks two armed bodies faced each other and the lives of peaceable citizens, as well as their property, were endangered. The only strength of the Carter faction was the support given it by the Federal officials and the belief that the national ad- ministration would back it with physical force. The gov- ernor communicated the facts about the use of the revenue cutter to keep the Senate from having a quorum, and the interference of the United States marshal to deprive the House of eighteen of its members. It was six days before the commander of the revenue cutter was ordered to return to his proper duties and to unship his freight of recalcitrant senators. The President, through the Attorney General, declined to take any part in the contest. In this he was undoubtedly right. It was a factional fight and he had no constitutional authority to interfere or to employ the troops. But this conservative view of his functions on this occasion should be marked and remem- bered in view of what followed a year later. Preparations were made on both sides for an armed conflict and Carter proclaimed that on January 22d he would move on the State House. The morning of that day General Emory informed the leaders of the two factions that he had received orders from Washington to suppress both sides if there was any fighting. This ended the Carter-Warmoth war and the latter remained master of the situation.

CHAPTER XVIII.

The quarrel of Warmoth with the Federal administration: The people's party: The election of 1872: The investigation by the Senate committee of privileges and elections: The Returning Board embroglio: The infamous conduct of the Federal judge, E. H. Durell: The scathing report of the majority of the Senate committee: The usurpation of Kellogg sustained by Federal troops: The conduct of Attorney-general Williams: Warmoth turned out: The people do not recognize Kellogg's government: The September revolution: The election of 1874: The verdict of the people again set aside: The conduct of the Returning Board denounced by a Republican congressional committee: The interference of the military: The speech of Mr. Evarts: The Federal administration denounced.

SOME efforts at reconciliation were made during the spring of 1872. What threatened to be a serious defection in the Republican party in the North had manifested itself upon the assembling of Congress in December 1871. A series of investigations followed into the conduct of the War and Navy departments. The opposition which the attempt on San Domingo had created among Republican senators was strengthened by the disclosures in connection with the sale of arms to France by Belknap, Secretary of War, and the payment of the Secor claims by Robeson, Secretary of the Navy. A formidable attack was begun, and followed up with great persistence, by several leading Republican newspapers. The administration and its friends in Congress desired to bring the disunited party in Louisiana together and to establish harmonious relations between the Warmoth and anti-Warmoth factions. But overtures to Warmoth were met by the demand for the removal of Casey. The President would not agree to sacrifice his brother-in-law and Warmoth would not yield. He had already entered into negotiations with the democrats of Louisiana, and believed that the Independent Republican revolt at the North would be sufficient to secure the defeat of Grant whose nomination was a foregone conclusion.

A coalition was formed between Warmoth and his followers and the democrats. The people's party nominated John McEnery for Governor and D. B. Penn for Lieutenant Governor. A legislative ticket, Congressmen, and an electoral ticket for Greeley and Brown, were also agreed upon. There was to be an important municipal election in New Orleans and a judicial ticket was to be elected also. For the important eighth district court, otherwise known as "the Political Court," the fusionists nominated Judge Elmore. The Custom House republicans nominated Kellogg for Governor, C. C. Antoine, a colored man, born in Hayti, for Lieutenant Governor, legislative, congressional, and electoral tickets, and for the eighth district court judgeship, Judge Dibble, who had gone over to the enemies of Warmoth.

The election was held on the fourth of November. It was conducted strictly in accordance with the laws enacted in 1870. The supervisors of registration were appointed by the governor and the revision of the registration lists was completed in due time and form. The commissioners of election were appointed by the supervisors, and the polling places designated. The law was strictly observed in the count of votes and the return thereof to the governor, and the deposit of duplicates with the clerks of parish courts.

22

It was not denied that every form of law was strictly complied with. The committee on privileges and elections of the Senate carefully investigated this election in connection with the rights of certain persons, claiming to have been elected senators of the United States. Four reports * were made from the committee, a majority report by Senators Carpenter, Logan, Alcorn, and Anthony, all republicans, one by Senator Trumbull, then a republican, one by Joshua Hill, senator from Georgia, elected as a republican, and one by Senator Morton. The majority report claims that " the colored population of that state largely outnumbered the white, and in the last election the colored voters were almost unanimous in support of the Republican ticket." They admit, however, that " the election was generally conducted in quiet, and was, perhaps, unusually free from disturbance or riot." Their opinion was that "Governor Warmoth, who was the master spirit in the whole proceeding, seems to have relied upon craft, rather than violence, to carry the state for McEnery." On the other hand Senator Trumbull found that " the census of 1870 shows that there were in the state one hundred and fifty-three more white than colored males over twenty-one years of age," and that it was proved "that from eight to ten thousand colored persons voted the fusion ticket, while the number of whites who voted the Republican ticket is not believed to have exceeded half that number." He insisted that " it was confessedly one of the most quiet and peaceful elections ever held in the state, and the evidence shows it was substantially free and fair." Senator Hill maintained that " while it must be conceded that the election in certain parishes was not conducted with entire fairness, and in others frauds were committed, it is nevertheless true,

* Senate Report No. 457, 42d Cong. 3d Sess. pp. 1 to 80.

according to the evidence before the committee, that on
the whole, the election was as fair and certainly as peaceable, as the people of Louisiana are accustomed to hold."
Senator Morton contended that the Republican ticket had
been elected although the election "was an organized
fraud of the largest dimensions."

The majority for the fusion ticket was, according to the
returns of the commissioners of election, several thousand
votes. The testimony taken by the Senate committee
demonstrates to an impartial mind that there were in all
not exceeding 5,000 white voters in the state who favored
the custom house ticket, and that a very large number of
negro votes were cast for the fusion ticket. It is capable of
the clearest proof that the colored voters of the state were
not in excess of the white electors. The census of 1870
gives 153 more white males, of twenty-one and over, than
colored males of like age. That census was taken by the
appointees of men who were interested in swelling the
colored population of Louisiana to the largest possible
proportions. They had deliberately concocted their scheme
to maintain themselves in power by controlling the negro
voters and to make the Northern people believe that the
colored population was much larger than the white. They
had provided the machinery for taking a census every four
years for the very purpose of enabling the seemingly fair
registration of a large majority of negro voters. The census
of 1880 shows that there could not have been in 1870 the
number of negro males of twenty-one years and upwards returned in the state. The excess of white males, of twenty-
one years of age and more, in Louisiana, over Negroes,
Chinese, and Indians, of like age was 833. There were of
Chinese 460 males, and of Indians 441 males. Deducting
the usual proportion, one-half, for Indians under twenty-one,

would leave 220. The Chinese immigrants may safely be assumed to be, as a rule, over the voting age. Hence in 1880 there must have been 1,513 more male whites of twenty-one years of age and over in Louisiana than there were negro voters. The same proportions must have held approximately in 1870 and, therefore, the excess of white males of twenty-one years and over, was, probably, nearer 1,550 than 153 as the census of that year gave it.

The returns of the election from the election officers came, as the law provided, to the governor who with the lieutenant-governor, secretary of state, and John Lynch and T. C. Anderson were the Returning Board to canvass and compile them. But the lieutenant-governor, Pinchback, and T. C. Anderson, having been candidates, were disqualified. Warmoth could not depend on Herron whom seven months previous he had appointed secretary of state vice Bovee removed. On the day the Returning Board was to begin its work, Warmoth removed Herron and appointed Jack Wharton. The authority claimed for this act, was first, the office was vacant, because Herron's commission expired with the adjournment of the legislature, and, second, the power of the governor to fill all vacancies happening during the vacation of the legislature, and, third, that Herron was ineligible to hold the office because he had been a defaulter. Here was a complication. Herron disputed the right of the governor to remove him and claimed to be a member of the Returning Board. Warmoth, Lynch, Wharton, and Herron met at the hour appointed November 14, for the assembling of the Returning Board. Warmoth and Wharton proceeded to fill the vacancies, caused by the ineligibility of Pinchback and Anderson, by electing Hatch and DaPonte. Lynch and Herron elected Longstreet and Hawkins.

There were thus two boards. But Warmoth had the returns and the others had nothing. They might have obtained certified copies of the duplicate returns deposited with the clerks of the courts, but this did not suit them.

Both boards appealed to the eighth district court, "the Political Court," Judge Dibble, as it alone had jurisdiction. Dibble promptly issued injunctions restraining both boards from canvassing, compiling, and declaring the result. He was personally interested, because having been defeated, two to one, by Elmore, he could only hope to hold on by preventing a legal determination of the result of the election. In this dilemma Warmoth took from his safe a bill which had been passed by the legislature in the previous spring but never approved by him. It could not become a law until it had his approval. He approved it Nov. 20th, 1872. It changed the election law in two important particulars—the constitution of the Returning Board which was to be "five persons to be elected by the Senate from all political parties," and the repeal of all existing laws. The Senate was not in session, and the governor, under the provision of the constitution, empowering him to fill all vacancies, in the vacation of the Senate, appointed De Feriet, Wiltz, Isabel, Austin, and Taylor, as the Returning officers.

In the meantime Kellogg had begun proceedings before Durell, Judge of the United States District Court, against the Warmoth, Wharton, Hatch, and Da Ponte board, to restrain them on the ground that they were about to deprive 10,000 citizens on account of their race, color, and previous condition, of their suffrages by having already deprived them of the right to register and vote. This falsehood was to give the judge color to assume jurisdiction under the Fifteenth Amendment and the act of Congress of May 31,

1870, with reference to depriving citizens of their suffrage on account of "race, color, or previous condition of servitude." The promulgation of the new election law, and the appointment thereunder of a new Returning Board, of course, invalidated the proceeding before Durell even if he had had jurisdiction. The majority of the Senate Committee on privileges and elections say of this proceeding, "conceding, however, that the bill did present a case within the jurisdiction of the court, that jurisdiction was limited by the scope of the bill, and gave no warrant to the extraordinary proceedings which were subsequently had in the case." However, a restraining order was issued against the old Warmoth, Wharton, Hatch, Da Ponte board. This board was out of existence, and the report above quoted says "it is difficult to see what was left of the case made by Kellogg's bill in the United States court." Accordingly the new Returning Board not being complicated by restraining orders proceeded to canvass and compile the votes from the returns turned over thereto by the governor, and to declare the result. This being done Warmoth issued his proclamation "making known the result of said election aforesaid," and commanding "all officers and persons within the State of Louisiana to take notice of and respect the same."

The only irregularity about Warmoth's proceedings, which can possibly be excepted to, was the original removal of Bovee in March 1872 from the office of secretary of state. But it may very plausibly be argued that the legislature had condoned that act by declining to notice it. Warmoth claimed that Bovee had been guilty of a misdemeanor in office in promulgating an act which he had not approved and which by a trick was made to appear to have been received by him, when in fact he had not,

and, not being returned with his objections, was held to
have become a law. The bill created a monopoly and in-
flicted great hardships on the people. Moreover, the eighth
district court, Judge Emmerson, in which Bovee began
suit against Herron under the "intrusion act," held that
the governor had authority to suspend him and to fill the
vacancy thus created in the office. All the other acts of
Warmoth were clearly within the law and the scope of the
extraordinary authority conferred upon him by the constitution and laws of the State. Undoubtedly the entire
fusion State ticket, and a majority of the members of the
legislature, were elected by the ballots in the boxes which
were counted in strict compliance with law and return
thereof legally made to the governor. The canvassing,
compiling of these returns and the declaration of the result
by the Returning Board, and the proclamation by the
governor were all in due form of law. That there was
constitutional power resident anywhere to lawfully undo
the result of the election no one has ever dared to assert.
But nevertheless it was undone; the history whereof consti-
tutes the most disgraceful chapter in even the annals of
carpet-bag rule in Louisiana.

There had been no amendment of the bill filed by
Kellogg in Judge Durell's court; his injunction issued in
pursuance thereof had no one to operate against, because
the promulgation of the new law made all boards created
under prior acts *functus officio.* It could not apply to one
not in existence and uncomplained of at the time the writ
issued. Nevertheless late the night of December 5th, 1872,
at his house, out of court, without application by any party,
Judge Durell made an order in which he assumed that
Warmoth and others were in contempt by reason of the
promulgation of the result of the election, as found by the

De Feriet board, and directed the United States marshal to "forthwith take possession of the building known as the Mechanics' Institute, and occupied as the State House for the assembling of the legislature therein, in the city of New Orleans, and hold the same subject to the further order of this court, and meanwhile to prevent all unlawful assemblage therein under the guise or pretext of authority claimed by virtue of pretended canvass and returns made by said pretended Returning Officers, in contempt and violation of said restraining order."

Senator Carpenter and four other Republican senators declared that,* "it is impossible to conceive of a more irregular, illegal, and in every way inexcusable act on the part of a judge, conceding the power of *the court*, to make such an order. The judge, *out of court*, had no more authority to make it than had the marshal. It has not even the form of judicial process. It was not sealed, nor was it signed by the clerk, and had no more legal effect than an order issued by any private citizen."

There are circumstances connected with the issuance of this illegal order by Judge Durell, which lays a heavy burden of responsibility on the Federal administration. If the Attorney-general and Secretary of War were not a party to the conspiracy, which culminated in Durell's outrageous act, the facts, as they subsequently appeared, bore very strongly against them. They were as follows: The night before Durell's order was issued, Attorney-general Williams telegraphed to Marshal Packard,† "you are to enforce the decrees and mandates of the United States courts, no matter by whom resisted, and General Emory will furnish you with all necessary troops for that purpose." It did not then,

* Senate Report, No. 457, 42d Cong. 3d Sess. p. 17.
† Ibid p. 54.

and has never since been made to appear that any application had been made to the President for troops. And yet two companies of artillery had been ordered from Fort Barrancas, Florida, to New Orleans, and they arrived there the night Durell issued his infamous order, and they were the troops, which under Packard's direction, occupied the State House. The remarkable coincidence of the Attorney-general's telegram to Packard, and the arrival of the troops, with the action of Judge Durell, very naturally excited comment at the time. Scores of men have been convicted, in courts of justice, of capital offences, and condemned to death, on circumstantial evidence little less conclusive. There was never any explanatian of the occurrences offered, either by the Attorney-general, or the Secretary of War or by any of their defenders in Congress. There had been no application for troops, and General Emory had not asked for reinforcements. The inference is irresistible that it was known to the Secretary of War and the Attorney-general that some extraordinary "decrees and mandates" were to go forth from Durell and preparation was made accordingly.

The Attorney-general was advised of the application to Judge Durell by Kellogg for an injunction against Warmoth and his colleagues of the first board. He was advised of the promulgation by Warmoth of the new election law on November 20th, and he was lawyer enough to know that the repeal of all existing laws swept away all offices and officers thereunder. Therefore, long before December 3d, he knew that, if the United States district court had jurisdiction in the first instance, and authority to enjoin, the board enjoined had ceased to exist. Where then was the case in which "decrees and mandates" could issue from the United States courts? If it is claimed that he was without this specific knowledge he is in no way relieved.

But it is inconceivable that the Attorney-general was not fully and accurately informed of all that was transpiring.

It is certain that they were advised of all the facts immediately after Durell's order was enforced. Both sides made their statements. The infamy of Durell's order could not be glozed over. It was as patent as the sun at noonday in a clear sky. The wrong could have been righted. Decency, self-respect, would have impelled men not privy to the conspiracy to have acted in order to clear themselves of the suspicion of complicity which the Attorney-general's telegram to Packard would create. They stood firmly by the stand they had taken, and when a committee of one hundred of the best citizens of Louisiana asked permission to wait upon the President and lay before him all the details they were brusquely told by the Attorney-general that they need not come because the President had made his decision and would not change it.

There was no halting or hesitating by the Custom House party. The Lynch-Herron board proceeded, without any returns, with no official data of any kind before it, to count in Kellogg and the whole state ticket and a large majority of senators and representatives. They made Kellogg's majority 18,861. They might as well have made it 88,861 while they were about it — they drew upon their imaginations for their figures. Three days thereafter the State House was seized by United States troops. Warmoth was impeached and ousted and Pinchback made governor. These proceedings were one and all revolutionary. Even the forms of law were not observed. Nobody in the state, outside the Custom House and the State House where they were protected by the troops, respected the sham government which had been set up. Durell's court was kept busy fulminating orders and Collector Casey and Pinchback sent almost hourly telegrams to Washington informing the President and Attorney-general of the progress of the conspiracy and clamoring for the approval of all that had been done. They frankly told their masters—their co-conspirators(?) — that unless this was done immediately that their fabric would fall to pieces. One week after Durell's order — a week which compassed more outrageous violations of law than were ever before chronicled in a land of constitutional liberty — Attorney-general Williams telegraphed to Pinchback — " Let it be understood that you are recognized by the President as the lawful executive of Louisiana, and that the body assembled at Mechanics' Institute is the lawful legislature of the State, and it is suggested that you make proclamation to that effect, and also that all necessary assistance will be given to you and the legislature herein recognized to protect the State from disorder and violence."

Well might Senator Trumbull have exclaimed after reviewing these proceedings * — " the history of the world does not furnish a more palpable instance of usurpation than that by which Pinchback was made governor, and the persons returned by the Lynch board the legislature of Louisiana ; nor can a parallel be found for the unfeeling and despotic answers sent by order of the President to the respectful appeals of the people of Louisiana." And Senators Carpenter, Logan, Alcorn, and Anthony declared that " viewed in any light in which your committee can consider them, the orders and injunctions made and granted by Judge Durell in this cause are most reprehensible, erroneous in point of law, and are wholly void for want of jurisdiction ; and your committee must express their sorrow and humiliation that a judge of the United States should

* Senate Report, No. 457, 42d Cong. 3d Sess. p. 17.

have proceeded in such flagrant disregard of his duty, and have so far over-stepped the limits of Federal jurisdiction."

It was these orders and injunctions made in "flagrant disregard of his duty" by Judge Durell which made, what Attorney-general Williams said, was the lawful executive and legislative power of the State of Louisiana! It was by this mockery of justice, for which four Republican senators expressed "their sorrow and humiliation," that William Pitt Kellogg was made Governor of Louisiana. For two years his government had to be sustained by the troops of the United States and the instant they ceased to be the guards of the State House the whole fabric fell to the ground. It required no display of force on the part of the opposition to accomplish this. The sham government had no friends among the white people, except its pensioners and hirelings, and even these began to desert as rats do a sinking ship because state warrants, the only currency the Kellogg government could command, were at an enormous discount. The tax-payers would not contribute to the treasury of the usurping power, notwithstanding they could not bring suit, or be a witness for, or in their own behalf, unless they could exhibit tax-collector's receipts! Outside the city of New Orleans there was no pretense of obedience to, or respect for, the authority of the so-called governor, or any of his minions. The whole body of the intelligent and self-respecting people preferred anarchy to a rule imposed by partisan power in Washington. There was no show of opposition to Federal authority in its legitimate sphere and to its illegal exercise in imposing upon and maintaining over them an usurping local government — there was only determined non-recognition of it. The limit had been reached. If the people could not have local self-government they would support no other. The interest upon the enormous indebtedness of the State, in large part illegally created, could not be paid, and forty per cent of the principal was repudiated.

In September 1874, nearly all the Federal troops having been withdrawn from New Orleans, Kellogg's metropolitan police attempted to seize without process of law arms belonging to private parties. This brought on a conflict between the people and the mercenaries. It was of short duration. Before the day closed the usurping government disappeared and the officers who had been elected in 1879 quietly assumed power. They were everywhere recognized throughout the state. After the brief struggle between the police and the citizens there was no necessity for even the display of force by the McEnery government. But orders came immediately from Washington to the commander of the Federal troops to restore Kellogg and upon the appearance of a few soldiers the people yielded quietly. It was the grandest example of an outraged and cruelly wronged people submitting to illegally exercised national authority ever witnessed !

An election occurred the succeeding November. The whole power of the Federal administration was exerted through the United States marshal to secure the triumph of the Custom House and Kellogg candidates for Congress and for the State legislature. There was an entire registration anew of the voters as provided by the election law. To bolster the frauds of this new registration a fraudulent census was prepared. Under the Federal election laws, supervisors of election were appointed for every polling place almost, and swarms of deputy marshals spread over the state, to rally the negro voters. Troops were stationed throughout the state as Kellogg and his friends dictated. The entire election machinery was in his hands. He ap-

pointed the supervisors of registration and dictated the appointment of commissioners of elections.   There was no
possibility of intimidation or frauds on the part of the
people's party.   The election resulted in the overwhelming
triumph of the people's candidates at the ballot-box.   It
was a fair, peaceable, and honest triumph.   All efforts to
prove the contrary had to be abandoned, and resort was
had to the pretext that prior violence and intimidation prevented the negroes from voting the Republican ticket.
How remote was this intimidation?   The minority of a
Republican Congressional committee went back *eight years*
to find causes for the admitted defeat of Republican candidates at the polls!   The ingenuity and eloquence of
Messrs. Hoar, Frye, and Wheeler were taxed to the utmost
to make out a plausible case for their side, but they reluctantly admitted that the campaign and election of 1874 was
one of peaceable methods on the Democratic side.   With
great rhetorical effect they revamped, with increased partisan coloring, stories of riots, alleged political outrages, and
intimidations, occurring from 1866 to 1872.   The desperate
character of their cause is evidenced in every line of their
report.   They were fully sensible of the fact that there had
been a revulsion of popular sentiment at the North.   A
great uprising of the people had occurred, and a tidal wave
of public indignation had carried into power a Democratic
House of Representatives.   " The bloody shirt " was no
longer the oriflamme of Republican victorious hosts.   The
maladministration of carpet-baggers in the South, their
wholesale plundering, their general official immorality, and
private rascality, could no longer be concealed, or glozed
over, by ancient stories of alleged barbarities to colored
men.   The northern people, devoted to the sacred principle
of local self-government, would have preferred almost any

calamity to the deprivation of a right which had come down to them from their remotest ancestors. And when ten years of peace had cleared away the fog of sectional distrust and prejudice, and they could see, with eyes no longer blinded by passion, the real situation in the South, they placed their seal of emphatic condemnation on those who were responsible therefor. Undoubtedly, the multiplied exposures of the misdeeds of high officials, the clearly proved betrayal of trusts by Republican office-holders, the gigantic Crédit Mobilier fraud, and multifarious peculations and plunderings in every branch of the public service, the impeachment of a Secretary of War, the demonstrated rottenness of the Navy department, and the wholesale corruption of the customs houses, had a powerful effect in hastening the conviction that a political reformation was necessary. But it was unquestionably true that the great mass of the people were disgusted with the indefensible conduct of the President, in the employment of the army to impose a lot of usurpers upon a peaceably protesting community.

It is not strange that two Republican members of the Hoar Committee should have declined to join in the report prepared by him. The confessions he was compelled to make neutralized his eloquent recital of stale outrage stories. * Neither is it singular that Mr. Phelps, of New Jersey, and Mr. Foster, of Ohio, refused to unite with their party associates in reasserting the exploded fiction about the large majority of negro voters in Louisiana. It was too palpable a falsehood to be any longer accepted by intelligent people, and they did not propose to be set down as wanton falsifiers. They, therefore, drew a report which was accepted by their Democratic colleagues and by a Republi-

* H. R. Mis. Doc. No. 26. 43d Cong. 2d Sess. pp. 1 to 4.

can House of Representatives. * It asserted and proved
that the election of 1874 in Louisiana was free and fair;
that if there was any fraudulent registration and voting it
was on the Republican side; that the official data showed
that in 1870 the voters were nearly equally divided between
white and black, and that the registation of 4,000 more
negro voters in 1874 than were shown by the census of
1870, and 10,000 less white voters, could not be satisfacto-
rily accounted for; that the returns of the votes cast, com-
pared with the registration figures, showed a fair election;
that "it was idle to assume that the disturbances so vividly
pictured by the minority could have kept up throughout
this State such a feeling of intimidation as would justify the
assumption that but for that feeling the State would have
gone Republican;" that they "understand the committee to
be unanimous in finding that the action of the Returning
Board has defeated the will of the people as expressed by
them at the polls on the 3d of November, 1874;" that
"the people then elected to the lower house of their legislature a majority of conservative members;" that " a portion of the conservative members thus elected were refused
their certificates."†

What was "the action of the Returning Board," thus
unanimously denounced by republicans and democrats?
It had taken the returns of the election forwarded by
the supervisors of registration, which showed the election of a majority of Democratic representatives, and
deliberately counted out enough democrats, and counted in enough republicans to make a Republican majority in the lower branch of the legislature.   This
was done notwithstanding the returns of the commis-

* H. R. Miss. Doc. No. 26, 43d Cong. 2d Sess. pp. 2, 3.
† Ibid, p. 3.

sioners of election did not certify that there had been riots, disturbances, acts of violence, intimidation, bribery, or corruption whereby a fair and free election had been prevented, and notwithstanding the supervisors had not protested that a full, fair, and free registration of voters had been prevented by like acts. There being no evidence of this kind before the Returning Board even Republican members of Congress were compelled to find that the counting out and counting in were in violation of the election law. Bear this in mind. Bear in mind also that a Senate committee, only one Republican senator disagreeing had held in 1873 that the Louisiana Returning Board could under the terms of the election law obtain jurisdiction in no other way than by the regular compliance with these forms. Remember, too, that the majority of the House Committee in 1875 reported that with months of time, and all the machinery of government at their command, the Kellogg party could not, outside their dependants in office, produce " more than half a dozen persons to testify to anything impeaching the freedom and fairness of the late election."

When the constitutional time for the meeting of the legislature arrived, Kellogg by the approval of the President ordered the United States troops to forcibly eject Democratic members of the assembly, and with the hall of the House filled with soldiers the Republican members organized that body. This unwarrantable, illegal use of Federal troops, the indecent delegation of command over them to Kellogg — raised a storm of indignation at the North which made the President and his hitherto unswerving defenders in Congress quail. Spontaneous gatherings of citizens irrespective of party in various cities of the North denounced the outrage in unmeasured terms. A mass-meet-

ing held in New York City and addressed by Wm. M.
Evarts, resolved that this interference of the military was a
monstrous outrage and deserved the condemnation of all
lovers of constitutional liberty. The administration appealed to its friends in Congress to help it out of its dilemma.
The Senate had persistently refused to recognize the crime
of 1872 by seating persons claiming to have been elected
by the legislature counted in along with Kellogg and maintained by Federal forces. This was a *quasi* condemnation
of the President and his illegal acts. The Republican senators who united with their Democratic colleagues to prevent
an approval of the President's unconstitutional performances could not rise to the height of the great occasion, and
flinging aside party trammels, put on record their *open* condemnation of what they knew to be subversive of free institutions. The majority of the House Committee which
reported in 1875 recommended the recognition of Kellogg
as *the defacto* governor of Louisiana for the remainder of
his term and a compromise was agreed upon whereby the
democrats were given control of the lower house of the
legislature.

APPENDIX.

THE following extracts referred to in the note on page 30, are given as fuller proof of the statement made in the text — to wit : " It might seem incredible that General Grant could be so enthralled were it not for the concurrent testimony of his most intimate friends and supporters which is contained in the eulogiums and reminiscences published since his death."

George W. Childs in the Phila. *Press*, Aug. 2, 1885.

" Gen. Grant," Mr. Childs went on to say in conclusion, " in the simplicity and honesty of his character, trusted all men who seemed to be friends and often stood by them long after their duplicity had been discovered by other people."

In his " Memoirs of Grant," published in the Phila. *Ledger*, Sept. 5, 1885. Mr. Childs said :

" When he was mistaken there was no man more ready to acknowledge a mistake. He showed a great tenacity in sticking to friends longer than he ought to have done. When I spoke to him about this he would answer, ' Well, if I believed all I hear, I would believe everybody was bad.' General Grant would say there was nobody who came in contact with him but that he was traduced, and secondly, he very often had to depend upon his own judgment in the matter. One of his expressions was, ' Never desert a friend under fire.' "

Hon. Hamilton Fish, Secretary of State for nearly eight years under President Grant, said in the New York *Independent*, July 28, 1885, of his former chief :

" His knowledge of men was generally accurate; but he was apt, in this respect, as in others, to reach his conclusions rapidly, and was thus not infrequently led to give his confidence where it was not deserved, and it was from the abuse of his confidence thus reposed that arose most of the censure which, after the close of the war, was visited upon him. Where he gave his friendship he gave it unreservedly — whether friendship or confidence, he gave it unreservedly—and was slow to believe anything to the discredit of those of whom he was fond."

Jesse Seligman said of General Grant in the New York *World*, July 27, 1885:

"He was a man noble in many ways, yet very weak in many others, and his weak points grew out of his noble qualities. He could not think that one whom he thought was a friend of his could deceive him. He was so honest himself that he took the word of those about him as fact without question."

Hon. Chauncey Depew, in his reminiscences of General Grant, published in the New York *World*, July 27, 1885, said:

"His great fault as President — and in that lay the difficulty which overthrew him as a politician — was his selection of confidants, When a man had once got into the confidence of Gen. Grant, no other man except himself could shake that confidence. Nothing that he could do except to Gen. Grant himself, could disturb it. There is no more admirable trait in personal and social relations than this, but in politics and in business it always brings overwhelming disaster upon the honest and confiding possessor of the faculty, as Gen. Grant has discovered to his cost.

"It was this which furnished the key-note to his connection with Ward in the late business firm. When he had taken a man into his confidence he trusted him with everything he had — his money, his honor, his everything. It is this which makes it so difficult for the man of business training and habits to understand him when the story of that failure is told."

Ex-Secretary Robeson published in the Phila. *Press* his reminiscences of General Grant and said:

"The next quality which attracted attention was his want of suspicion. Direct, brave and unaffected himself he never seemed to realize any pretence or subterfuge in other persons or to dream that they would allow their judgment of any question of conduct in regard to it to be influenced by outside considerations. He always assumed that people were honest in their convictions as well as their practices, and believed that honest men differed only from want of judgment or lack of information.

* * * * * *

"The fact is that this great man, experienced in the direction of large affairs and familiar with the principles which governed them, was at the same time utterly ignorant of commercial details. Not accustomed to these transactions and wholly unsuspicious in his nature, he was, notwithstanding his great qualities, perhaps by reason of them, the most likely man to be deceived in such business that I have ever known."

Hon. John A. Logan, in his recollections of General Grant, published in the New York *Independent* of July 28, 1885, says:

"He was a most confiding man; was strictly honest and truthful, and believed implicitly in the honesty and truthfulness of every one until the contrary was made to appear. If to have such confidence be a fault, it was a grievous one in him, it being the cause of all the serious trouble I ever knew him to have."

The New York *Tribune* of July 24, 1885, in its editorial article on General Grant, said:

"It is to be added as a vital fact in General Grant's political history, that he never acquired the faculty of valuing men for their devotion to principles. Thus he lost one great safeguard against error in selection. Nor was he always ready to appreciate criticism in the light of the principles by which he was guided. To him a friend was a friend, whether agreeing with him wholly or not, and a foe was a foe.

* * * * * * *

"Since he did not question his own judgment, and had learned to trust without reserve the men of his choice, he was many times placed in false positions by his errors of selection and by confidence misplaced, and in matters of vital public policy found his high aims defeated by the unworthiness of persons he had trusted.

* * * * * * *

"He was easily deceived, and was the ready prey of designing flatterers. Whoever wished could gain his confidence by adulation, and could then turn him vehemently against another by the flimsiest of misrepresentations."

The Albany *Evening Journal* in its obituary notice of General Grant, said:

"The only fault the most critical could find was the rugged obstinacy with which he clung to his friends through evil and through good report. He never betrayed a friend."

Rev. James S. Chadwick, pastor of the Forty-third Street Methodist Church, N. Y., in his sermon of July 26, 1885, on the character of President Grant, said:

"But I believe that the purpose and heart of President Grant were ever with the right, although the glory of some of his movements was obscured by the attitude and sayings of some men who seemed to be very near the seat of power."—N. Y. *Herald*, July 27, 1885.

Surgeon-General Gunnell, of the U. S. Navy, speaking of the influence those about General Grant had, says:

"Then came a long struggle with political enemies and false friends who abused his confidence. After his political career was ended he made another mistake by entering Wall street. Always confiding he placed his all in the hands of disreputable men who robbed him."—N. Y. *World*, July 26, 1885.

The New York *Evening Post* of July 25, 1885, speaking of General Grant and the Republican party, said:

"The Republican party, its best friends must confess, abused, through its leaders, Gen. Grant's inexperience and trustfulness, and thus prepared early in his first Administration for that gradual withdrawal of popular confidence in it which finally led to its loss of power."

In its issue of July 23, the same paper said:

"The President refused to believe evil of his personal friends and dependents; his tenacity of purpose and of affection was successfully appealed to, to prevent his abandoning them 'under fire,' and the scandals only grew in number and in proportions. The appointment of Mr. Bristow to the Treasury Department was, however, accepted as proof that thorough work was meant with the suspected irregularities there. When prosecutions were begun, and Babcock was indicted, the President's words, ' Let no guilty man escape,' were again hailed with delight by all who wished well to the country. Yet Babcock was not convicted, and the Secretary found his position intolerable. The managers of the whiskey ring had the effrontery to claim that they levied their assessments upon distillers and cheated the Treasury to raise a fund to insure a third term to the President, and that the end justified the means. When some of them were convicted and sent to the penitentiary, they even alleged an understanding that they were to be pardoned out."

Ex-Governor Bedle, of New Jersey, said July 27, 1885, to the New York *World*, of General Grant :

"He made many mistakes in life. The one most prominent was his over-confidence in the integrity of his friends. This fault may have cast a shade upon his usefulness in public life and it remains a question for mature historians to discuss."

The New York *Tribune*, of July 24, 1885, in its obituary notice, said :

"The chief event of Mr. Bristow's administration, which lasted for two years, was his attack upon the Whiskey Ring, by which many corrupt combinations for defrauding the Government were broken up, large sums of money recovered, and a large number of convictions obtained. Mr. Bristow apparently had the hearty support of President Grant in this course, but for some cause a coolness grew up between them which led to Mr. Bristow's leaving the Cabinet. This was supposed to be partly due to the fact that General O. E. Babcock, the President's private secretary, was in the course of these prosecutions indicted for conspiracy. The jury, however, failed to convict him. During a House investigation which followed the trial, Secretary Bristow, when placed upon the stand as a witness, declined to state what had passed between General Grant and himself with regard to the matter, taking the ground that it was a privileged communication. The President addressed him a letter, absolving him from any such restraint. The President ultimately pardoned most of the leading members of the Ring who had been convicted, and most of the officials who had been prominent in the prosecutions withdrew from the public service or were dismissed. The entire episode was one of the most important in the history of the Administration. One of the pardoned members of the Ring had confessed to frauds amounting to a quarter of a million of dollars, suffered only a nominal imprisonment, and paid back only $10,000.

*   *   *   *   *   *   *

"At times he would delight his well-wishers by some appointment of such ideal fitness that it served to recall the cool sense he had always displayed in selecting men for various posts in the war; and then he would disappoint and mortify them by some appointment made on purely personal reasons and without any apparent regard to the public interest. He appointed so many of his connections of one degree and another, to places that his came to be called 'a brother-in-law Administration,' and the charge of 'nepotism' was the one most frequently made against it. Casey at New Orleans, Leet at New York, Babcock and 'Boss' Shepherd at Washington, and Belknap in the War Department were among the relatives and intimates who brought discredit upon his Administration."

George C. Bates. ex-U. S. District Attorney for Utah, in the Denver, Col., *Opinion*, said:

"In life and in death he suffered more from the false pretenses of scurvy politicians and such men than he ever did from his worst enemies, if any he had; but in truth and in faith he had no enemies, save false and pretended partisans, 'who sought to use him and his memory for their own aggrandizement and advancement'—dead moons, with no light in themselves, that circled around him while President and clustered at his grave in death.

"It was the Belknaps, the Bories, the Babcocks, the Luckeys, the McDonalds, *et id omnes genus*, that beclouded his Presidential career.

* * * * * *

"I have lived to mourn over the disease and death and misery of one of the greatest heroes and military chieftains and one of the purest and truest patriots that the world has ever yet produced—one eminently worthy and well qualified, duly and truly prepared, to sit down with Washington and Lincoln in that 'house not made with hands, eternal in the heavens'— and yet who, in his last Presidential term, was so blinded by his pertinacious devotion to those whom he thought were his friends, that his Administration was one of the most corrupt and infamous of any ever recorded in the history of this nation. And yet the President himself, although blind to the crimes committed all around him was as pure and as honest as Lincoln himself."

FAC-SIMILE OF THE CARD

GENERAL GRANT GAVE MR. MADDOX.

I wish the dr. of the Int. would see Mr. Maddox Spl. Agt. of the Treas. who has just returned

from New Orleans and has valuable informat'n

U. S. Grant

Nov. 24 '76

JEWETT'S STATEMENT.

COPY of a brief left with General B. F. Butler by Col. D. J. M. A. Jewett, of Louisiana, for use in his examination by the Potter committee. Jewett was the secretary of the Republican state committee on registration and canvassing in 1876. This brief being made by a partisan of the most virulent kind, a champion of the carpet-baggers— Jewett being himself a carpet-bagger — is important because of the admissions it makes. It is unnecessary to say that his interpretations of the election law are wrong in those instances where he was directly interested on account of rulings he had made.

REGISTRATION AND ELECTION LAWS.

An elector shall be not less than 21 years of age ; a citizen of the United States ; shall have been a resident of the state not less than one year and of the parish 10 days.

Registration shall close 10 days before election, and a person who moves into the parish on the last day of registration may register, as on the day of election the 10 days' residence will have been complied with.

Registration shall be supervised by a supervisor of registration, who shall be appointed not less than sixty days prior to election, shall have two clerks, shall personally make the registration, for which purpose he shall successively open his office at not less than three nor more than twelve points in the parish other than the seat of justice.

The supervisor decides all disputed rights under the registration law, without appeal but subject to the civil penalty of $500, for refusal to register a duly qualified person. Courts are prohibited from interference with him in the discharge of his duties by mandamus, injunction, or otherwise.

The law imposes upon the supervisor the duty of erasing from the registration book the names of all who have become disqualified for any reason, or who have obtained registration fraudulently, limiting his powers in this respect only by the provision that he shall not erase the name of any one in his absence, except upon the affidavit of two respectable citizens registered electors of the parish.

To the supervisor is committed the duty of making arrangements for election. He locates the polling places, his discretion being limited in this respect by the provision that there shall be one poll for each justice-of-the-peace ward. He appoints the commissioners of election, he furnishes to these last the ballot-boxes (which he may demand from the clerk of courts for this purpose,) the stationery, poll lists, and other requisites, and instruct them verbally or otherwise in their duties.

At this point all his discretionary powers appertaining to ELECTION *cease and determine, and his remaining duties become strictly* MINISTERIAL.

From the opening of the polls at 6 A. M of the day of election, to the close of the count and the delivery of the statement of votes, the commissioners of election decide all cases appertaining to election without appeal. (An appeal remains during the day of election to the supervisor, but on questions of *registration* and *erasure* only), the commissioners' powers are limited only by the power of the supervisor *to close the poll* for notorious and open violations of law, within the same or in its immediate neighborhood.

The commissioners of election count the vote, and make the statement of votes without there being in the supervisor any power of supervision or interference. Their statement of votes is made in duplicate, one copy and the box (the ballots having been replaced therein) resealed, they deposit with the clerk of courts, the other copy they deliver to the supervisor, together with any protest appertaining to the election which they may have seen cause to make in duplicate, and which if made shall be corroborated by the oath of three respectable citizens, registered voters of the parish, and may be accompanied by such other written evidence as may exist.

These duties it is provided shall be performed and completed within 24 hours after the close of the poll, this however on the ground that the law never requires impossibilities, has been construed* to be

* This construction was made by Jewett, Blanchard, McArdle & Co.

declaratory, only, and that the duties are to be performed and completed as soon as it is physically possible. These duties performed the commissioners become *functus officio*.

The supervisor shall now from the several statements of votes which have come to him from the several polls, compile the consolidated statement of votes, in duplicate. These he shall submit to the clerk of courts, and obtain his certificate that they correspond with the duplicate copies of the statements of votes filed in his office by the commissioners of election. To the consolidated statement he shall attach his protest (if any) appertaining to *registration* in his parish. The original with his original protest attached, and accompanied by all the original statements of votes from the several polls, the original protests of the commissioners of election, all tally sheets, lists of voters, and memoranda of election from each poll, and any evidence in the shape of affidavits or depositions affecting registration or election, he shall *forward by mail* to the returning officers of the state at New Orleans. The duplicate consolidated statement of votes he shall deposit with the clerk of the courts, and at the same time shall deposit with the same officer, the duplicate of his protest of the registration and the duplicate protests of election (filed with him by the commissioners of election) for the use of the district attorney. This done he becomes *functus officio*.

To the five returning officers of the state are limited all powers as returning officers of election and there can be no returns of election except those made by them.*

The law gives them unlimited powers to enquire into any and all violations of law; which have affected the freedom and purity of registration, or the freedom and purity of election, in any parish, or at any poll in the state and to apply the remedy; and the return of election which they may, after such enquiry, make, is not subject to review by any other authority.

The law, however, is express in its terms as to the manner in which these officers may acquire jurisdiction in any particular case.

It was made in view of the probability of having to manufacture affidavits *after* the returns from the parishes came to New Orleans. If it was necessary to throw out a few votes in order to bring in some candidate they would not be foreclosed by the 24 hour clause of the law.

* This provision of the election law is in direct conflict with section 48 of the Constitution of Louisiana. It has been held by the supreme court of the state to be unconstitutional. Senator Edmunds held the same in the Senate of the United States March 16, 1875.

A protest affecting the registration shall emanate from the supervisor and affects the entire parish, a protest affecting the election shall emanate from the commissioners of election and affects only the particular poll. These shall be made and forwarded to the board with all the formalities detailed herein; upon the receipt of the protest in the form and in the manner provided by law, the board acquires jurisdiction in the particular case affected thereby. *This jurisdiction can be acquired in no other manner.* In the absence of the protest received, in form and manner prescribed by law, the duties are purely *ministerial* to canvass and compile the statements of votes as received, and no evidence may be received or enquiry made except respecting the authenticity or form of the documents before them.

I am unable to recollect that in any case, except that of Caddo, protests were forwarded to the board *in form and manner prescribed by law.* Farther, if a strict construction of law, as affecting supervisors were raised, and that of my circular of October 15 were admitted, it remains that the protests received were those of supervisors appertaining to the election, *while it is expressly provided that these shall be made, if at all, by the commissioners of election and by them only.*

CONSPIRACY.

There was no conspiracy existing prior to the election in La., between Packard, Kellogg, Dibble, Blanchard, Morey, Ray, Wells, Anderson, Cassannave, Kenner, myself and others to obtain a fraudulent return by the board if the election went fairly against us.

All matters touching registration, election, and returns were freely and fully discussed by and between Gov. Kellogg, Judge Dibble, Mr. Blanchard and myself from time to time. No one concealed his opinion that the bull-dozed parishes so called would be carried heavily against us by fraud and violence, and that the proper means must be taken to give the board jurisdiction in these cases.

That due evidence must be obtained of all facts which would enure to our partisan advantage after the election and before the Board. Gov. Kellogg seemed to rely chiefly upon Mr. Blanchard and myself to attend to this department. I, on several occasions during the campaign, especially on two or three occasions in October, communicated to all supervisors likely to be interviewed upon this subject, and impressed upon them the great importance of lawful evidence of all violations of law in their several parishes, affecting or likely to affect the purity and freedom of registration and election. Mr. Blanchard and myself being in practical control of the office of late registrar of voters, draughted and sent out over Gov. Hahn's signature, various instructions to supervisors and commissioners of election, intended to preserve such freedom and purity, or to secure evidence of illegalities if they could not be prevented. If all these several instructions had been duly obeyed and enforced there is no question but that the return of the Republican ticket would have been obtained in strict accordance with law.

AFTER THE ELECTION.

After the election when it was found that the White league tactics had been more successful in the bull-dozed parishes, and that by the just fears of some supervisors, and the inattention and stupidity of others, the instructions had not been carried out, or the evidence of fraud and violence obtained as required by law, the officials named and others concurred (without any special agreement however to that effect) in an endeavor to supply the requisite evidence in a *colorable* shape. Having anticipated, in part, what actually happened, I had recently, before election, issued a circular calling attention to the fact that, if unable for any sufficient reason to attach protests and evidence to their returns in accordance with Sec. 26, election act, they might forward the same to the board in separate packages under Sec. 43. This *was a strained construction of the law*, sent out to meet a possible contingency which actually arose. This construction was, of course, found very useful after election. As the time approached for the board to close its labors and the utter unscrupulousness of the opposition became more manifest, still more unscrupulous means were used to circumvent their frauds and perjuries. Though, at no time was any formal agreement come to by and between any of the Republican managers and myself or with my knowledge, to go outside the law.

Mr. Packard was not in the city until the evening of Nov. 4th, and neither then or after was any consultation had with him respecting details.

Nov. 8, and several days thereafter Mr. Packard, Mr. Pitkin, Mr. Blanchard and myself were at the custom house in receipt by telegraph and otherwise of the result of the election. Our gain in the city had been large (2,400) and the first advices from the country were favorable, and it was not until about Nov. 13 that we knew that the state had gone against us by the ballots in the boxes.

The Returning Board were by law to meet Nov. 17: about Nov. 12, a committee of counsel was selected to attend to the interests of the party before the board.

This was composed of Dibble, Gorham, Hardy, Harris, Morey, Blanchard, Campbell and myself. Each member took charge of evidence from localities with which he was most familiar. I appointed Mr. Hagin, a young lawyer of N. O., attorney for the committee on registration and election, and made him chief clerk. I detailed one of my confidential clerks, Jas. P. McArdle, as his assistant and others as occasion required. Campbell, Harris, Hardy, and Gorham chiefly draughted the affidavits and protests while Blanchard and myself reserved to suit ourselves the examination of all witnesses from localities with which other members of the committee were unfamiliar and the decision respecting the value or availability of their evidence. In the collection and reduction of such a mass of evidence in a few days, it was manifestly impossible for one man to even read it all but I kept myself informed of all that was of importance.

After the arrival of the Congressional committees the committee was enlarged to include

and the following sub-committees were organized:

Again at the special request of Mr. Packard I took charge of the preparation and collection of evidence, as chairman of the committee for that purpose.

DE SOTO PARISH.

C. L. Ferguson, supervisor, mailed his returns per registered package to New Orleans from Mansfield, Nov. 14th; he reached New Orleans in person about the 23d; on the 24th I received from Geo. L. Smith, in person, or from some person in his interest, a notice that my presence in the private office of the post-office would be desirable about 9 or 10 P. M. that night. On my arrival I found there Geo. L. Smith, candidate for Congress, 4th district, D. D. Smith, cashier post-office, C. L. Ferguson, supervisor De Soto parish, T. H. Hutton, supervisor Bossier parish, Jno. S. Morrow, supervisor, Fred. E. Heath, candidate for House of Representatives, and Sam'l Gardner, citizen of Webster parish, with one or two others I think, whom I do not now remember. I had detailed Mr. McArdle to attend, and he was there, but on account of objections on the part of Geo. L. Smith he was sent away. The fact whether protest, had been made or not, etc., having been considered, D. D. Smith unlocked the post-office vault and produced therefrom the returns of De Soto, Bossier, Caddo and Webster. Caddo, it was stated that he had brought down himself. Bossier and Webster he had, as I understood. On the De Soto package I noticed the post-mark of Mansfield and that it bore evidence of registration. It was, however, already open. It was unrolled and examined by Smith and myself. It was not possible to create a Republican majority except by throwing out polls 1, 3, 5, 7 and 8. These were selected for protest and Ferguson was asked for facts. I draughted a protest based on such facts as he had knowledge of, either personally, or from information received, or as were suggested by Geo. L. Smith, or by the well-known conditions of the parish. This Ferguson copied and was directed to take the same before F. A. Woolfley for administration of the oath.

It was suggested by me, that of course it was not possible to attach this protest and various affidavits in hand affecting the same parish (taken before commissioner Levissee in Shreveport) to the consolidated statement of votes, this having come forward by mail and there being a disagreement of dates, but they should be handed, or sent in under Sec. 43, as per my circular letter of instructions.

Notwithstanding, the unbounded stupidity of somebody, rolled these up in the original package, which restored apparently to its original condition, went forward by carrier to the board Nov. 25.

BOSSIER PARISH.

The returns of Bossier were handed by Capt. Hutton, the supervisor, to G. L. Smith for safe-keeping upon his (Hutton's) arrival in the city and were by Smith placed in the vault of the post-office.

T. H. Hutton, had on Nov. 13, (the day that he started from Bellevue for New Orleans) sworn his consolidated statement of votes (popularly known as the return) before Geo. B. Abercrombie, clerk of court, and had deposited with said clerk a copy as required by law, at the date named and when the returns were examined by me in the post-office. This document bore in the space for remarks a protest of the Atkins Landing box (No. 1) and no other.

In my presence in the private office of the post-office, the supervisor interpolated in the same space under the protest noted above, and above the jurat, a second protest affecting the Red Land box (No. 3.) There is no question in my mind but that the protest and exclusion of this box was an afterthought which first took shape at this time (Nov. 24).

WEBSTER PARISH.

Jno. W. Morrow, supervisor of registration, forwarded his returns by mail to New Orleans as I now believe. If I am mistaken herein he had deposited them with Geo. L. Smith for safe-keeping.

On the night of Nov. 24 I saw them taken by Smith out of the post-office vault (see De Soto), at this time they were unrolled and examined. Those present took the view that it would be highly convenient to get rid of about 250 votes in this parish. An affidavit made in Meriden, (Nov. 20), by W. L. Franks was at hand affecting poll No. 1. Sam'l Gardner then present made another, then and there, affecting poll 5, (Meriden.)

I draughted a protest for Morrow on this occasion based on facts stated in the affidavit, and by F. E. Heath and Jno. W. Morrow. This protest Morrow copied, or it was copied for him by F. E. Heath, and he signed it in the clerks office, U. S. Circuit Court the following day. This protest and these two affidavits were forwarded to the board with his returns.

MOREHOUSE PARISH.

F. M. Grant, supervisor, brought his returns to New Orleans about one week prior to Nov. 20th. No protest accompanied his returns. In conversation with Mr. Blanchard and myself he stated (immediately after his arrival) that while he was of the belief that there had been intimidation affecting both registration and election, he knew nothing important of his own knowledge and could not see his way clear to make a protest. He also called attention to the dangerous consequences to himself, as a property-holder and resident of the parish, should he do so.

The evening of that or the following day, at the governor's request, Blanchard and myself drove him out of the governor's residence where we had a conference respecting his parish and testimony. This being without effect the governor took him apart, into an adjoining room, and they conferred together some time. The next day he was again interviewed by Kellogg at the custom house and was (as I was informed), taken to see the visiting statesmen. Blanchard informed me, that Grant was bull-dozed by these and other parties for several days before he would make the protest which he made Nov. 18th.

At this time I purposely avoided even seeing the visiting statesmen except as I met them casually at Kellogg's, and it was arranged between myself and Mr. Blanchard that he should do everything which would require the slightest connection with them.

This was done because it was not proposed that Mr. Blanchard should testify before either committee of Congress when they came, as was expected, and I desired to be, myself, incapable of answering any inconvenient questions which might be propounded to me touching these gentlemen and their connection with our affairs.

OUACHITA PARISH.

M. J. Grady, supervisor, was extremely reluctant to protest the election. He stated that he had sent in considerable testimony in the shape of affidavits but assigned as a reason for not making the protest, which would confer jurisdiction upon the board, that many facts alleged were personally unknown to him, and that he feared the future consequences to himself. He was so reluctant to formally protest facts which were notorious and indisputable that I recollect being somewhat severe in my language to him as betraying his principles, his friends, his party, by his refusal. He finally made the affidavit or protest.

I am informed by Mr. Blanchard that Mr. Grady was bull-dozed by Kellogg, Sherman, Garfield, and others for a week before he would sign the protest. He admitted to myself that he could not stand the pressure. I do not charge or believe that any fact stated by Grady was untrue or unknown to him, at least by common report. The evidence was simply obtained in a manner which deprived it of any legal value.

EAST BATON ROUGE.

F. A. Clover, supervisor, reached New Orleans with his returns complete about Nov. 11 or 12. It is already in evidence that his protest was written in upon his consolidated statement above the jurat which he made in Baton Rouge. His protest dated Nov. 18, (258 Sherman) stated facts no doubt, and no dishonesty is charged in connection therewith.

The fraud in this parish was committed by his refusal to compile the statements of the votes cast at polls 5, 6, 7, 8, 9, and 13, on the ground of technical informalities of proceeding upon the part of the commissioners of election.

The judicial powers of returning officers of election is confided by the Louisiana law to the returning officers of the state and to them alone, and it was Mr. Clover's duty to compile and forward to the board all statements whatever, and all memoranda connected therewith, to call attention to all frauds and irregularities connected with any poll, in order that the board might obtain jurisdiction to apply the remedy provided by law. (See sec's 26 and 43, act 98, 1872.)

This Mr. Clover refused to do and was sustained in his refusal by Kellogg, Campbell, and others, to whose advice he would have yielded. Mr. Clover undoubtedly did this with the promise or expectation of reward.

I do not by any means charge that Mr. Clover committed an intentional fraud. `He was a man not especially qualified to construe a statute. Under a construction, which he adopted, and which was upheld by parties fully aware of his error, (those named), he attempted to remedy one wrong by the commission of another.

It may be said that I ought to have corrected him. This it would have been useless for me to do against the influence of those named and, while Mr. Blanchard and myself were practically in control of the state registrar's office, and while Gov. Hahn would have undoubtedly signed an order (drawn by either of us) to Mr. Clover, the law has expressly excepted supervisors from obedience to the rulings or orders of the state registrar of voters, who is at the same time deemed their administrative chief.

EAST FELICIANA PARISH.

Jas. E. Anderson, supervisor, refused, upon his arrival in New

Orleans, to make any protest, alleging as a reason his fear of being murdered if he did so. This, in his case, I did not believe, having been convinced by his then secret conduct that he was a corrupt scoundrel, who would protest or not, betray one party or the other (he was unquestionably in the employ of both) as he might conceive to be for his interest.

As Gov. Kellogg was responsible for his being in his parish to go through the farce of an election I abandoned to Gov. Kellogg the task of getting him to testify to notorious facts unquestionably within his knowledge and washed my hands of him and of his affairs. I was present on two occasions at Kellogg's house, when Anderson and the Governor were in conference respecting his testimony.

On the 10th of November, immediately after his arrival, Anderson had signed a protest drawn by Hugh J. Campbell which the following day he distinctly repudiated, and which he stated to be at least in part untrue. This protest was not finally accepted by him again until, as I was informed, Anderson had been promised the position of deputy naval officer or something that should be a full equivalent. Anderson himself informed me while under the influence of liquor (about November 20) that " he had got what he was after," by which remark and its context I understood that he had received pledges of reward for his testimony.— I have also been informed that Messrs. Sherman and Garfield assisted in bringing Mr. Anderson " to listen to reason."

RICHLAND PARISH.

J. F. Kelley, supervisor, brought consolidated statement to New Orleans in person, waited upon Gov. Kellogg (before delivering returns to board) and reported to him certain facts respecting registration and election.

The Governor then and there draughted a protest for Kelley who having disappeared meanwhile, Kellogg handed the draft to me with the request that I would see that Kelley signed something like that, and that he filed the same with his returns.

Upon meeting Kelley the next day, he declined to sign a statement such as the governor had draughted, assigning as a reason, that he did not personally know the facts stated to be true. Mr. Kelley returned to his parish without making any protest.

Kelley returned to New Orleans with witnesses about November

25th when I handed Judge Campbell a substantial copy of Kellogg's draft and requested him to take charge of the matter. I think the judge afterwards told me that Kelley still refused to sign. About November 30th Mr. Kelley signed an inconsequential affidavit respecting the election in Richland which was shown to me, whereupon I drew up the protest which appears with his returns (460 Sherman) and handed it to Mr. Hagin I think for Mr Kelley's signature. This Mr. Kelley signed 16 or 17 days after his returns were in the office of the board.

SECOND WARD, ORLEANS.

A. J. Brim, supervisor, refused to compile and forward statement of votes from poll 6 contrary to law and was sustained in his refusal by Kellogg, Hahn, and others.

See remarks upon East Baton Rouge.

PARISH OF LAFOURCHE.

Marcelin A. Ledet, supervisor, refused to receive and compile and forward to the board the statements of votes, tally sheets, and memoranda of election from polls No.

His error was the same as that of Capt. Clover and was sustained by the same parties. In this case also the returns were withheld a very long time after their arrival in the city.

Mr. Ledet was perfectly honest in his error; had no intention of defrauding anyone, and the neglect did not change any result in the parish or in the senatorial or congressional district.

CLAIBORNE PARISH.

Capt. J. E. Scott, supervisor, forwarded his returns by mail to the board. His commissioners of election were all democrats. No protests were made by them. No protest was made by him and forwarded with his returns according to Sec. 26, election act.

Upon his arrival in New Orleans he stated that he had no personal knowledge of any facts which would justify a protest although he had no doubt of the existence of such, his belief being based upon information received. November 24 Mr. Hagin drew up, under my instruction, a protest in the presence of Capt. Scott which he signed and which was forwarded to the board. This protest stated no facts which, under a fair construction of the law, would have given the board jurisdiction, and affected polls 1, 2, 3, 5, and 11. No. 3 was thrown out.

VISITING STATESMEN.

I expect to prove that protests and evidence, such as it was, which had been received and filed up to November 27, excluded votes for Packard 1,620 and for Nichols 9,700, leaving Mr. Packard elected by a clear majority, with a Republican majority in the Senate and House, and also elected 3 Hayes and 5 Tilden electors.

That thereafter, in pursuance of a conspiracy between J. M. Wells, Thos. C. Anderson, Jno. Sherman, and J. A. Garfield, and others, polls were excluded in the parishes of Caldwell, Natchitoches, Richland, Catahoula, Iberia, Livingston, and Tangipahoa, with the result, and for the purpose, of returning as elected 5 Hayes electors who were otherwise defeated. That the consideration of this conspiracy was the absolute control of the Federal patronage within the State of Louisiana by the said Wells and Anderson, that the evidence used to effect the object of the conspiracy was manufactured without regard to actual facts and with the knowledge of the several conspirators, and that the consideration to be given to said Wells and Anderson has been delivered up to date.

INDEX

ARRANGED ACCORDING TO VOWEL LETTERS, A, E, I, O, U, Y.

25

INDEX. 393

PAGE
MATHEWS, Stanley, correspondence of, with Jas. E. Anderson:
Defense of, by Hon. Henry Watterson : Accepted charge
of Nash-Anderson agreement, ... 148
Relations of, to R. B. Hayes 205
Letter of, to S. B. Packard 206
Custodian of the Nash-Anderson agreement : Election of,
to U. S. Senate : Made justice of U. S. Supreme Court. 207
Pledges of, to representatives of Nichols 228
Agreement of, that Hayes should recognize Nichols' gov-
ernment 229
Relations of, to Jas. E. Anderson 303
Watterson's defense of, ... 307
Interest of, in Jas. E. Anderson 308
MAXWELL, E. W., sent to Florida 65
MEMBERS OF CONGRESS, the Democratic, timidity of, in 1876 ... 34
MERRICK, Hon. R. T., indictment of Kellogg secured by, ... 261
MILLER, Mr., justice, admissions made by, ... 48
MILLS, George D., services of, and reward of, ... 110
MILITARY FORCE, ordered to Washington : Purpose to intimidate
representatives of the people 33
MISSOURI, disappearance of alien government in, ... 8
MISSISSIPPI, disappearance of alien government in, ... 8
MITCHELL, Amy, testimony of, about affidavit, ... 140
Affidavit of, draughted by Jas. A. Garfield : Made to say
what she did : Husband of, killed — did not know who
killed him 141
MONROE COUNTY, Florida, polls of, rejected, ... 83
MOORE, W. J, supervisor of registration, 7th ward, New Orleans 119
Places held by, in New Orleans custom house 290
MOORE, W. B., letters of, to J. H. Maddox 216
MORTON, Oliver P., senator, ... 12
Report of, on Electoral-count bills 14
Partisan character of bills of, ... 16
Drives Electoral-count bill through Senate : Provisions of
Electoral-count bill: Change of front by: A representative
of desperate men 23
Opposition of, to Electoral-commission bill 29
Maintains that President of the Senate has power to count
electoral votes 35
Appointment of, on committee to prepare for counting elec-
toral votes 36
Information given to, by Kellogg about forgery of Louisi-
ana electoral certificates.. 191
Motion of, to Electoral Commission to count electoral votes
of Louisiana 195
Knowledge of, when motion was made 196
Information received by, from Kellogg 254
Report of, on Louisiana election of 1872 339
MORTON, Alfred, post-office inspector, sent to Florida 65

ANTON GIULIO BARRILI.

A Whimsical Wooing, from the Italian by Clara Bell, one vol. paper, 25 cts., cloth, 50 cts.

The Devil's Portrait, from the Italian by Evelyn Wodehouse, one vol. paper, 40 cts., cloth, 75 cts.

The Eleventh Commandment, from the Italian by Clara Bell, one vol. paper, 50 cts., cloth, 90 cts.

LA MARCHESA COLOMBI.

The Wane of an Ideal, from the Italian by Clara Bell, one vol. paper, 50 cts., cloth, 90 cts.

Mme SOPHIE COTTIN.

Matilda, Princess of England, from the French by Jennie W. Raum, two vols. paper, $1.00, cloth, $1.75 per set.

Mme AUGUSTUS CRAVEN.

Eliane, from the French by Lady Georgiana Fullerton, one vol. paper, 50 cts., cloth, 90 cts.

FELIX DAHN.

Felicitas, from the German by Mary J. Safford, one vol. paper, 50 cts., cloth, 90 cts.

GEORG EBERS.

An Egyptian Princess, From the German by Eleanor Grove; authorized edition, revised, corrected, and enlarged from the latest German edition, two vols. paper, 80 cts., cloth. $1.50 per set.

A Question, from the German by Mary J. Safford; authorized edition, one vol. paper, 40 cts., cloth, 75 cts.

GEORG EBERS. Continued.

A Word, Only a Word, from the German by Mary J. Safford, one vol. paper, 50 cts., cloth, 90 cts.

Homo Sum, from the German by Clara Bell; authorized edition, one vol. paper, 40 cts., cloth, 75 cts.

Serapis, from the German by Clara Bell; authorized edition, one vol. paper, 50 cts., cloth, 90 cts.

The Burgomaster's Wife, from the German by Mary J. Safford, one vol. paper, 50 cts., cloth. 75 cts.

The Emperor, from the German, by Clara Bell; authorized edition, two vols. paper, 80 cts., cloth, $1.50 per set.

The Sisters, from the German by Clara Bell; authorized edition, one vol. paper, 40 cts., cloth. 75 cts.

Uarda, from the German by Clara Bell; authorized edition, revised, corrected, and enlarged from the latest German edition, two vols. paper, 80 cts., cloth, $1.50 per set.

Ebers' Romances, 12 vols. in half calf extra, Matthews' binding, in neat case, $24.00.

ERNST ECKSTEIN.

Prusias, from the German by Clara Bell, two vols. paper, $1.00. cloth, $1.75 per set.

Quintus Claudius, from the German by Clara Bell, two vols. paper, $1.00, cloth, $1.75 per set.

The Will, from the German by Clara Bell, two vols. paper, $1.00, cloth, $1.75 per set.

A METHOD FOR THE

IDIOMATIC STUDY OF GERMAN
BY
OTTO KUPHAL, Ph. D.
—PART ONE—
LESSONS, EXERCISES, AND VOCABULARY.
Large 12mo. — 536 pages. Price $2.25.

This Method is based on the principles of modern philosophy. Gradual progress and spontaneous development are its leading features. The sentence is the unit. Natural language precedes literary language. The example teaches the rule.; language teaches grammar. The work is printed entirely in the Roman character.

"Spoken language is to written language what the real object is to its description.

"The knowledge of language is based on sound. Sound is the soul of language; without it language is dead. Sound imparts life ; vividly and forcibly it impresses *facts* upon the mind, and *facts* are the *absolute basis* of *all* knowledge. *No true, no real knowledge* of language has ever been attained, unless it was founded on this solid basis which *the living voice* alone has the power to create.

" The study of language must conform to the process of nature. Language was spoken many ages before letters or books were even thought of, and no one ever attempted to read or write his mother-tongue before he was able to understand and to speak it. *To go counter to the sequence in which the faculties naturally and spontaneously develop, is to oppose the precepts of nature. We must understand a language before we can speak it; we must speak a language before we can read it. Reading* is indirect *hearing.* In reading we mentally *pronounce* the author's words and these mental *sounds* are reported to the brain. If we cannot *pronounce,* we cannot *read.* When we begin to read our mother-tongue, we recall to our mind *known* sounds and *known* ideas. Must the process not be the same when we begin to read a foreign tongue? To make reading *the starting-point* in the acquisition of a foreign language is contrary to reason and the student, after fruitless efforts, invariably abandons his task."—*Extract from Author's Preface.*

William S. Gottsberger, Publisher, New York.

A PRACTICAL METHOD

FOR

LEARNING SPANISH

BY

A. RAMOS DIAZ DE VILLEGAS

"Spanish is not under any circumstances a difficult language to learn. It has in its construction and pronunciation an encouraging directness very unlike the grammatical involutions of German and the delicate sound-shadings of French. Working in accordance with the rules of almost any 'system,' a diligent, student can in a very little while acquire a fair mastery of the language; though it is true that some of the 'systems' are much more difficult than others. One of the simplest and best of them all is 'A Practical Method for Learning Spanish,' by Señor A. Ramos Diaz de Villegas, just now published by William S. Gottsberger, New York. The 'method' of Señor de Villegas comprehends a collection of anecdotes arranged in short lines with an English translation, similarly arranged, on the corresponding opposite page; familiar phrases, with idiomatic renderings in English in parallel columns; a vocabulary of words in common use, and a complete list of the Spanish irregular verbs. It will be observed that this method hardly can be called original; that it is more or less that of Morales, of Velazquez, of Prendergast, and that some of its features are found in Ollendorff and in Ahn; but in simplicity of arrangement and directness of purpose it is superior to all of these—Prendergast possibly excepted. It certainly is what it is called—a practical method for learning Spanish. With a relatively small outlay of mental exertion it produces exceptionally good results."—*Philadelphia Times, June* 24, 1882.

ONE VOL., 12MO.—PRICE 75 CENTS.

Sent by mail, post-paid, on receipt of price.

WILLIAM S. GOTTSBERGER,
Publisher,

11 Murray Street,   New York.

MATILDA, Princess of England, by Mᵐᵉ Sophie Cottin, from the French by Jennie W. Raum, in two vols., paper, $1.00. Cloth, $1.75 per set.

"A good old-fashioned novel with a good old-fashioned hero and heroine, possessed of superhuman strength and virtues, is rare enough in the present day to be refreshing. 'Matilda, Princess of England,' would have been thoroughly satisfactory to our forefathers. It is crowded with incidents, has an exciting plot, is not sparing in sentimental love scenes, and describes the romantic times of the crusaders. The heroine is a sister of Richard Cœur de Lion, a novice in a convent, who desires to go with her brother on his pilgrimage to the Holy Land. The hero is Malek Adhel, a Mussulman and brother of the famous Saladin. The passionate love of the Eastern prince for the Christian maiden, and the chivalrous devotion which eventually won Matilda's heart, are but a part of the romance. After love on both sides is felt and acknowledged comes the long and terrible struggle of the lovers to be true to their different faiths. The agonizing efforts made by the Christian maiden to convert the Saracen, his loyal fidelity to his country and his people, and the subsequent tragedy, make the novel exceedingly powerful and interesting. The descriptions of scenery in the East are very fine; the situations are dramatic, and the language is highly colored and Oriental, perhaps too much so to be always agreeable. One may wish that Mme. Sophie Cottin had condensed her work and given us only one volume of 'Matilda;' but the novel as it is will be a valuable addition to the historical pictures of the days of the crusades. The boys and girls who have followed Richard Cœur de Lion's fortunes so gladly in 'The Talisman' and 'Ivanhoe' will rejoice to find him again foremost in battles and generous alike to friend and foe; while those who remember the venerable William, archbishop of Tyre, will find his life and character portrayed with wonderful truth and beauty. The first few chapters of any historical novel require a certain effort of the will to accomplish, but after the reader has left these behind he will find 'Matilda' as stirring and absorbing as a tale of modern times."—*Evening Transcript, Boston, July* 16, 1885.

William S. Gottsberger, Publisher, New York.